Looking Beneath the Surface

CURRENTS OF ENCOUNTER

STUDIES ON THE CONTACT BETWEEN CHRISTIANITY AND OTHER RELIGIONS, BELIEFS, AND CULTURES

VOL. 48

Looking Beneath the Surface
Medical Ethics
from Islamic and Western Perspectives

Edited by
Hendrik M. Vroom, Petra Verdonk,
Marzouk Aulad Abdellah, and Martina C. Cornel

Amsterdam - New York, NY 2013

R

Cover illustration: Wilma IJzerman

Copy editor: Henry Jansen

The paper on which this book is printed meets the requirements of
"ISO 9706:1994, Information and documentation - Paper for
documents - Requirements for permanence".

ISBN: 978-90-420-3730-4
E-Book ISBN: 978-94-012-0983-0
© Editions Rodopi B.V., Amsterdam - New York, NY 2013
Printed in the Netherlands

Table of Contents

Preface

This volume is outcome of a project that started with a conference on medical ethics organized by staff members of the medical and theological faculties of VU University Amsterdam and the Islamic Universities League in Cairo. The incentive for collaboration between medical and theological faculties emerged from the fact that Martina Cornel and Hendrik Vroom were the two final candidates for the Senior Societal Impact Award 2009 given by VU University. Cornel (Department of Community Genetics of VU University Medical Center) and Vroom (Center of Islamic Theology, VU University) decided to collaborate on a common project. The conference, which included the authors and a few guests, led to a very interesting exchange. Among the obvious differences between the academic paradigms of the Arab-Islamic and Western/post-Christian cultures, we also looked for shared values and common practices. One of the things we had in common is that medical ethical issues are interdisciplinary: medical scholars work together with scholars in ethics/*fiqh*, and the Western professors of medical ethics have some training in theology as well. Some of the chapters in this volume have been written by scholars in cultural anthropology, law, and comparative studies.

This discovery of differences in paradigms and commonalities has become the main line in the process of editing the chapters and putting the volume together. The aspect of intercultural comparison is central to this book as a whole. Therefore, the chapters have to be read on two levels: first on the level of *what* they say about the particular ethical issue in the medical practice dealt with, and then on the level of *how* they argue their point. Given the structure of the book as a whole, readers can read the chapters on both levels—reading them as they are and digging below the text: "Looking beneath the surface: medical ethics from Islamic and western perspectives."

Each chapter describes the ethical dimensions of a particular topic. The editors have highlighted both dimensions in their introduction to the book as a whole, first drawing attention to the differing paradigms of accountability or moral reasoning and then introducing the chapters around the ethical themes: genetics, embryos and abortion, organ donation, and palliative sedation and euthanasia. The last chapter of the book returns to the comparative issues indicated in the introduction.

One of the most prominent differences between the Arab-Islamic and Western secularized culture(s) is Western individualism over against the more communalist thinking in the Arab and Islamic world, which we discuss in the introduction, especially in relation to different forms of accountability or moral reasoning. One remarkable indication of this difference is that Western authors write as individuals and Arab-Islamic authors as members of the Islamic academic community that honors authorities. Western academic life prefers—or seems to prefer—originality and creativity; the Islamic community prefers—or seems to prefer—harmony and the acknowledgement of authorities. Nonetheless, "beneath the surface," Western authors strive for the assent of their readers and the Arab-Islamic authors try to find their own specific path "between" the points of views given by the authorities. Nevertheless, the chapters by the Arab-Islamic authors reflect the courses taught in their university faculties in a way that those by Western authors will never do. The contributions on the treatment of fetuses, embryo selection, and abortion from the Islamic perspective present what students are taught. The contributions by Western authors as such do not say what other professors in their or other medical faculties teach—although, as stated, the Western authors also account for their position in discussion with other writers and look for consent. Therefore, the contributions vary with respect to style and content as well.

Because of the Islamic paradigm of accountability, the Arab-Islamic scholars begin with an overview of their sources in the *Sunnah*. Consequently, the first parts of their contributions had much—too much—overlap on the one hand and were too short for many Western readers who are not familiar with Islam. The contributors from Cairo thus gave the editors a free hand in the editing process. The parts on the *Sunnah* were shortened; two contributions that overlapped a great deal were forged into one chapter. Instead of the various short introductions on Islamic moral reasoning, the Muslim editor of the volume, himself an acknowledged *fiqh* scholar, provided a broader introduction to the Islamic way of accounting for an ethical position as Islamic. Also, because of the variety of the styles of transcriptions from the Arabic, and the intention of this volume to stimulate comparative studies and interreligious and inter-cultural dialogue, the editors have decided to omit diacritical signs that would hinder the transcultural exchange they hope to make possible.

The editors hope that the present volume will help scholars and students of medicine, ethics, theology, and religious studies read these texts by Arab-Islamic and Western/post-Christian authors on moral medical problems. They hope that these scholars and students will learn to read those texts as chapters on a specific issue *and* see the underlying structures of moral reasoning against their respective worldview backgrounds. Readers can thus skip the phase of making oversimplifications of "the other's" culture and see commonalities and points of contact "beneath the surface" for further and fruitful discussions.

CHAPTER I: INTRODUCTION

Looking Beneath the Surface

Commonalities and Differences
between Islamic and Western Perspectives
in Medical Ethics

Introduction

This volume contains contributions on medical issues that are
the subjects of heated ethical debates: community policies on
genetics in health care, preconception genetic testing, the treatment of embryos, abortion, organ donation, palliative care, and
euthanasia. Other contributions deal with the juridical question
of who has the right to make decisions about treatments and
the practical issue of how patients and their families actually
make difficult decisions. The authors are Islamic medical
scholars and theologians, and Western scholars in medicine,
ethics, and theology—some are Christians, some have a secular
view of the world. They come from Egypt, Kuwait, the Netherlands, and Belgium. In the second part of this introduction we
will summarize the content of each chapter; here we will
introduce some of the parameters of this project in interdisciplinary comparative ethics. In the final contribution, "Observations," we will compare the various approaches and look for
commonalities and differences, discuss individualism, autonomy and forms of communalism since they are basic to the arguments found in this volume, and compare the paradigms of
Western and Islamic moral reasoning, such as the dignity and
autonomy of the individual in the West and the obligation in
Islam to live in accordance with the will of God.

The aim of this volume is to offer descriptions of the state
of health care in Western Europe and the Middle East in relation to the medical ethics issues mentioned above and descriptions of the ethical considerations of the medical staff and medical ethicists that play a role in these heated debates. The contributions on the same medical issues from different perspectives

are printed side by side in one section of the book, allowing the reader to compare the descriptions on the state of the art in the Middle East and northwestern Europe and to see commonalities and differences between the Arab-Islamic and Western (post-Christian and Christian) approaches. Given so many misunderstandings and prejudices between "the" Arab and "the" Western world, it is important to reflect calmly on the medical care and moral reflections in both "worlds" and see if and in how far the outcomes of ethical reflections actually differ.

Those who read some of the contributions will notice subtle and sometimes substantial differences in the approaches to medical ethics issues. The parameters of the argumentation of the different authors clearly differ. With respect to the ethical issues, some contributors refer to sacred texts while others do not, but all do refer to some basic values like health and the value of the human being—otherwise it would be impossible to make decisions. Nevertheless, the question arises as to how exclusive the basic values in the different traditions are. It is quite possible that there are basic human values "beneath" the references to the authoritative "public" values that people who live in the same culture or in different cultures could acknowledge.

Therefore, other arguing could lead to similar conclusions or to different outcomes. That is what we want to investigate. This volume can be read as being more than "just about ethics." Rather, the contributions show our often less conscious, prejudices and the ways in which "we" are trained to account for our decisions. We can study what is said, but we can also study the framework within which that something is said. Patients and medical practitioners have to evaluate medical facts before they make decisions, but they also have to look at the values that help determine what is best when they are applied in concrete circumstances. In this volume we have to compare both the content (ethical views) and the methods to account for such views and learn to understand "the other"—either Arab-Islamic or Western-(post)Christian—in his or her own perspective. To make it somewhat more complex—and "true to life"—some of the Islamic contributors live in the West. Because of these complexities, we will make some introductory remarks that may help us to understand the approaches of the different contributors and the paradigms in which medical ethics decisions are made and accounted for. The contributors come from different cultures, each with its own variations and accents. Cultures differ in the ways scholars develop their ideas and set them down in sentences and arguments. We should not overlook the fact that both cultures are diverse as such, and contributors whose methods seem similar need not be similar in the elaboration of their argumentation. In what follows, we first will deal with intercultural comparisons—here comparisons of two larger paradigms of moral reasoning—and then describe two paradigms, the Islamic and the "Western."

Comparisons, Differences, and Commonalities

When comparing cultures, it is tempting to compare whole cultures, just as scholars compare whole traditions, either secular or religious. Muslims could then easily read articles by Westerners who do not refer to the Bible and think that those authors are not Christian or, if their references to the Bible are rather marginal, not true Christians. Western culture as a whole is then viewed as secular—certainly its public domain with its large health institutions. But that conclusion is superficial because the ways in which Christian scholars express their views may not be explicitly Christian, enabling them to also reach other, non-Christian people. Furthermore, Christian values may have become so integrated into Western culture that—even without explicit reference—implicitly "secular" medical ethics may incorporate those values. Conversely, Western readers looking at a contribution in which Muslims derive their moral principles from the Qur'an and quote the Qur'an while discussing bio-ethical issues might think that all Muslims share the same views and take the Qur'an as the basis for their argumentation and thus preclude further dialogue with others. When one party speaks from a secular perspective and the other from an Islamic perspective the ethical dialogue ends up being a conversation between people who cannot understand each other. Actually, in the conference at which most of the contributions in this volume are based (after an elaborate editorial process), the various contributors found many overlappings or similarities in the practical ideas of the others despite their different paradigms.

To get past the easy comparison—and putting a stop to dialogue before it starts—we want to read more carefully. The method of comparative philosophy is to study worldviews and determine insights that are basic to a worldview, to see if commonalities can be found in specific parts of argumentation and to determine how—within those traditions—general statements are applied in specific situations. Here is an example of this an area other than medical ethics and another religion. Classical Hinduism teaches that one's next life is determined by the karma—the balance of good and evil—one has built up during his or her life. People live a great many times and have to try to live perfectly in order to get rid of bad karma so they can be liberated from karma as such and thus from the ties that prevent people from attaining eternal happiness. Classical Christianity and Islam teach that God will judge people according to whether they have lived according to his will or not. The quick conclusion is to state that these views are opposed: one party believes in reincarnation, the other in the Last Judgment. But if we delve a bit deeper, we can see that both parties believe that deeds have consequences beyond one's current life. Thus, on the practical level, both parties have a lot in common: for instance, people have to live responsibly, not selfishly, and further the common good. In concrete matters, it is usually counterproductive to make so-called "clear" oppositions. Collaboration between people with different worldviews requires that people establish what insights they have in common as opposed to emphasizing their differences, start a discussion, and thus attempt to find a way out of conflict to collaboration.

Such a position implies that we have to get past general descriptions of Worldview A and Worldview B and break down the easy, counterproductive and even dangerous oppositions of beliefs. Instead, we need to look for analogies and commonalities. Perceived differences need to be investigated and debated and may lead to a better understanding. In this respect, it is interesting to analyze the contributions in this volume that deal with research on fetuses and abortion and how they distinguish several phases in the development of the embryo. It is possible for Muslims to say that "the West" does not reckon with the will of God and for Westerners to say that the Muslims try to derive biological facts from Qur'anic texts, but those are "half-truths," as the reader will discover in the contributions on abortion from both sides. An important tenet of comparative studies, therefore, is to look beneath the surface at differences and commonalities.

In dialogical and comparative studies of religious and secular worldview traditions, we have to drop all sweeping judgments about "the West" and "Islam" and "Christianity." The term reification (from *res*, Latin: thing) was used for this already in 1962 (Smith 1963). "The" West does not exist; it is as much an instance of reification as "Islam" or anything described in such sweeping terms. North American culture differs from northwest European and south European culture—surely in medical ethics. The USA is divided: its two political parties, the Republican and Democratic parties, differ widely in their views of health care and issues like abortion and care at the end of life. The health care system in the USA is very different from that in western Europe. The states in northwest Europe have much in common, such as extended public solidarity. The broad medical and care systems are based on this notion of solidarity, which has its roots in *caritas* (charity) that was part of the way of life of the earliest Christian communities. The meaning of charity has been extended by the "convergence" of Christian and socialist thinking. At present, part of the population of western Europe is Christian and part is secular, but a large part is also post-Christian in the sense that they share originally Christian values like charity and solidarity, responsibility for others, and righteousness in a much broader sense than justice, and the basically biblical idea of the dignity of all humans. Many Muslims conceive of "Europe" as completely secular, but this "reification" is also mistaken. It is much more complex and diverse. Ideas are shared across the borders of (sub)traditions. People have influenced one another—just by living together and coping with the same problems. Secular humanists honor one of the most important Christian thinkers of his time, Desiderius Erasmus, by viewing him as the father of humanism. Many Christians are influenced by the humanist ideas of personal responsibility (which in turn has strong Protestant roots). What is "real" Christianity? What is "complete" secularism?

Nor is there anything that qualifies as "real" Islam. Muslims differ in their application of the rules. Islam has a set of common beliefs and practices, but how people pray and how they practice giving alms (*zakat*) in small villages in the desert differs from how those practices are carried out in big cities like Casablanca and Paris. It is easy to think that all Muslims have the same rules, but is it right to equate someone living in a village, with almost no electricity, in a faraway place in Pakistan with someone living in Brussels or Istanbul? In this respect, the same rule applies: look for commonalities and differences. The "same practice" may have a somewhat or even radically different meaning in another religious and cultural environment. We should not deny commonalities in the Western view of being human nor in the Islamic view of the good life, nor should we overlook nuances and differences. Cultures are not uniform; they change over the centuries, not least through migration. Christians have lived in Cairo, Egypt since the year 100 (Copts), and Muslims have lived in Cairo since their arrival in the seventh century. Things do change in history, including in the West. Currently, about 5% of the population of many western European countries are Muslims, living in a Christian and post-Christian culture, and are beginning to see themselves as Muslim citizens of the West.

Nevertheless, we can distinguish Western and Islamic paradigms of argumentation in the contributions in this volume. Therefore, we will discuss both paradigms briefly.

The Arab-Islamic Paradigm of Accountability

The sources for Islamic ethics are the Qur'an and the early oral traditions on how the Prophet Muhammad and his comrades lived. Muslims believe that the Qur'an is the report of the God's revelations to Muhammad. Because God guided Mohammed in various circumstances, the prophet and his comrades are the most important examples for Islamic life. Therefore, accountable Islamic ethics has its sources in the Qur'an and early traditions (*hadiths*). The more technical details of the use of these sources will be explained in this volume. Here we will restrict ourselves to hermeneutical and comparative issues and especially to how this particular paradigm works.

The Arab-Islamic contributors to this dialogical and comparative volume start with explaining their frame of reference: on the one hand, the Islamic sources and, on the other, the medical facts and dilemmas in medical treatments. These Muslim contributors are part of a centuries-long tradition and do not have to work out from scratch how to apply their sources in later—and their own—circumstances: they make "use" of examples in the classical sources and apply them to new situations.[1] Therefore, the approaches of the Arab-Islamic scholars look quite similar. In actuality, however, we have shortened their expositions of their "use of original sources" and added, as stated above, a chapter devoted as a whole to the paradigm of moral reasoning in Islamic ethics and jurisprudence. To the Western reader who is unaccustomed to the Islamic frame of reference, these approaches look very much alike, which—in part—they are. For instance, when discussing the development of the fetus, the contributors refer to the same Qur'anic texts and give more or less the same explanations. As in Christian theology in the past, a "system" has been developed in which some main biblical texts were taken as authoritative for each ethical question. Those texts were so-called "proof texts": if someone's view was in line with those texts, it was accepted as accounted for within the Protestant paradigm. The official declarations of the Roman Catholic Church had the same function in Catholic theology: they provide frameworks of accountability for the opinions of Catholic ethicists. Such "systems" may become ossified, but, time and again, they will be broken open to create "hermeneutical space" for application under new circumstances like new medical treatments and possibilities for research. Previous generations of Islamic scholars were wise to

---

[1] We use the terms paradigms, frames of references, systems of accountability as equivalent, although one difference is that the first two terms refer to "tacit knowledge"—to use a term coined by Michael Polanyi—and the third term refers to an explicit Islamic moral system that has been developed over the centuries. Thomas Kuhn used the term "paradigm" for this cluster of ideas and examples of good practice within which results of research can be evaluated as true and useful (Kuhn 1970: 181-91).

create openings for divergent explications and adaptations of "the same texts." The Islamic paradigm does allow for such openness to diversity. The authoritative and classical texts of Islam show more openness to diversity than traditionalists are prepared to acknowledge. Therefore, students who study the contributions by the Arab-Islamic writers may wish to compare their content carefully and note the different emphases they make.

The Western Paradigm of Accountability

When accounting for their views, most Western contributors do not refer to religious sources for their views but to values that are considered fundamental for being human—apparently taking it for granted that these values are shared. Consequently, the basic insights behind their views are less obvious in their contributions: they are not introduced in the same way that the Islamic paradigm is. The most central values on which Western contributors base their conclusions in cases of medical ethics are the dignity of human beings and autonomy—the dignity of each human being the main and most central category. This dignity is considered an intrinsic dignity that each person "possesses," independent of his or her qualities and limitations.[2] This inherent dignity can be accounted for from different perspectives, such as a theistic belief that all human beings have been created by God and have equal worth and deserve care from other people, from a humanistic belief in the value of humanity, and/or on the basis of the preamble of the *Universal Declaration of Hu-*

---

[2] Dignity is not an empirical term but a value term that helps people orient themselves in the world; its meaning depends on practices and experiences and is not derived from empirical research (cf. Kadushin 1972: 30-45). Because the dignity of human beings is not derived from a broader (abstract) concept of "dignity," it is wrong to speak about "human dignity" (Dalferth 2012: sections 3 and 12). Since dignity is intrinsic, people cannot lose it or develop it, and people should not be used as means to an end (Kant 1785: 63 [BA70]; see Copleston 1960: 119-20).

man Rights. The value of the dignity of each human person sur-
passes all differences between human beings and is accepted as
a common value beyond diversity. This notion of dignity functions in the background in various contributions on the use of
embryos in research, just as it does in the discussions on abortion. In a sense, this basic value is taken for granted; even when
a contributor does not refer to it explicitly dignity is the back-
bone of the argument.

The second main value at the background of all argumentation is the individual autonomy of those persons in particular
that have not been declared incapable of performing legal acts.
The contribution, "The Right to Moral Independence," describes how legislation works: the patient has the right to accept
or reject medical care; the medical practitioner has to provide
the necessary information to the patient and to ask the patient
to accept or reject the proposed medical care. This ruling of the
lawgiver seems inevitable: Who else could decide but the legislative body? In various contributions we see how such a notion
of autonomy works out in counseling described by medical specialists who have added more concrete rules to this main Western value. Nevertheless, if we look beneath the surface of the
contributions and investigate the actual process in which decisions are taken, we can see that the various authors accentuate
different issues and thus introduce nuances to the concept of individualism in the abstract notion of autonomy. Some emphasize the social structures in which patients live (individuals
are members of families) and that play a role in how patients
reflect on the screening or treatment before they decide. Several
contributions describe the counseling and the implied advisory
work that is based on the experience of the medical staff, as
well as the professional rules that have to be observed in counseling. The patient has to trust their advice—they are the experts. But, especially in difficult ethical decisions where there
are differing opinions, medical professionals may not want to
adopt the position of "expert" but only want to assist patients
in making an informed decision in line with their moral values
and worldviews. The hospital chaplains, spiritual counselors,
and imams in the West do not dictate what patients should
decide but help them find an accountable decision on the basis
of their religious or secular worldviews and the medical advice

of the doctors. Therefore, we cannot take the notion of autonomy at face value but have to see how it works out in medical
practice and how its actual meaning is determined by the faith
and worldview of those concerned and the people closest to
them.

Both notions, dignity and "autonomy," are not secular in
themselves or, as some Muslims say, "man-made" over against
the "God-made" origin of Islamic values. For most Westerners,
"inherent dignity" refers to transcendence; inherent or intrinsic
dignity calls to mind the profound mystery of life in general
and human life in particular. This reference to transcendence
expresses the conviction that dignity transcends all that we can
make as humans. Because of the Western freedom of religion
and its related diversity in worldviews, the implications for
health care with respect to, for instance, fetuses and embryos
and the care of persons in the last phase of their lives may vary
widely. In some contributions the authors refer to ecclesiastical
opinions and reports; in others they just refer to the basic values
mentioned. The reader may find other basic values that the contributors use to account for their conclusions in medical dilemmas.

The Law, Religious Reasons, and Medical Codes

We mentioned the role of state law above. Whatever the autonomy of the patients and the dignity of the fetuses and unborn children may be and whatever the professional responsibilities of the medical staff, in the end the law of the state determines the boundaries of which treatments are allowed and
which are not. In several contributions we see the ways in
which the medical staff and ethicists search a way between the
letter of the law, the letter of the sacred texts, the medical (im-)
possibilities, and the needs of patients. Some contributors refer
explicitly to medical codes that have been formulated by international medical professional organizations. Medical standards,
guidelines, and examples of good practices that the medical
staff follows for diseases and in situations of crises play a role in
the background. There are "mediating structures" between the
law and the practical treatment of patients that help people decide what is morally right or wrong to them. Therefore, in health
care we have to take six elements into account: 1) laws; 2) the

ethical codes of the societies of medical professionals; 3) the rules of the hospital that are the result of deliberations of all personnel involved; 4) the informed opinions of the individual medical staff members; 5) the secular or religious convictions of the individual patients and the rules or advice of their religion or counselors; 6) the views and values of other persons or communities that are important in the life of the patient. Within this framework, the patients have to decide what treatment they choose from the possibilities that are open. The least we can say is that laws, rules, and medical opportunities correct the patient's "individual autonomy." Nevertheless, the patient should not be treated as an object—neither in health care nor genetic research—and therefore not be treated against his or her will.

The Contributions

We will now briefly introduce the contributions in this volume. The *second chapter* is an introduction to the *parameters of Islamic ethics*. Marzouk Aulad Abdellah describes the sources of Islamic ethics and the methods used to derive basic insights from these sources and apply them in different and often new contexts in which people live. The editors decided to add a special introduction because these sources and methods are introduced in several of the contributions by Muslim contributors as well in this volume. Because these overviews are short, the readers are not given the full picture of Islamic moral argumentation. Therefore, we asked a scholar in Islamic religious obligations and moral rules (*fiqh*) to give a separate introduction to Islamic ethics and valid moral reasoning in Islam. When Muslim contributors included quite extensive overviews of Islamic ethics in their original papers, the authors and editors decided to shorten these sections.

Aulad Abdellah describes the sources of Islamic ethics and rules of life, and therefore the relation between the Qur'an as the revelation of God's will and the later authoritative traditions in the Sunnah. He explains how *fiqh* works—the term is often translated as "Islamic jurisprudence" but is not to be confused with state law. As we have already seen above, a distinction should be made between state law and Islamic rules for life. Islam follows mosque-state separation. Aulad Abdellah describes the role of the authorities in the development of Islamic rules (*muftis*). The ruler (who can take whatever he thinks wise from Islam) enacts state law, whereas *muftis* enact Islamic law, and, as this contribution shows, each Muslim is religiously justified in following the *fatwas* of whatever *mufti* in the world he chooses. Thus, Aulad Abdellah describes the structure of Islamic moral reasoning that is in the background of the contributions by the Islamic scholars. The reader may notice the differences between the Muslim contributors who live in Islamic states and those who live in northwestern Europe.

Genetic Research, Treatments, and Counseling

Following Aulad Abdellah's introduction are *five chapters that deal with moral aspects of genetic research and treatment*. This is a wide topic. Knowing that people are genetically predisposed to serious conditions can help them, but such knowledge can also be a source of great concern. The mapping of the human genome and detecting the effects of genetic mutations is an area of real progress because diseases can be discovered at an early stage and some of them—but not all in all circumstances—can be treated to remove the danger of the effects or help patients adjust their lives so that the consequences of genetic vulnerabilities can be diminished. The topic is morally loaded, and counseling plays a major role.

In the *third chapter*, *Martina Cornel* describes, from the perspective of a Western medical school, the state of the art in this area: major developments and high expectations, but, as often, research findings point to a complex biological phenomenon of genes that do not work in isolation but can influence one another and may predispose people, though not with complete certainty, to specific developments. Cornel describes the methodical and moral issues that arise in clinical genetics: how to invite people to collaborate in genetic health care that might indicate that they and their family members are carriers of a certain predisposition? Is it fair to establish risk for suffering from conditions and diseases for which there is no treatment to date? What should be done with unintended insights into someone's condition? She explains the development of professional codes in the Western medical communities and the role of counseling individuals whose genes will be or are being screened or tested. She also describes the dilemma between the interests of the individual versus the community in large-scale genetic research projects.

In the *fourth chapter, Ahmed Ragab* and *Gamal Serour* pose the question how medical facts in genetics research might play a role in moral argumentation. As staff members of the medical faculty of Al-Azhar University in Cairo, the largest intellectual center of Islam, they refer to the principles of Islamic ethics. They deal quite extensively with the tension between scientific research that, if possible, studies causal relations and theistic religion that believes that the world has been created as ordered at least in some way and holds that human persons can normally be held responsible for their acts. Does genetic research show that genes determine who we are and what we do, or do they predispose people to certain behavior and diseases, and does what actually happens depend on other factors as well? It is interesting to see how this contribution deals with these questions in comparison with Martina Cornel's. Such a comparison is also interesting in relation to the description of genetic engineering and gene therapy, preimplementation diagnosis and genetic counseling in both papers, and the moral questions involved in the collaboration of persons in genetic research. Specifically, Ragab and Serour draw attention to the moral side of public expenditures on genetic research because in poorer countries research into the prevention of disease and starvation will have more effect on reducing morbidity and mortality than genetic research that can predict the risk of hereditary diseases. They end their chapter with ideas on the compatibility of modern medical science and Islam.

The *fifth chapter* gives an overview of the medical and moral decisions in counseling people in consanguineous marriages from a Western perspective. With the progress in "technological" possibilities, experts are increasingly able to determine the risk of consanguineously married parents for offspring with a genetic disease. *Pascal Borry, Marieke Teeuw,* and *Martina Cornel* first describe various processes of genetic testing—which differs of course from the treatment of patients who have actually developed a condition. Then they describe the procedures for counseling individual people and discuss the complex moral questions of the outcomes of genetic population research. In the second part, they draw conclusions about the often mistaken views of consanguinity in the public sphere in the West and the possible consequences for the relatives of the patients who have been found to be carriers of hereditary illnesses. By definition, genetic information provides information about how people are related to their ancestors. Hence, what does confidentiality mean in this context: How does sensitive genetic information about a family member relate to confidentiality and what is the responsibility of the medical doctor to other family members who could develop illnesses? The answer to this question touches on the crucial issue of what the medical world understands by the "autonomy" of the person.

The *sixth chapter* gives results from the anthropological research carried out by *Oka Storms and Edien Bartels* on consanguinity in northern Morocco—which is part of a wider Arabic culture in which cousin marriages are quite common. For centuries, such marriages provided social security: they kept the individuals in the care of the whole family instead of handing women over to other extended families. The pros and the cons of this "binding the extended family together" are understood. This chapter presents a nice summary of the thoughts and even conversations between women who understand those risks and the experiences of educated women who live between "two cultures": traditional villages with their extended families and modern urban mass society with its individualism. This social dimension—the common care in extended families—is also in the background of the papers of Islamic contributors when they touch on *in vitro fertilization,* abortion, and organ donation with organs from non-relatives.

Embryos and Abortion

The next five chapters deal with the status of the embryo, the treatment of embryos, embryo research of any kind, and abortion. The *seventh chapter* describes the approach taken by the Clinique of Al-Azhar University, which is attended by Muslim students from all over the world and where patients from Cairo and the surrounding area are treated. As is already clear from the contributions by Aulad Abdellah and Ahmed Ragab, the basis for the Islamic paradigm of accountable decisions lies in the revelation to the Prophet Muhammad and the earliest *hadiths* (traditions). Therefore, the medical writers, *Ayman M. Nas-*

sar and Gamal I. Serour (both work in obstetrics and gynecology) and *Serag el Din Mansour* (population studies), give an account of their medical treatments with reference to the sources of Islamic rules for life and the laws of the state. Then they describe the status of the embryo in its development through three stages of 40 days each. They discuss the question of research on embryos and describe a consensus among Islamic medical specialists: all research on preembryos should serve therapeutic treatments. They state that most ethical commissions accept a rather broad spectrum regarding embryo research and discuss the legitimacy of constructing embryos for research. Then they explore the question of the conditions under which surplus human embryos can be treated and "used" in preimplantation genetic diagnosis, fetal sex selection, gene therapy, and cloning, and discuss research on fetal tissue obtained from abortions. From the Qur'anic emphasis on the importance of marriage, Muslims conclude that adoption is not acceptable as a solution to the problem of infertility because children should be raised by their genetic parents or relatives. So Islamic medical ethics respects the embryo: after it has developed its higher brain the embryo should be treated as a person, thus, during pregnancy.

In the *eighth chapter, Egbert Schroten* describes the *sources of Western and Christian ethics*. Aristotle's view that the soul is what makes an embryo a living being was basic for much Western thought for two millennia. Schroten discusses the controversy concerning the time of the soul's arrival in the embryo, during fertilization or later—although this difference did not play a major role in the evaluation of the moral status of the embryo. The book of Exodus in the Bible distinguishes between the killing of an unformed fetus and that of a formed fetus. The early church opposed the wide practice of abortion, infanticide, and certain forms of contraception. Against this background, Schroten describes the later developments of Christian ethics and its internal variety of views. He briefly discusses a Catholic, an Anglican, and two Protestant reports on the status of the embryo. More recently, medical developments have made it possible to use cryopreservation (preservation by deep-freezing) so that research can be done before any conception takes place. An ovum researched in this way is not intended to develop into a human being. Such developments force us to rethink old positions and find new understandings of the various sorts of embryos that exist or can be developed. Schroten argues in favour of the view that speaks of the "increasing protectability of the human embryo."

Leo ten Kate elaborates on the *termination of pregnancy on the basis of genetic or non-genetic disorders* in the *ninth chapter*. He has conducted research in clinical genetics for a long time and counseled patients who wrestled with genetic or disorder questions, wondering whether they should or should not allow a fetus to develop. The contribution begins with further discussion of genetic counseling. Ten Kate stresses the autonomy of the patient in the sense that the patients themselves should be able to make informed decisions and consider the consequences of possible reproductive options. Both, patients and medical specialists, should follow the law. As in other secularized post-Christian countries, the law is a compromise between the moral values of people with a wide variety of worldviews. Ten Kate summarizes the conditions that have to be fulfilled to allow for abortion under Dutch legislation (i.e. only before the 24th week). He provides the options that people with hereditary deviations have. In an overview of three concrete cases of counseling, Ten Kate shows the important role that ethical considerations and emotional feelings of patients play in the process of counseling and their decision making.

In the *tenth chapter*, *Guido de Wert* shows how medical researchers and ethicists wrestle with the new moral questions that arise in the further development of medical knowledge and technical possibilities. De Wert sketches the state of the art in present medical research and possibilities of treatment. Next to embryo selection *in vitro*, research of maternal plasma can gain information about the embryo—which has broadened the possibilities of getting information about various aspects of the genetic constitution of the fetus and the risks on illnesses for "it" and its lineage, without the risk of fetal loss. First, he describes the state of the art in research into fetuses and fetus-like entities composed from human genomes—that can help the progress in standard medical treatments of *in vitro* fertilization and possibly treatment of some serious illnesses of the potential child. Then, he summarizes the complex ethical questions that are under discussion or should get more attention in circles of medical researchers and ethicists. Pointedly, he sketches the two moral views that embryos have no special moral status or share in the dignity of the human but argues for the (most widely accepted) view that they do not have a very special status. However, because research will affect human beings, it should reflect potential consequences carefully—partly against the pressure in the field to research what can be researched. At the end of the chapter he gives his own conclusions. This contribution is very informative for non-specialists in this area of research and contains a warning against easy judgments of whatever sort.

Moustafa Hegab discusses *abortion from the perspective of Islamic ethics* in the *eleventh chapter*. He begins with the authoritative sources to see what hints they give for distinctions in the process between fertilization and birth. In these references to the sources of Islamic anthropology and ethics, we see again the paradigm of Islamic moral reasoning, as we have encountered it in the other Islamic contributions. The Islamic tradition acknowledges various ethical schools that use different methods to reach accountable decisions. Hegab lists their views on abortion. In addition to the Qur'anic texts that are quoted by all schools, Islamic ethics has a large basis of stories that can be interpreted to indicate the basic insights that help people make decisions about abortion. Then Hegab deals with the prohibition of abortion in cases of pregnancy outside marriage or caused by rape—although he also points out that some Islamic states allow abortion after rape. The author gives a short introduction into the discussions among Islamic scholars on the possibility of abortion in case the fetus is deformed.

Organ Donation

In the *twelfth chapter Ahmed el-Gindi* points out that the Islamic sources themselves have no clear message on *organ donation*. The main objection is that it is an assault on the body of the person or the deceased to take one of its organs. God has given the body and its organs to a person. Therefore, the integrity of the body should be preserved, so that organ donation needs a higher religious obligation for transplant to be allowed. This can be the case if the harm done to the body of the organ donor is less than the harm that threatens the recipient. If organ donation is acceptable in the case of organs of *deceased* persons, the most difficult question is to determine the precise moment of death of the donor. Medical specialists have to define the moment of death in such a way that an organ can be removed before the organ "dies" as well. The definition of brain death has to be so clear that ethicists and lawyers can accept it as a sufficient condition to declare persons dead while their hearts are still beating and their lungs still breathing. In this contribution we see how medical specialists and Muslim ethicists, i.e. authorized scholars in *fiqh*, collaborate in the formulation of the religious rules. Ahmed el-Gindi describes how the Islamic Organization for Medical Sciences (IOMS) organized symposia on "the end of human life" and the definition of death already in 1985 and 1996. The criteria and safeguards that were formulated in the 1996 symposium are presented in the text of the contribution; an appendix presents the form that has to be filled before a brain death certificate can be given. Next, el-Gindi discusses the general rules for making incisions in the body for retrieving an organ from a *living* person after obtaining his consent and summarizes the discussion on whether or not a person has the right to donate part of his body. He shows how, in Islamic moral reasoning on organ donation, medical possibilities for treatments are related to arguments from Islamic sources and together lead to criteria for organ donation. El-Gindi reports results from long and careful discussions in the international meetings of Muslim scholars.

The *thirteenth chapter* concentrates on *Muslim immigrants in the Netherlands and their ideas on organ donation and receiving*. The authors of this contribution are *Karen Schippers, Mohammed Ghaly, and Tineke A. Abma*—a team of Islamic and non-Islamic Western scholars. Based on a broader research project, they sketch a specific case in which a young man had developed kidney problems and received a kidney transplant after a few years of dialysis. This kidney, however, had to be removed after eight years. They outline the deliberations of a Turkish immigrant who consults his Turkish specialist back home as well and wonders if he, as a Muslim, is accountable to God for accepting the kidney of another person. This contribution shows the roles the Western and Turkish specialists play, and the differences between "autonomous" Western patients and medical staff as advisors at the one hand and the more traditional Muslim culture with its paternalistic doctors and patients who trust what their doctor thinks best on the other. At stake again is the Western "autonomy" of the patient and the superior knowledge of the specialists with their experience of the (im-) possibilities and risks of transplantation. The authors point out that among Muslims who live "between two cultures" (as the expression goes) the doctors have to find out how they can maneuver between acting as paternalists or as informants. They state that research shows that a large majority of Muslims living in the West accept organ donation and give Islamic grounds to hold organ donation accountable.

Euthanasia, Palliative Sedation, Islamic Counseling, and the Right to Decide for Oneself

The next chapters discuss *euthanasia, palliative care, Islamic counseling, and the right to moral independence*. Theo Boer explains the background of Dutch law in the *fourteenth chapter*. On the one hand, Dutch law has been profoundly influenced by the biblical Christian value of the dignity of each human being. On the other hand, the freedom of conscience and religion implies that each person should decide for him- or herself how to live—and how to die. Therefore, the principle of autonomy has become a basic value. Nevertheless the state law stipulates conditions under which medical treatments like sedation and euthanasia are or are not allowed—and thus restricts human freedom. In addition to state law, the Royal Dutch Medical Association (RDMA) has provided guidelines for these and other procedures around life and death. Practitioners who violate those guidelines run the risk of losing their license. Because of the biblical background of the dignity of the human being and the legal criteria for valid and invalid reasons for euthanasia and palliative sedation, many Christians speak of the value "system" of western European society as post-Christian.

Boer begins his discussion of palliative sedation with the statement that most Christians and others have accepted it. Most doctors feel that the number of euthanasia cases should be reduced as much as possible; palliative sedation, then, is a solution that reduces the patient's pain. Euthanasia is bringing about the voluntary death of the patient whose suffering is unbearable and hopeless by medical means. Dutch law stipulates very strictly the cases in which and the procedures along which medical practitioners are allowed to apply euthanasia. One definition of palliative sedation is "the monitored use of medications intended to induce varying degrees of unconsciousness, but not death, for relief of refractory and unendurable degrees in imminently dying patients." Patients will be placed in a comatose state in a degree that corresponds to their pain. The intention of the treatment is not to cause death but to suppress unbearable pain that cannot be treated in other ways.

In principle, medical treatments are aimed towards maintaining life. Boer argues from a Christian perspective but does not refer extensively to Christian sources. To make rules in a pluralistic culture, all parties in the public debate have to be as understandable as possible to one another. Boer thus puts his arguments in more general terms so that other Western persons can agree with him as well.

In the *fifteenth chapter*, Arslan Karagül, a mufti and Islamic spiritual counselor, describes the process of decision making among Muslim immigrants in Dutch hospitals. He discusses three cases from his experience among Muslims and in one case his own experience. He refuses to give *fatwas* because he wants patients to follow their own conscience in the choices that they make during their medical treatment. Karagül discusses cases of abortion, organ donation, euthanasia, and palliative care.

He first shows the complex relation between religious and moral beliefs on the one hand and the state laws and ethnic usages—in his case Dutch and Turkish—on the other. In the case study on abortion, he shows how, in Islam, wisdom connects the rules to the practical situation; common sense can help interpret the tradition. In relation to organ donation, he shows the extreme complexity of a person in emergencies when his or her organs function badly but transplantation entails complications. After a sketch of the treatment of euthanasia in *fiqh*, he discusses, from his Islamic point of view, the Dutch law on euthanasia with its strict criteria, and rules for euthanasia. In the last section, he deals with "stopping treatment, palliative sedation, and counseling in dying." In concrete cases, the strict individual autonomy of patients may be far beyond the reality of the patient's situation: the advice of experienced doctors and nurses, the care from families with their wisdoms, anxieties, and (mis)understandings of their own religious traditions, and the role of spiritual counselors. Against the background of the enormous technical medical possibilities, secularization, and the need to organize care efficiently, modern medical treatment and regulations tend to take precedence over religious faith, rules and deliberations, stress the individual conscience, and easily forget the social context of the individual.

In the *sixteenth chapter, Mostafa Salem* describes the *system of fiqh and its application to euthanasia and organ donation.* His main question is if and to what extent Islamic law and the practice of Muslim states are in line with the attitude towards such issues in other parts of the world. First, he briefly describes the sources and methods of Islamic ethics and jurisprudence (*fiqh*). He raises the question whether the whole body of *shari'ah* — given how basic it is for all Islamic thought and especially ethics — is a "unified and well-defined body of rules that direct Islamic life" in different situations *or* a body of texts and practices that in itself is diverse, uses complicated methods of reasoning, and is "not necessarily coherent or authorized by any single body." Salem stresses the role of customary law in the various countries and cultures in which Islam has become the primary religion and refers to the distinction between state and mosque: rulers have provided their own interpretations of *fiqh* when making laws. Their freedom is limited, however, while recognized religious scholars interpret *shari'ah.* Islamic ethics, on the one hand, is not one solid, unified whole, although Muslims do have much in common. As far as euthanasia is concerned, Islam takes a stand on principle. Salem relates why Islam rejects euthanasia. In the second part of his contribution Salem uses organ donation to compare the Islamic approach with the regulation of organ donation under the Egyptian Law on Organ Transplantation (2010) and warns for criminal trafficking in organs. As in other contributions, the fundamental Islamic rules that "necessity makes the prohibited lawful" and "the argument of the lesser evil" play a role in his argumentation.

In the *seventeenth chapter, Arend Soeteman,* a philosopher of law, discusses the issue of autonomy in western countries with their freedom of religion and conscience, and, therefore, "the right to moral independence." These fundamental human rights prevent legislators from steering people's lives into certain directions, forcing them to grant them as much moral freedom as possible: "Laws should be restricted." Soeteman discusses John Stuart Mill's no harm principle, i.e. prevent harm to others, and interprets it as "a wrongful setback of interests." Nevertheless, we all accept that some acts are prohibited although they do not harm other people. This leads to a distinction between hard paternalism (telling or even forcing people to live in a certain way) and soft paternalism (protecting people from behavior that will have harmful consequences), with restrictions on euthanasia and palliative sedation as examples. In the end, the right of people to live as much as possible according to their own religion and worldview—either Christian, secular, or Muslim—depends on the dignity of the human. If all humans have intrinsic dignity, there can be no coercion in their basic beliefs—only conduct that does not meet the dignity standards is inacceptable. "[P]olitical communities in particular should be organized such that all its citizens are treated in accordance with their dignity." After a discussion of the conservative and liberal interpretations of which rights follow from inherent dignity, he raises the question how much freedom the law should grant people to decide for themselves in medical issues. The medical doctor should not treat a patient against his will. Therefore, patients can refuse some treatments. But patients do not have the right to every medical treatment available in a technical sense. Here, the medical staff has the expertise to decide. If the medical practitioner does not want to take responsibility for a treatment—like euthanasia—that is allowed in principle, the patient has the right to ask another medical doctor and find out if he would be willing to do so.

In *chapter eighteen* the editors of this volume give some final reflections on comparing the "Western" and Islamic views with their religious and cultural backgrounds.

Bibliography

Copleston, Frederick. (1960). *Kant*. A History of Philosophy. Vol. 6, Part 2. New York: Image Books.

Dalferth, Ingolf. (2012). "Religion, Morality and Being Human: The Controversial Status of Human Dignity." Paper read at the 2012

Conference of the European Society of the Philosophy of Religion, Soesterberg (NL), in September 1.

Kadushin, Max. (1972). *The Rabbinic Mind*. 3rd ed. New York: Bloch Publishing Co.

Kant, Immanuel. (1983) *Grundlegung der Metaphysik der Sitten* [1785]. In: Immanuel Kant, *Schriften zur Ethik und Religionsphilosophie*. Ed. Wilhelm Weischedel. Darmstadt: Wissenschaftliche Buchgesellschaft. Pp. 7-102.

Kuhn, Thomas S. (1970). *The Structure of Scientific Revolutions*. 2nd enlarged ed. Chicago: University of Chicago Press.

Smith, Wilfred Cantwell. (1963). *The Meaning and End of Religion*. New York: Mentor Books. Originally published 1962.

CHAPTER II

The Sources of Islamic Ethics and *Fiqh*

Marzouk Aulad Abdellah

Introduction

Islamic ethics deals with the main rules for how Muslims should live. These rules do of course need to be worked out concretely for various situations. This discipline of Islamic theology is called *fiqh*, often translated as (Islamic) jurisprudence.[1] It should not be confused with the study of the laws of Islamic states. Islamic *fiqh* scholars reflect on how people should live. While they do have spiritual authority, they have no authority or say over people in the same sense that governments do. In this volume a good treatment of the difference between Islamic ethics and *fiqh* on the one hand and state legislation on the other can be found in the chapter by Mostafa Salem on Islamic ethics and Egyptian laws concerning organ donation.

Islamic legislation has two sources: the Qur'an and the *Sunnah*. The Qur'an comprises the revelations by God to the Prophet Muhammad. In addition to this central sacred text, there are countless traditions on how Muhammad lived and made decisions in complex situations. Traditions have been passed on about his closest followers as well. There are collections of these *hadiths*, which constitute a second source for Islam.

In this chapter I will first discuss the two sources in Islam for ethics and *fiqh*: the Qur'an and the *Sunnah*. I will then look at how rules and insights from these sources were and can be ap-

---

[1] Al-Bardisi: 1987, 23, writes that, linguistically, *fiqh* means "the understanding." The corresponding verb occurs in the following Qur'anic verse: "They say: O Shu'ayb, we do not understand a great deal of what you are saying ..." (Hud (11):91). It thus concerns having proper insight into something, the knowing and understanding of what someone says and means. *Fiqh* legal scholars thus had to try to understand how God wanted people to live.

plied in other times and new contexts. Islam has rules for those who are authorized to issue (juridical) opinions on how people should act: religious authority. There are two reasons why such opinions (*fatwas*) are not obligatory. In principle, every individual is answerable to God for his or her own acts: people may choose which of the various *fatwas* they want to follow. In practice, this means that *fatwas* carry no legal force. The state can set down Islamic rules and norms in law, and in that respect it can happen that state legislation will forbid acts that are permitted according to many *fiqh* scholars.

Fiqh includes *criteria* for a responsible development of Islamic ethics in new situations. After a discussion of these criteria for Islamic jurisprudence, we will turn to one of the most crucial subjects for the study of Islamic law and ethics: the analysis of the *objectives* of *fiqh*. One objective of ethical rules is to make society good and decent. The objectives of ethics must always be kept in view in the application of the criteria for valid ethics. Traditional or new acts that do not correspond to these objectives cannot be justified.

The Difference between Fiqh and Shari'ah

Fiqh is the study of the rules for living properly that are found in both the Qur'an and the *Sunnah*. That collection of revealed rules for living is called *shari'ah*. Because *shari'ah* is a corpus of texts, it is unchangeable as a source text. Discussions can arise about its interpretation, but the history of *fiqh* shows how scholars worked out the insights and rules in connection with the moral questions confronting Muslims. The heart of *shari'ah* is generally valid to a large degree: these rules deal with basic principles, whereas the rules determined by *fiqh* are directed at specific situations. The basic principles of *shari'ah* that were concretely applied and the methods people considered responsible are clear in the history of *fiqh* (Philips n.d.: 21).

The Two Sources

The Qur'an
The Qur'an is the collection of the revelations that descended to the Prophet Muhammad (the praised one), and Islamic theology is done on the basis of these revealed texts. Muhammad was the son of Abdallah, his father, and of Amin Binto Wahb,

his mother. Both died young, and he was subsequently raised by his grandfather and later his paternal uncle, Abu Talib, who was a merchant. Muhammad lived in Mecca in the western part of the Arab Peninsula. He lived there from 612 to 632 (Western calendar), and died in Medina, a city a few hundred kilometers to the north. Muslims view these revelations to Muhammad as the literal word of Allah (God) (Ibn Hishaam: 224; Brugman 1985: 22-23). That is why the Qur'an is the most important source for faith knowledge about God, humans, and the world in Islam.

The revelations were recited in their entirety or in part already during the life of the prophet, and this example was followed in all later generations and is still done so today. The recitation is done in a peculiar sing-song tone that has to meet certain criteria (Al-Zarqani 2006: 43-52; Mellema 1958: 34).

The first five verses of the Qur'an that the prophet received through revelation, called "Read," are:

> Read aloud in the name of your Lord who created,
> Who created man from a drop of blood.
> Recite for this Lord, the highly revered,
> Who taught by the pen,
> Who taught man what he did not know
> (Surah Al-Alaq (1): 1-4; Von Glasenapp 1980: 15)

The Qur'an is perfect with respect to both style and content. It was revealed in Arabic and is an Arabic text with 114 *surahs* (chapters). A *surah* is divided into *ayat*, the singular of which (*ayah*) can be translated as "verse" or "sign." Each *surah* has a title, and those who know the Qur'an by heart use this title (many printed versions of the Qur'an number the *surahs* as well). Surah 4 is called "The Women" because it deals with marriage and divorce. Surah 2 is called "The Cow" because verse 63 mentions the cow that Allah commands be sacrificed. Aside from chapters and verses, the Qur'an is also divided into 30 more or less equal parts, *juuz*, that are in turn subdivided into *hizb* (parts) (Al-Sayyuti n.d.: 184-98). One *juuz* is recited during the evening prayer in the 30 days of the month of fasting, Ramadan.

The *Hadiths*

The meaning of moral rules and opinions about the intention of the rules becomes clearer if we see how people apply them in practice. That also obtains for the Qur'an, which is why the stories about how the Prophet lived and the decisions he made in complex situations are very important for the development of Islamic ethics and faith in general. He was guided by God: in various situations God revealed to him what he was to do or how he could have improved on what he did. The traditions (*hadiths*) about Muhammad and his closest companions were passed on orally and only later gathered into collections. There are a number of authoritative classical *hadith* collections.

Because Muhammad and those companions who succeeded him were thus guided by God, these caliphs were called the Rightly Guided Caliphs. Their judgments and way of life are exemplary and authoritative within Islam. That is why the *hadiths* are the second source, after the Qur'an, of Islamic theology. The *hadiths* provide insight into the context of the revelation and can be used in moral questions that the Qur'an does not make any statements about so that sound ethical positions can be taken. A *hadith* consists of the text with the situation and the statement (*matn*) that is preceded by a chain of transmitters (*isnad*). *Hadith* studies determine what authority a certain *hadith* has by the length of the chain and the reliability of the transmitters: the more reliable the witnesses and the shorter the chain, the more authoritative the tradition. The text itself is usually short, often much shorter than the chain of transmitters. A *hadith* can be about anything—from very practical matters to ethical dilemmas (Al-Sayyuti 1985: 21-25; Abu Shohbah 1985: 111-20; Douwes 2003: 60).

The *hadiths* have been used to compile biographies about the Prophet that reconstruct his lifestyle. The traditions about the Prophet constitute the heart of the *hadiths*. In Islamic theology at present, the *Sunnah* is understood almost universally as the imitation of the exemplary life of the Prophet—thus, that is what the *hadiths* are about. The Arabic term *Sunnah* means "path" or "way." There are different categories of traditions in the *Sunnah*: statements (*kaul*) by the prophet, his actions (*fi'l*) and behavior that indicate approval (*takriq*) (Hasabo 1997: 30). I will give one or two examples of each.

An example of a *hadith* about a statement of the prophet is: "The Prophet said: 'Allah has forgiven my community [*Ummah*] what they did by mistake, through forgetfulness, or under coercion'." The following tradition is attributed to Aisha, the Prophet's wife:

> Aisha, the Prophet's wife, said that Hind bint Utba said: "O, emissary of God, Abu Sufian [her husband] is a skinflint; he does not give me enough for me and my children. But I take it from him without his knowledge." Then he answered: "You may take what is enough for you and your children."

An example of how the Prophet lived is found in the following tradition about the *salat*:

> Abu saidal-Cherdi said: "It was overcast once and rained so hard that the water poured through the roof—which was made of palm branches. Then *Salat* began and I saw the emissary of God (God bless him and give him salvation) throw himself to the ground in the water and the mud; I even saw a splatter of mud on his forehead."

Other *hadiths* tell of situations that indicated his silent approval:

> Rubajji bint Mu'awwidz ben Afra said: "We were involved in a campaign with emissary of God. We gave the people something to drink, took care of them, and brought the fallen and wounded back to Mecca."

Such traditions obtain as supplementations and further specifications (of the revelation in the Qur'an) (Waardenburg 2000: 76). That is why they are the most important source of faith for Islam next to the Qur'an.

Levels in the Obligations and Commands

As stated, *fiqh* deals with how people should live. Life has many aspects, and it is not always fixed as to what one should do. Thus, we can also understand that Islamic "law" does not determine every aspect of life but prescribes a number of acts, recommends or advises against others, and forbids yet others. Islamic "law" is thus a description of the culture, the ways of life that are considered good from the perspective of Islam. This range can be found in the classical division of acts into the following five categories.

What is Obligatory (Wajib or Fard)

People will be punished by God for transgressing his commandments. What is obligatory is described in two ways: as individual obligations (fard ayn), such as the fixed prayers and fasting, almsgiving, the pilgrimage, and social obligations (fard kifaya), such as attendance at the funeral of a member of the community to which one belongs. With respect to the latter, it is enough for a number of friends and acquaintances to attend the prayers for the deceased and his burial. It is enough in other communal duties as well for a few people to carry out the obligations on behalf of the community. If these obligations are deliberately left unfulfilled, each individual of the community will be held accountable.

What is Recommended (Mandub, Sunnah)

Whoever does not do what is recommended is not punished, but people are rewarded in the hereafter if they do. Examples of these acts are voluntary offerings or free prayers.

What is Neutral or Permitted (Mubah, Sunnah)

People are not punished for these acts, but they are not rewarded either. This category includes, of course, all acts of which no statement can be found in tradition and have not been included in any of the four other categories during the development of fiqh. These acts are permitted: they have no consequences. An example of this is fasting or not fasting while on a journey.

What is Advised Against (Makruh)[2]

People are not punished for doing these acts, but whoever does not do them is rewarded.

---

[2] Jaad Al-Haqq n.d.: Part 3, 400; Al-Razi 1997: I, 104; Al-Zohaili 1998: 46-92; Al-Faozan 2003: 21-24; Al-Isanwi 1980: 74-81.

What is Forbidden (*Haram*)[3]

Whoever does what is forbidden is punished by God; whoever lives properly is rewarded. Theft and murder are examples here. Most forbidden acts in this category are followed by a punishment according to the procedure and in the measure set by the rules of the four Islamic law schools.

Religious Authority

The Islamic Scholars (*Ulama*)

Religious authority is constituted by the Islamic scholars (*ulama*). Consensus (*ijma*) among the recognized Islamic scholars is one of the criteria that ethical opinions (*fatwas*) have to meet. According to the authoritative legal scholar Ibn Qudama Al-Maqdisi, *shari'ah* has four "roots": "The roots of *Shari'ah*, of which there are four, are: the book of Allah, the tradition of the prophet, *ijma*, and reasonable proof."[4] The scholars are the theologians, such as Imam Shatibi and Imam Al-Ghazali, who, after having studied for several years, were declared authorized through *usul al-fiqh* to interpret the religious source texts. According to Sunni Islam, it is the responsibility of every Muslim to practice his faith in the right way: Muslims are free to seek out scholars of their choosing for consultation. Because there is no recognized and official power relation between clerics and believers, the *ulama* cannot enforce their authority unless they are assisted in certain matters by political rulers. Every person is personally responsible before God.

There are different kinds of religious clerics, and each kind has its own function. The *mufti* is the juridical expert who— usually at the request of a believer—issues a *fatwa*. A *fatwa* is religious-juridical advice, but it is non-binding. I will return to this below. An *imam* has an entirely different function. He is the one who leads the prayers in the mosque, and his education is usually not as extensive as a mufti's. In some cases, however, depending on his education, an imam is also authorized to is-

---

[3] Al-Razi 1997: 101

[4] Ibn Qudama (*Al-Moghni*) (541 AH/1147 CE) was a well-known Hanbalite scholar on Islamic law.

sue theological opinions. A third type of cleric in Islam is the preacher. Like an imam, he is authorized to preach during Friday prayers. The sermons often concern issues in life and concrete problems (Kalaji 2006: 308; Shatannawi n.d.: I, 92).

The *fatwa* is the most important factor for medical and political issues. Karrafi describes the *fatwa* as follows: an opinion that an act is obligatory or permitted by God or not.[5] Thus, a *fatwa* is more general in import than a legal opinion; it is advice and not a court order. To obtain a court order or a binding judgment in a dispute one would need to go to a judge, a *kadi*, who has been appointed by the caliph. Islam thus distinguishes among authorities in Islam and also distinguishes those from authorities from or of the state. A *fatwa* does not have any legal status. Both the mufti and the *kadi* can follow the sources of Islam—the judge insofar as the caliph or the state has established that as law and sees to it that his verdict is implemented. After its initial period, Islam made a distinction between the religious organization and the state.

Requirements for the *Mujtahid*

Issuing *fatwas* is thus reserved for the *mujtahid*. Someone can be recognized as a *mujtahid* and thus be authorized to issue *fatwas* if he meets the following requirements (المجتهد): 1) knowledge of the Qur'an and the *Sunnah*; 2) knowledge of *usul al-fiqh*; 3) knowledge of *ijma* issues; 4) mastery of the Arabic language; 5) mastery of logic; 6) mastery of one or several other modern languages, such as English (Shabaar 2007: 135 -36; Hasabo Allah 1979: 82).

The Law Schools (*Madahib*)

Since the rise of Islam in the seventh century of the Christian or "common" calendar, Islam has spread over a large part of the world and has undergone various developments. The law schools arose around the eighth century. The most prominent

---

[5] Ahmad Ibn Idris Al-Maliki, originally from Egypt, was a well-known scholar in jurisprudence and in the foundations of *fiqh*, theology, exegesis, and other disciplines. He died 682 AH/1283 AD. See, e.g., Al Al-Dahabi 1978: I, 51; Ryad 2010: 186-87.

are the Hanafite, Malikite, Hanbalite, and Shafi'ite schools. The school that most Shi'ites follow, the Jafarite, is also recognized as a fifth law school (*madhab*); this law school goes back to the sixth imam, Jafar al-Sadiq, who taught Abu Hanifa. This school was also recognized by, for example, the faculty of law of the Sunni Al-Azhar University in Cairo (Musa 1953: 48).

The law schools (*madahib*) arose when the classical traditions about the prophet and his companions began to gain form. The plurality of texts made the practice of *fiqh* impossible, and a consensus had to be found on how to deal with the Qur'an and the traditions. Certain methods that had met with general acceptance therefore had to be used in *ijtihad*. One of the most important individuals to give impetus to the formation of such methods was al-Shafi'i, a student of both Malik ibn Anas and Abu Hanifa.[6] He held that the Qur'an had to be interpreted on the basis of the *hadiths*, i.e. the traditions about the Prophet and his companions, whereas it had been previously held that the *hadiths* had emerged from the Qur'an. It was through al-Shafi'i's agency that the first *madhab* as we know it arose. Although there had been various types of thinking and directions in thought before that, from that time on people were subject to the authority of an imam and one of the law schools.

At first, the various schools strove for recognition among believers and authorities. Over the course of time the schools lost a great deal of their regional character and their ideas became generalized. The schools slowly grew closer to one another. That four different schools on the interpretation of the religious laws within Sunni Islam exist alongside one another does not mean there are schisms. There is little hostility between the schools; rather, what can be observed is a cross-fertilization of ideas and debates that serve to refine the teachings of the different schools. It is thus also not unusual for an individual to follow a certain school but at the same time adopt the position of another school on a certain issue (Al-Askar 1998: 41-86). The chapters on Islamic ethics in this volume sometimes

---

[6] Malik ibn Anas and Abu Hanifa were the founders of the Malekite and the Hanafite schools, respectively.

point to the fact that the law schools can have differing positions on a certain issue.

Fiqh: Jurisprudence

The application of Islamic law is thus a matter for *fiqh* scholars. They describe *fiqh* as follows: the study of Islamic ethics and Islamic law that arrives at properly reasoned opinions on the basis of knowledge of the Qur'an, the *Sunnah,* and the rest of the tradition. Properly reasoned opinions entail proof from the Qur'an, the *hadiths,* and continuing discussions among *ulama.* For *fatwas,* a strong argument of course is a strong consensus (*ijma*) among the *ulama.* Unanimity is a sufficient argument (Al-Jasas 1993: 47-48; Hasabo Allah 1979: 95), but *fiqh* does differentiate between various forms of consensus:

> *Silent consensus.* In some cases the *fiqh* scholars are of one mind. If a case has not been discussed for some time, one can appeal to the silent consensus if it is clear that people are aware of the means of acting in question and tacitly agree (الاجماع السكوتى; Al-Zohaili 1998: 552)
> *Clear consensus.* In other matters the scholars who have looked at an issue have clearly stated their view. In that case one speaks of a clear consensus.[7]

For Islam, it is important that law scholars strive for consensus (*ijma*), for the collective nature of the decision guarantees the continuity of the developments of *shari'ah* and prevents cracks in the Islamic community as a whole.

In addition to consensus, one can also appeal, in the case of a *fatwa,* to customary law (*'urf*). A custom is what people are used to doing and saying and is allowed if it is not in conflict with unambiguous religious texts (the Qur'an and the *Sunnah*). A distinction is made between universal and local customs. A universal custom (عرف عام) is what people in all times and locales do, such as (at that time and still the case in many areas) paying to make use of a bath house. A local custom (عرف خاص)

---

[7] (الاجماع الصريح); every scholar or *mujtahid* clearly states his own opinion about the specific event; see Al-Jasas 1993: 33-34; Al-Zohaili 1998: 552.

is what is done as a matter of course in a certain area (Al-Razi 1997: 20, 153). If no clear statement can be found in the Qur'an or the tradition of the Prophet, a scholar can make a decision on the basis of custom.

In the event of new questions one cannot, of course, appeal to a consensus or customary law but only to core moments from the tradition and the objectives of Islamic ethics. Here the central insights of the Qur'an, the *hadiths*, and the authoritative views of scholars from the later developments of Islam are of great significance, but an assessment must be formed through rational argumentation (*ijtihad*) that will then be discussed in *ulama* circles. In this light, we can understand why the society of experts in the field of Islamic medical ethics has organized conferences. Medical ethicists still rely on the pronouncements that have emerged from any conferences that were organized.[8]

Ijtihad

Just as in all areas of life, the progress of medical knowledge and technical possibilities yields new questions about what is wise and morally and religiously permitted or forbidden. In the chapters on Islamic medical ethics in this volume we see that the contributors fall back on statements in the Qur'an and the *Sunnah* that deal with ethical questions or are of indirect application in the new issues that are the subject of reflection. They connect the fundamental ideas with knowledge of the current state of medical ethics and thus arrive at an assessment of which medical actions are permitted and which are not from the perspective of Islam. In *usul al-fiqh* (foundations of *fiqh*) scholars reflect on how one can arrive rationally at normative judgments in new issues that occur in current developments or suddenly in special cases: What obtains as a rational argument and accounting (*ijtihad*) (Shabaar 2007: 40; Hasabo Allah 1997: 68)?

---

[8] See especially the chapter by El-Gindi, assistant to the secretary-general of the Islamic Organization of Medical Sciences (IOMS). The findings of the conferences on and the speeches of the chairman of the IOMS at those conferences, Prof. Serour, carry a great deal of weight.

The Islamic community has to make sure that there are experts in every age who are able to practice *ijtihad* with authority, according to Imama Shafi, the founder of one of the law schools. The basic meaning of the word *ijtihad* is diligence: diligence to live, in all circumstances, as much as possible as people who live in the presence of God (Al-Sayyuti 1985: 22-23). Shafi expressly forbade acting without thinking (diligently) by doing what others do or tell one to do (Al-Sayyuti 1985: 22-23). *Ijtihad* is thus what in Christian theology is called hermeneutics: the process of understanding and explaining holy scripture and applying moral insights and rules in the changing contexts in which people live.

The fundamental source is the Qur'an, supplemented by the *Sunnah*; thorough knowledge of the classic *fiqh* texts in connection with the purposes of *shari'ah* is required, and thereafter knowledge of the field in which one has to act (Al-Ihyaa 2007: 107). One has to arrive at an assessment using rational analysis, reflection, and argumentation. The basis for accepting *ijtihad* can be found already in the *hadiths* of the Prophet. The emissary of God, Muhammad, sent a prophet named Mu'aadh ibn Jabal to Yemen with the task of acquainting them with service (*Islam*) to God. People converted to Islam there, but they brought their own life situations and customs with them. Islam began to spread in other directions as well and was confronted already from the start with new situations and moral issues. This required consultation with the Prophet and his companions and decisions on how to deal with new situations.

Ijtihad goes back to how the Prophet himself arrived in practice at further assessments. This task was given to the *mujtahid*, the *fiqh* scholars. The enormous developments in the world have raised new questions to which Muslims attempt to provide answers via the fundamental Islamic norms and values. Within Islam internationally, it is urgently necessary to bring the demands of modern life and religious values together and to help people live dignified and righteous lives in the world. New social developments and innovations in such divergent areas like social life, health, medical possibilities, and financial limitations, economic policy and legislation, ecological changes, and the shortage in raw materials—all these issues are topics of discussion not only in Western culture but in all countries and thus also among Muslims: What policy merits preference from a religious perspective?

The Objectives of Shari'ah

In our explanation of Islamic ethics and legislation, we have seen that the traditional patterns of acting are not enough in changing circumstances and in new situations. One must look within the sources of ethics for fundamental notions; in that connection I have pointed several times to the intentions of the commandments and the objectives of *shari'ah*.

The purpose of *shari'ah* is to protect and safeguard the interests of people and to provide a check against everything that can harm them. *Shari'ah* has been sent to serve the interests of people both in this world and in the next and to protect and look after them. I am convinced that all religions are never directed against people but are intended to serve people and help them in their lives. On the basis of this fundamental idea, the whole *shari'ah* legislation strives to deal with the following five matters.

1) *Protection of religion.* The authenticity of religion must be protected against high-handed changes and additions and against misuse by people who put their own interests or the interests of their people above those interests.

2) *Protection of people's souls* by seeing to it that they lead a dignified existence, with no lack of housing, food, drink, and clothing. The soul of the human being must be protected against what can ruin and disfigure it. All kinds of human rights flow from this fundamental idea of *shari'ah*: the right to protection of the right to live and to exist, the protection of the dignity of life, of human freedom of action, thought, opinion, and the right to housing.

3) *Protection of property.* Because everyone may and must be responsible for him- or herself, everyone must have the means to exist and to manage his or her own possessions him- or herself. *Shari'ah* condemns all forms of expropriation of another's property and all forms of aggrieving or deceiving others. The government should make this impossible and punish transgressors. Ulti-

mately, all possessions beyond what one needs for one-self are to be used in service to the community (Atayah 2001: 142-47).

4) *Protection of the mind of the human individual.* Human dignity, independence, and responsibility are central Islamic values. Humans depend on their cognitive abilities to achieve this. God judges the individual on the basis of his deeds and considerations. That is why it is forbidden to harm someone's mind. The purpose of *shari'ah* is to promote and preserve physical and mental health.

5) *Protection of marriage and offspring.* Shari'ah has extensive regulations for marriage, in particular for choosing a partner, the marriage contract, the nature of the relationship between spouses, the rights and duties of both spouses, and the care for and rights of children (Ibn Moahemed 2010: 70; Ryad 2010: 280-81; Atayah 2001: 146; Najar 2006: 146).

Conclusion

The above description of the classical view of the development of Islamic ethics and *fiqh* seems to be contradicted by the actions of radical and traditional Muslims. Indeed, there is a great distance between what people make of a religion and the heart of that religion. Hopefully, this chapter will contribute to showing what, in our view, is the classical and responsible view of ethics in Islam. A similar approach to the one described here in a somewhat broader way can be found in the chapters by the Islamic contributors to this volume.

The reality of the Muslims in the West requires a careful and effective *ijtihad*. This obtains for both reflection on and the articulation of faith, as well as for the commandments and morality. On the one hand, the old and unchangeable texts must be known and studied as well as, on the other, the peculiarities and details of specific situations. Each new question can be approached anew from the central objectives of *shari'ah*: true humanity, equality, mercy, and justice.

Bibliography

Abu Shohbah, Mohamed. (1985). *Difaa Ani Sunnah*. Cairo: Majma Al-Bohot Al-islamyyah.

Al-Askar, Umar Sulayman. (1998). *Al-Madgkhal Ila Dirasat Al-Madhahib Al-Fiqhya*. Beirut: Dar al-Nafa'is.

Atayah, Jamal al-din. (2001). *Nahw Tafiel Maqasid*. Damascus: Dar al-Fikr.

Al-Bardisi, Mohammed Zakarya. (1987). *Usul Al-Fiqh*. Mecca: Al-fa-yalya.

Brugman, J. (1985). *De zuilen van de Islam*. Amsterdam: Meulenhof.

Al-Dahabi, Al-Imam. (1978). *Tarikh al-Islam*. Part 1. Beirut: Dar al-Fikr.

Dermendhem, Emile. (1991). *Mohammed*. Kwadraat Monografie. Transl. Remko J.L. ter Laan. Utrecht: Kwadraat Monografie.

Douwes, Dick. (2003). *De islam in een notendop*. Amsterdam: Prometheus.

Al-Faozan, Abdo Allah Ibn salih Abdo Allh Ibn Sali. (2003). *Jam Al-Mahsol Fi Sharh Risalat Ibn Sadi Fi Al-Usul*. Riyadh: Dar Al-Moslim.

Hasabo Allah, Ali. (1997). *Usul Al-Tashri Al-islami*. Beirut: Dar Al-Fikr al-arabi.

Ibn Moahemed, Mohamed. (2010). *Al-Nadar Al-Maqasidi*. Alexandria: Dar al-Salam.

Ibn Hishaam. (n.d.). *Al-Sirah Al-Nawawiyah*. Vol. 1. Beirut: Dar Al Jil.

Ibn Qudama Al-Maqdisi, Imam Mawaffaq Al-Din Abdullah Ibn Ahmad. (n.d.). *Al-Moghni*. Vol. 7. Beirut: Dar Al-kutub Al-ilmyah.

Al-Ihyaa, Ijtihad Al-Moeaser Wa Istia. (2007). *Dat Al-Waye Bi Siyyaq*. Rabat: Al-Rabita Al-Mohamadyyah Lilulama al-Magrib.

Al-Isnanwi, Imam Jamal al-dien Abi Mohamed Ibn Al-Hasan. (1980). *Al-Tamhid Fi Takhrij Al-Furuh Ala Al-Usul*. Cairo: Moeasasat Al-Risalh.

Jaad Al-Haqq Ali-Jaad al-Haqq. (n.d.). *Buhuth wa Fatawa Islamiya fi Kadaya Mu`asira*. Part 3. Cairo: Al-Azhar University.

Jabaar, Said. (1981). *Alijtihad: Wa Al-Tajdid Fi Al-Fikr Al-Islami*. Cairo: Al-Mahad al-Alami Lilfikr Al-Islami.

Al-Jasas, Abu bakr. (1993). *Al-Idjma*. Sana'a: Dar al-Montagab al-Arabi.

Kalaji, Mohamed Rawas. (2006). *Mojam Lugaa Al-Foqha*. Beirut: Dar Al-Nafais.

Mellema, R.L. (1958). *Een interpretatie van de islam*. Amsterdam: Royal Tropical Institute.

Musa, Mohammed Yusuf. (1953). *Al-Madkhal li Diraset Al-Fiqh Al-Islami*. Cairo: Dar al-Fikr al-Arabi.

Najar, Mohamed Abdelmajid. (2006). *Maqasid Al-Sharia'h Bi Abaad Jadidah*. Beirut: Dar al-Gharb Al-Islami.

Philips, Abu Ameenah Bilal. (n.d.). *De Ontwikkeling van Fiqh: De Islamitische Wet*. Transl. Aboe Yoesoef. Helmond: Momtazah.

Al-Razi, Fakhr Al-Din Mohamed Ibn Omar Ibn Al-Hasan. (1997). *Al-Mahsul Fi' Ilm Usul Al-Fiqh*. 3rd ed. Beirut: Moasasat Al-Risalah.

Ryad, Mohammed. (2010). *Usul Al-Fatwa Wa Al-Kada Fi: Al-Fiqh al-Maliki*. Damascus: Najah al-Jadidah.

Al-Sayyuti, Jalalo Al-Din Abdel-Rahman. (1985a). *Al-Ijtihad, Wall-Rado Ala Men Akhlada Ila Al-Ard Wajahila anna Al-Ijtihad Fi koli Asr Fard*. Cairo: Moasasat Shabab Al-Jamiha.

——— (1985b). *Tadrieb Al-Rawi Fi Sharh Taqrin Al-Nawawi*. Cairo: Dar Al-ktab.

——— (n.d.). *Al-Itqan Fi Oeloemi Al-Koran*. Cairo: Dar Al-Torat.

Shabaar, Said. (2007). *Ijtihaad wa al-tajdid fi al-fikr al-islami*. Cairo: Al-Mahad Al-Alami lilfikr al- islami.

Shatannawi, Meryam. (n.d.). *Islam in beeld: Kunst en cultuur van Moslims wereldwijd*. Part 1. Amsterdam: SUN.

Von Glasenapp, Helmuth. (1980). *De Islam*. The Hague: Kruseman's Uitgeversmaatschappij.

Waardenburg, Jacques. (2000). *Islam: Normen, ideaal en werkelijkheid*. Houten: Fibula.

Al-Zarqani, Shaikh Mohamed Abd AlAdim. (2006). *Manahel Al-Irfaan Fi Oeloem Al-Koran*. Cairo: Dar Ibn Hazm.

Al-Zohaili, Wahbah. (1998). *Usul Al-Fiqh Al-Islami*. 2nd ed. Damascus: Dar al-Fikr.

CHAPTER III

Genetic Medicine

Facts and Moral Issues
from a Western Perspective

Martina C. Cornel

Introduction

This chapter will give an overview of ethical issues in medical genetics from 2000 to 2010, the decade after the publication of the draft sequence of the human genome. In this decade the price of genome technology dropped very quickly. Ethical principles central to genetic health care on the one hand and research on the other will be explained, as well as the recent shifts in attention from the right not to know to the duty to inform in health care, and from the autonomy of the individual to more collective values in large-scale genetic research.

Genetics in Health Care

The first form of genetic medicine I will discuss is *neonatal screening*. Some children with mental retardation, fair hair, and blue eyes have a metabolic condition called phenylketonuria (PKU). With a diet containing a very limited amount of proteins starting soon after birth, they will develop normally. Around 1970 several Western countries started newborn screening programs to identify children affected by PKU. All newborns were offered a test in which some blood was taken, usually from the heel, dried on a card, sent to a laboratory, and analyzed (currently) in high-throughput tandem mass spectrometers. One of every 10,000-20,000 infants will turn out to have PKU, and his health gain can be enormous if the diagnosis is made before the symptoms occur.

A form of genetic medicine where questions of (family members of) patients are investigated and discussed is called *genetic counseling*. I will give an example. A couple married and wanted to have a child. But the husband's brother had had a severe condition which caused his death at the age of ten, and the couple wanted to know if their future children were at risk of having this condition. They visited a genetics clinic where the diagnosis of the condition in the brother was confirmed, and the couple's status as potential carriers of this genetic condition was investigated. He turned out to be a carrier, but she was not, and so their children were not at risk. For an increasing number of genetic conditions, a genetic test can be done to establish a diagnosis and investigate carrier status.

If the couple appears to be a carrier *couple* for an autosomal recessive condition (i.e. both are carriers) and each of their children has a 25% risk of developing that condition, they may consider several *reproductive options*: accept the risk, choose not to have children, adopt, choose a different partner, use donor gametes (such as artificial insemination by a donor's sperm), prenatal diagnosis and selective termination of affected pregnancies, and pre-implantation genetic diagnosis (embryo selection).

Pregnant women who have no family history of a serious condition may also undergo testing during pregnancy: prenatal testing. If the test is performed in a low-risk population, however, we speak of *prenatal screening*, while in high-risk situations we use the term *prenatal diagnosis*. Couples may want to know if they are carriers before getting married or before getting pregnant. In some countries they can ask for *preconceptional carrier screening*, for instance in the Ashkenazi Jewish population in the Dor Yeshorim program. In this community, a severe neurodegenerative disorder of childhood, Tay Sachs, used to occur much more frequently some decades ago until matchmakers started screening before arranging marriages.

Some genetic conditions are diagnosed in adulthood, such as hereditary forms of cancer and cardiogenetic conditions. Parents, siblings, and children are at an increased risk if one person is diagnosed with such an autosomal dominant condition with reduced penetrance (*autosomal dominant* means that on average half of the first-degree relatives have inherited the mutation; *reduced penetrance* means that some of the persons with the mutation will not have any symptoms). Since treatment or preventive interventions are available for several of these conditions, family members may profit from early diagnosis. A *cascade screening* approach may be used to inform family members (systematically inviting all first-degree relatives to be tested or, if first-degree relatives are not available, second-degree relatives). Each of these applications of genetics in health care raises specific ethical and moral questions.

From Research to Health Care

The rate at which genetic data have become available in the last decade is enormous. Genomics promises to have major consequences for our health care, including diagnosis, treatment, and prevention, and medicine will become personalized. The scientific promise is overstated, however. The challenge for the next decade is to translate knowledge from bench to bedside in a responsible manner. A general moral framework of genetic testing for health purposes is given by the Additional Protocol to the Convention on Human Rights and Biomedicine concerning Genetic Testing for Health Purposes (Council of Europe 2008). The primacy of the interests and welfare of the individual human being over the sole interest of society or science, non-discrimination and appropriate test quality are important criteria mentioned in this convention, as are appropriate information, counseling, and consent.

In this chapter we will first discuss some ethical and moral issues involved in various *health care* practices. The examples mentioned in the first part of this chapter all referred to genetic health care. For many issues in health care, a professional policy has been developed that will serve as a professional standard for treatment in a country and will be followed by many hospitals. These standards may differ among countries and cultures. This chapter will presuppose a Western perspective. Physicians and other health care workers in general have to follow professional guidance. Western thought is a composite of ideas from Christianity, Humanism, Judaism, etc. In the last decade, however, explicit reference to religion as a basis for medical ethical reflection has become rare in Western professsional guidance. Professional debate is influenced by legal guidance on the one hand and evidence-based medicine on the other. Basic ethical principles implicit in genetic professional guidelines are individual autonomy, privacy, beneficence and non-maleficence.

The second part of the chapter will discuss some ethical issues in genetic *research* where other questions may also play a role, such as the balance between hopes and hypes, transparency, and questions on informed consent and whether or not to report relevant findings to study participants. Finally, ethical issues related to translation from research to practice will be discussed.

Screening and the Availability of Treatment

Doing good while not causing too much harm has been the central issue in genetic screening. "All screening programs do harm. Some do good as well and, of these, some do more good than harm at reasonable cost" (Raffle and Gray 2007). This quote from Sir Muir Gray, former programs' director at the UK National Screening Committee, clearly shows the ethical challenge of balancing the pros and cons of screening. Testing newborns implies causing some pain to them and a period of stress and uncertainty for their parents. If all newborns are tested, some may be referred to the hospital and will turn out not to have the disease, the so-called false positives. However carefully done, tests do sometimes fail. Those that are missed by the screening program, the so-called false negatives—judged not to be affected although they are—will be diagnosed much later on the basis of symptoms, and the child's condition may have deteriorated because of the later diagnosis. Insurance companies aim to avoid financial risk and may base their risk assessment on screening, and employers may do so well. Thus, screening at a later age might lead to the loss of insurance or employment.

Intuitively, one feels that early detection improves health outcomes. The side effects and harms of screening programs can, however, be greater than their advantages. More than four decades ago, J.M.G. Wilson and G. Jungner (1968) were commissioned by the World Health Organization to study the growing practice of screening and provide support for it with clear evidence and principles. The screening criteria that they formulated was to contribute to the evidence on the pros and cons and make sure that the quality of screening programs offered by public health authorities would be optimal. Wilson and Jungner formulated ten principles, including the point that the condition sought should be an important health problem for which there should be an accepted treatment and for which facilities for diagnosis and treatment should be available. As in the additional protocol, the interest and welfare of the person screened are thus central.

Right Not to Know and the Duty to Inform

The double helix structure of DNA was discovered in 1953 by James Watson and Francis Crick. The DNA molecule carries the genetic information of cells and individuals. Before cells divide, this information is duplicated, which is how this information is passed on from one cell to another and from one generation to another. After the discovery of the structure of DNA, the mutations in genes causing genetic diseases were gradually discovered and tests developed. For many genetic disorders, however, there was and is no treatment available. A classic example is Huntington's disease, a progressive neurodegenerative disorder. If a parent suffers from this disorder, each child has a 50% risk of inheriting the mutated gene that causes the disorder. Persons at risk might want to know if they are going to develop the disease, since this might influence family planning as well as allowing them to prepare for the future.

Despite the discovery of the Huntington gene and the development of a test, many choose not to be tested. The uptake of predictive testing varied between countries from 4-24% (Tibben 2007). Since there is no treatment available, the advantages of knowing the diagnosis are less clear than in the case of PKU. The World Medical Association recommends

> that this type of diagnosis for a predicted condition be performed only when a therapeutic or prophylactic remedy is available or when an estimate of the risk of transmission can assist parents in making reproductive decisions. (World Medical Association 1995)

Generally speaking, testing for Huntington's disease does not satisfy this criterion. Because the advantages of knowing that one has Huntington's disease are not very clear, the right not to know must be respected. But the knowledge of being a carrier of an autosomal dominant genetic condition may be important for individuals for future planning. Some may choose to have children or not, based on the information on carrier status (a valid reason for a diagnostic test according to WMA), whereas others may want to plan their future life or career.

In families, testing one person may provide information on another. For Huntington's disease, some have argued that the "right not to know" of one family member overrules the "right to know" of another. Should a treatment alter the likelihood of survival, then the "right not to know" becomes less obvious. Effective preventive measures increase the moral relevance of the *right to know* (de Wert 1998). Treatment is available for an increasing number of genetic conditions. Thus, the "duty to inform" family members is felt increasingly (de Wert 2005). The more the benefits outweigh the possible harm, the more individuals may have the *right to know* and physicians feel the *duty to inform*.

Genetic Counseling, Non-Directiveness, and Autonomy

Until the end of World War II and shortly thereafter, eugenics practices were associated with unethical acts such as discrimination against certain racial groups and attempts to improve the gene pool by, for instance, forced sterilization. The development of human genetics in the post-war era was strongly influenced by these atrocities. Respect for research subjects together with the principle of full consent would become a central feature of research ethics (Harper 2008: ch. 17). In genetic counseling the "non-directive" nature clearly differs from the coercive aspects of eugenics. Patients seeking genetic health care deserve support and respect for their feelings and decisions and support in overcoming the various medical and other problems that their particular genetic disorder poses (Harper 2008: ch. 17). As we will see in the extensive definition below, non-directiveness became the guiding principle for genetics counseling that promotes the autonomy or self-determination and personal control of the client (Biesecker 2001). Two different goals could be distinguished: (1) preventing birth defects and genetic disorders and (2) improved psychological well-being in client adaptation to a genetic condition or risk. In the decades after the Second World War, a shift from the first goal to the second was described (Biesecker 2001). The first may be a consequence of individual choices, but it should not be the goal as that might lead to the coercion of individuals. Especially when thinking of reproductive choices such as refraining from having children or prenatal diagnosis and selective termination of pregnancies, the distinction between both goals is crucial.

The definition of genetic counseling by the American Society of Human Genetics has been cited by many:

> Genetic counselling is a communication process that deals with the human problems associated with the occurrence or risk of occurrence of a genetic disorder in a family. This process involves an attempt by one or more appropriately trained persons to help the individual or family to: (1) comprehend the medical facts including the diagnosis, probable course of the disorder, and the available management, (2) appreciate the way heredity contributes to the disorder and the risk of recurrence in specified relatives, (3) understand the alternatives for dealing with the risk of recurrence, (4) choose a course of action which seems to them appropriate in view of their risk, their family goals, and their ethical and religious standards and act in accordance with that decision, and (5) to make the best possible adjustment to the disorder in an affected family member and/or to the risk of recurrence of that disorder.

Non-directiveness is a guiding principle for genetic counseling that promotes the autonomy or self-determination and personal control of the client (Biesecker 2001). At times, autonomy has been misunderstood as a goal of genetic counseling. There are different views on the goals of genetic counseling, which usually includes gaining information and assistance with decision making. Evaluation of genetic counseling has often been performed on the basis of reproductive plans or reproductive behavior, but, according to its goals, it should involve a measure of informed decision making. There may be cultural differences in the interpretation of this goal. An individual informed choice may be at odds with collective values. Decision making in couples or families challenges this principle of reproductive autonomy of parents because they live in families and communities with partly shared values.[1]

Research

The human genome sequence was published in 2000. At a press conference, the then president of the USA, Bill Clinton, together with the leaders of public and private research groups Francis Collins and Graig Venter, announced this milestone: "Without a doubt, this is the most important, most wondrous map ever produced by humankind" (The White House 2000). The human genome sequence was described in religious terms: "Today, we are learning the language in which God created life. We are gaining ever more awe for the complexity, the beauty, the wonder of God's most divine and sacred gift." After uncovering the sequence, the function of the genome was further studied in genomics research. Clinton voiced his great expectations:

> With this profound new knowledge, humankind is on the verge of gaining immense, new power to heal. Genome science will have a real impact on all our lives—and even more, on the lives of our children. It will revolutionize the diagnosis, prevention and treatment of most, if not all, human diseases.

Almost ten years later, the results of huge investments remain rather modest (Manolio 2009). Hundreds of genetic variants associated with common diseases have been recognized, but they explain only a small proportion of familial clustering. The value of genetic variants in disease prediction is widely debated. Only a few rare variants have a high predictive value.

When the sequence was published, a metaphor used by journalists and scientists was *the genetic blueprint for human beings*. This may suggest that DNA contains the instructions for

---

[1] This communal aspect is discussed as well in the chapters "Can Facts about Genetic Research Play a Role in Moral Reasoning?" by Ragab and Serour (4) and "Islamic Care Ethics between Law and Conscience" by Karagül (15) below.

the body on how to develop, how to stay alive, how to grow, etc. Nowadays the genetic determinism implied in the metaphor is not supported by most scientists, so a new metaphor has been suggested by Rehmann-Sutter (2010): *systems*. In complex molecular systems mutual influences exist. Genes alone are not sufficient for the complete description of developmental pathways. Rather than considering nature responsible for writing our book of life, individuals have a responsibility to know about their risk and possible precautions.

The Large Scale of Research

Before the year 2000 genetic research often looked into the causes of monogenetic diseases in specific families. As soon as the participants from these families gave informed consent, the study could be performed. For genome-wide association studies on common complex disorders to be feasible, however, large numbers of participants were needed. DNA is stored in biobanks, coded, or anonymized. The increase in interest in population-based genetic research has led to calls to rethink the paramount position of the individual in ethics (Knoppers and Chadwick 2005). The WHO's report on genetic databases states:

> The justification for a database is more likely to be grounded in communal value, and less on individual gain ... it leads to the question whether the individual can remain of paramount importance in this context. (World Health Organization 2003)

After the publication of the human genome, genomics research was moving from rare monogenic conditions to common complex disorders, such as cancer, depression, diabetes, and cardiovascular diseases. Common genetic variants that originated many generations ago were supposed to increase the risk of these disorders. The type of study needed would involve large numbers of participants: thousands or even more. With high-throughput technology, many potentially associated variants could be studied hypothesis-free in many participants. In the decade after 2000 a shift in emphasis took place from autonomy to the ethical principles of reciprocity, mutuality, solidarity, citizenry, and universality (Knoppers and Chadwick 2005). Collective values gained prominence. *Reciprocity* is the notion of exchange: recognition of the participant and his or her contribution to a study, for instance, by safeguarding data and options for research, as well as prior consultation of and communication with specific communities. *Solidarity* has entered the debate on the right to know or not to know, insurance, and human genetic databases. An important issue is if individuals have a responsibility to know their genetic makeup so that they can then make responsible decisions. Human genetic databases as an infrastructure to understand the cause of diseases and develop better treatment can only be built if many people donate their DNA and information as a gift, knowing that it is unlikely that they will profit from the research themselves. The principle of *citizenry* is central in public consultation and debate for shaping the governance of the future of research. *Universality* is emphasized on the basis of the characterization of the genome itself as a shared resource of humanity. If the genome is our common heritage, its benefits need to be shared.

From Research to Practice

Many invested in genomics research and may want to see the knowledge translated into practice, either to the benefit of individuals and populations or to receive profits from their investments. Translation from research into practice should include the careful evaluation of pros and cons, implementation studies, the development of professional guidelines and studies to evaluate the compliance with these guidelines (Khoury *et al.* 2007). While large investments have been made in genomic science, the number of studies on the responsible translation from research to practice is limited. Ethical, legal, and social aspects of new techniques in health care are easily overlooked.

Commercial companies have meanwhile implemented genetic testing offers directly to consumers at a higher pace. Risk profiles for common disorders, tests for single variants, ancestry profiles, and paternity tests are all available on the internet,[2] and have been frequently criticized. Recommendations on direct-to-consumer testing have been made by several profes-

---

[2] www.decodeme.com; www.23andme.com; www.dnacenter.com.

sional bodies, including ESHG (European Society of Human Genetics 2010):

1) clinical utility of a genetic test is to be an essential criterion for deciding to offer this test to a person or a group of persons;
2) laboratories providing genetic tests should comply with accepted quality standards, including those regarding laboratory personnel qualifications;
3) information about the purpose and appropriateness of testing should be given before the test is done;
4) genetic counseling appropriate to the type of test and disease should be offered, and for some tests psychosocial evaluation and follow-up should be available;
5) privacy and confidentiality of sensitive genetic information should be secured and the data safely guarded;
6) special measures should be taken to avoid inappropriate testing of minors and other persons legally declared incapable;
7) all claims regarding genetic tests should be transparent; advertising should be unbiased and marketing of genetic tests should be fair;
8) in biomedical research, health care, and marketing, respect should be given to relevant ethical principles, as well as international treaties and recommendations regarding genetic testing;
9) nationally approved guidelines considering all the above-mentioned aspects should be made and followed.

From Research to Legal Practice

In the last decade as well, the genetics of mental health has been studied and genes have been identified that are associated with neurological and psychiatric disorders. Genes involved in behavioral genetics, for instance, impulsive and antisocial behavior, were identified. These findings have expanded the debate on how scientific findings such as these could affect criminal law and if such information should mitigate criminal responsibility (Forzano *et al.* 2010). If our genes are responsible for our behavior, does that imply that individual humans are less responsible? The debate renewed prominence after a sentence rendered by an Italian appeal court in the case of a murderer with a genetic predisposition. The convicted man was an adult male affected by schizophrenia who was actively psychotic at the time of the crime, having discontinued his psychotropic medication against medical advice. He was found guilty at his trial and was given a reduced sentence (9 years) owing to his mental illness. His initial prison sentence was reduced from 9 to 8 years because he was found to be a carrier of a few genetic variants thought to be associated with a predisposition to aggression.

The scientific evidence for these variants is weak, but the sentence does raise the question of responsibility. Judges worldwide will take it into account if an individual had the required state of mind to be legally responsible for his acts. The phenotype (in this case: an active psychosis) may be a reason for a reduced sentence. At present, genetic variants associated with schizophrenia do not add to the evaluation of the phenotype itself. We should be judged on what we are, not on what we might be. Although genetic susceptibility information (as in the case for violence and aggression) had a probabilistic nature, this type of information often tends to be interpreted in a deterministic sense. It is crucial to avoid simplistic causal relations between genetic variants associated with violence or aggression and actual violent or aggressive behavior. Whereas some people showing more aggressive or violent behavior might have these particular gene variants, others will have the same variants despite being perfectly law-abiding citizens. It should be clear that there is no such thing as a "criminal gene." We should be aware that labeling individuals with a "criminal gene" also leads to identifying them as being a risk to society. The unsound application of scientific findings would thus lead to stigmatization. Indeed, debate is needed on the implications of the identification of genes associated with (somewhat increased) risks of impulsive and antisocial behavior. Research results do not support determinism, however. Genes and environmental factors act together in a complex system. People with the same gene variants, actually do not act in the same way; Genetic information is probabilistic and does not determine with certainty which diseases people will have or which character traits they will develop.

Bibliography

Biesecker, B.B. (2001). "Goals of Genetic Counselling." *Clinical Genetics* 60: 323-30.

Bombard, Y. *et al.* (2010). "Reconsidering Reproductive Benefit through Newborn Screening: A Systematic Review of Guidelines on Preconception, Prenatal and Newborn Screening." *Eur J Hum Genet.* 18: 751-60.

Council of Europe. (2008). *Additional Protocol to the Convention on Human Rights and Biomedicine, concerning Genetic Testing for Health Purposes.* http://conventions.coe.int/Treaty/EN/Treaties/Html/ 203. htm.

European Society of Human Genetics. (2010). "Statement of the ESHG on Direct-to-Consumer Genetic Testing for Health-Related Purposes." *European Journal of Human Genetics* 18: 1271-73.

Forzano, F. *et al.* (2010). "Italian Appeal Court: A Genetic Predisposition to Commit Murder?" *European Journal of Human Genetics* 18: 519-21.

Grosse, S.D. *et al.* (2010). "Population Screening for Genetic Disorders in the 21st century: Evidence, Economics, and Ethics." *Public Health Genomics* 13: 106-15.

Harper, P. (2008). A *Short History of Medical Genetics.* Oxford: Oxford University Press.

Jong, A. de *et al.* (2010). "Non-Invasive Prenatal Testing: Ethical Issues Explored." *European Journal of Human Genetics* 18: 272-77.

Khoury, M.J. *et al.* (2007). "The Continuum of Translation Research in Genomic Medicine: How Can We Accelerate the Appropriate Integration of Human Genome Discoveries into Health Care and Disease Prevention?" *Genetics in Medicine* 9: 665-74.

Knoppers, B.M., and R. Chadwick. (2005). "Human Genetic Research: Emerging Trends in Ethics." *Nature Reviews Genetics* 6: 75-79.

Manolio, T.A. *et al.* (2009). "Finding the Missing Heritability of Complex Diseases." *Nature* 461: 747-53.

Pfleiderer, G., G. Brahier, and K. Lindpaintner. (2010). *GenEthics and Religion.* Basel: Karger.

Raffle, A.E., and J.A.M. Gray. (2007). *Screening: Evidence and Practice.* Oxford: Oxford University Press.

Ross, L.F. (2010). "Carrier Detection in Childhood: A Need for Policy Reform." *Genome Medicine* 2: 25.

(2006). "Screening for Conditions that Do Not Meet the Wilson and Jungner Criteria: The Case of Duchenne Muscular Dystrophy." *American Journal of Medical Genetics A.* 140: 914-22.

Tibben, A (2007). "Predictive Testing for Huntington's Disease." *Brain Research Bulletin* 72: 165-71.

Wert, G. de. (2005). "Cascade Screening: Whose Information is It Anyway?" *European Journal of Human Genetics* 13: 397-98.

(1998). "Ethics of Predictive DNA-Testing for Hereditary Breast and Ovarian Cancer." *Patient Education and Counseling* 35: 43-52.

Wilson, J.M.G., and G. Jungner. (1968). "Principles and Practice of Screening for Disease." *Public Health Papers*, No. 34. Geneva: World Health Organization. http://whqlibdoc.who.int/php/WHO PHP 34.pdf.

White House, The. (2000). Remarks Made by the President, Prime Minister Tony Blair of England (via satellite), Dr. Francis Collins, Director of the National Human Genome Research Institute, and Dr. Craig Venter, President and Chief Scientific Officer, Celera Genomics Corporation, on the Completion of the First Survey of the Entire Human Genome Project. www.genome.gov/10001356.

World Health Organization. (2003). "Genetic Databases: Assessing the Benefits and the Impact on Human and Patient Rights." Geneva: World Health Organization.

"World Medical Association Proposal on Predictive Medicine." (1995). *Bulletin of Medical Ethics* (November): 5-6.

CHAPTER IV

Can Facts about Genetic Research Play a Role in Moral Reasoning?

Muslim Perspectives

Ahmed Ragaa A. Ragab and Gamal Serour

Introduction

The rapid progress of genetic research and technology has led to new hope in the treatment of some genetic conditions and diseases, but these developments have also raised ethical and moral concerns in different societies. In this chapter we will look at several methods of genetic research and testing, their positive consequences, and the problems they raise. We will show how Muslim medical specialists deal with these problems, with their religious sources as their point of departure while taking the results of science seriously, and weighing the pros and cons of various methods of testing and treatments. In this introduction we will look at the Qur'an and the *hadiths* (*Sunnah*) as the foundational sources of Islam. Then, in the first section, we will discuss the idea that the characteristics of each person are genetically determined and raise the question of the freedom of choice. In the second section of this chapter we will explore genetic testing and population research.

Islamic moral codes are derived from *shari'ah*, which now obtains as a general law for humankind since its revelation by Allah to the Prophet Muhammad. *Shari'ah* regulates all aspects of human behavior; it is a comprehensive system of rules and regulations that practically covers all aspects of individual or collective human affairs, with the ultimate objective of assuring human welfare in this world and in the hereafter (Abdel-Ati 1975).

There are primary and secondary sources of *shari'ah*. The former are (in order of importance): the Qur'an, the very word of Allah, and the authentic traditions and sayings (*Sunnah*) of the Prophet. For Muslims, *Sunnah* is a form of revelation given to the Prophet, but not verbatim, as is the case with the Qur'an. As such, the authentic *Sunnah* is the second primary source of Islamic teachings, after the Qur'an. It plays an important role in defining, explaining, and elaborating on the Qur'an. Other primary sources are the consensus of Islamic scholars and analogical argumentation, i.e. intelligent reasoning in cases not dealt with in the Qur'an and the *Sunnah* from rulings in similar or equivalent cases in the past (Abdel-Ati 1975). *Fiqh*, Islamic jurisprudence, has various options, especially in new circumstances — as discussed in the chapter by Marzouk Aulad Abdellah in this volume.

Like other major religions and spiritual worldviews, Islam has been and is faced with difficult ethical questions and has had and has to formulate solutions derived from its sources. The most central question raised by the discovery of genes and how they work is whether moral judgments make sense in cases in which genetic research shows that some forms of morally objectionable behavior are caused by genetic factors without any volitional component. If there is complete genetic determinism, no one can be blamed or praised for what they do, since their behavior is determined. Could violence or crime be punished?

In general, there is no conflict between science and Islam: research on human subjects is acceptable in Islam. Therefore, Muslims will look carefully at the question whether scientific research can explain all human conduct concisely and uniquely on the basis of causal genetic factors, with the result that humans cannot be held morally responsible for their conduct. Genetic determinism and the Islamic view of moral responsibility cannot both be true. Therefore we will deal with this subject first.

Genetic Research and Morality

The human genome project is possibly the most important human achievement in the field of genetic research. The genetic codes are basic for the entirety of humankind's existence; this information is increasing in importance and is already widely used (Bendell 2001; Hawly and Mori 1999; Elmer-Dewitt 1994).

Although the term "genetics" first appeared in 1909, Sir Francis Galton (1822-1911) was the first to study heredity and human behavior systematically. Since then, a substantial body of knowledge has been discovered in the field (Manage and Manage 1999; Elmert-Dewitt 1994; Singer 1985). For instance, researchers in the field of behavioral genetics claim to have found a genetic basis for numerous forms of physical behaviors, such as violence and aggression. The quickly growing body of scientific research on the relation between genes and behavior will contribute to the resurgence of the belief that genetics is not only a real factor in human potencies but fully determines behavior (genetic determinism) (Clark and Grunstein; 2000).

The Nature versus Nurture Debate

The search for "behavioral" genes is the subject of constant debate. The issue whether heredity or environment plays a major role in determining or shaping an individual's behavior has been dealt with in many studies. It is known as the nature versus nurture debate. Some scientists think that people behave as they do according to their genetic predispositions. This is known as the Nature Theory of Human Behavior. Scientists have known for years that traits such as eye and hair color are determined by specific genes encoded in each human cell. The Nature Theory stipulates that intelligence, personality, aggression, and sexual orientation are also encoded in our genes (Reiss and Straughen 1966). Others believe that people think and behave in certain ways because they are taught to do so. This is known as the Nurture Theory of Human Behavior (Bouchard 1998).

Islam acknowledges the role of heredity in shaping human characteristics; there are many examples from the sayings of the Prophet Muhammad to support this argument. Islamic teaching acknowledges the role of inheritance as a contributing factor in human characteristics. In addition, it does not deny other factors such as upbringing and the surrounding environment as important contributing factors. Over the last decades, the nature versus nurture debate has concluded that both influence the development of human behavior. In the 1960s, researchers from both sides began to study the interaction of genes and environment (Bouchard 1998). The quickly growing understanding of the human genome has recently made it clear that both sides are partly right. Nature endows us with inborn abilities and traits; nurture takes these genetic tendencies and molds them as we learn and mature (Bouchard 1998).

The Role of the Spirit

Surprisingly, there are fewer human genes than anyone predicted. This clearly shows that there is something other than the number of genes that make us human. Muslim scholars believe that this other component is the spirit that has been given to us by Allah (Surah El-Esraa (17):85). For instance, all cells—skin cells, brains cells or heart cells—inherit exactly the same set of genes because all cells originate from one single zygote (Ahmed 2000; Hawly and Mori 1999; Reik and Surnai 1997). It is safe to assume that the spirit is the manual that tells genes when to become active and to carry out their proper functions.

Muslim Scholars and Genetic Discoveries

Muslim scholars are at the forefront of those giving their views on scientific discoveries, especially those that lead to ethical conflicts. This opens the door for Muslims to benefit from these discoveries since religious opinions play an important role in the lives of Muslims. In this section we will give some examples of such discoveries and the opinions of religious leaders.

Genetic Engineering and Gene Therapy

Genetic engineering and gene therapy have been discussed widely among Muslim scholars. Since Islam enjoins the alleviation of pain and the healing of disorders, there are no serious objections to therapeutic procedures applied for prevention, delaying the onset of a disease, or carrying out appropriate care for genetic disorders (El-Hazmi 2004). Hathout (2006) argued that genetic engineering that involves the introduction of a gene of one species to another is not permissible except to cure illness and alleviate suffering. Non-therapeutic manipulations are controversial, and the majority of scholars are cautious regarding its implications on the societal and global level (Bayaumi and Ali 2001). Gad El-Hak (1992) argued that human gene therapy should be restricted exclusively to therapeutic applications. Somatic cell gene therapy is encouraged since it involves remedying and alleviating human suffering. But enhancement genetic engineering or eugenic genetic engineering will have unforeseeable consequences and thus bring about changes in God's creation that may lead to imbalance in the universe as a whole and should be prohibited. Gene therapy to manipulate hereditary traits such as stature, beauty, or intelligence would be examples of manipulation that might cause imbalances in human life (Serour 2001). In relation to stem cell research, Hathout (2006) and many other scholars are of the opinion that stem cell research on preimplantation embryos may be justified if the aim is to save actual patients who are suffering from serious illnesses on the basis of the juridical rule that it is justified to choose the lesser of two evils. Research and use of stem cells taken from adults are accepted by the vast majority of Muslim scholars.

Preimplantation Genetic Diagnosis (PGD)

Islam ascribes great importance to the prevention of congenital abnormalities. Seeking to protect the well-being of children, couples are advised to choose their partners with great care. The Prophet said: "Select your spouse carefully in your offspring's interests because lineage is a crucial issue." Islam has also determined the rights of the fetus; the mother is not to harm or expose the fetus to harm. Currently, a portion of the embryo can now be removed and analyzed for a specific gene defect (McLaren 1999; WHO 1992). Embryo transfers after a PGD are done successfully (Grifo *et al.* 1998). Islamic scholars differentiate between a PGD for medical purposes, which is currently a routine practice offered to high-risk parents to help them have healthy children, and the controversial preimplantation genetic manipulation that aims at enhancement. As a result of PGDs, gender selection for either medical or social purposes has been debated and there are some conflicting views. While the vast majority of Islamic scholars approve of gender selection for therapeutic purposes or, in selected cases, for social reasons if there is a need for a fetus of a specific gender (Serour 2001), a minority of scholars approve of gender selection for social reasons without any restrictions.

Cloning

In 1997, the world was surprised when I. Wilmut and his colleagues produced a lamb by transferring the nucleus of an adult mammary cell from a sheep into an emptied egg cell and implanting it (Wilmut *et al.* 1997). This largely unanticipated development demonstrates that asexual reproduction of mammals can be done; over time it might be possible for humans as well.

In relation to cloning a human being, we have to distinguish between reproductive cloning aimed at the birth of identical individuals and non-reproductive cloning limited to the *in vitro* phase. Human reproductive cloning has been completely banned by almost all organizations. In the same vein, Hathout (2006) argued that cloning is outside the bounds of religious permissibility if used for reproduction. Its use for purely research purposes is permissible during the stages in which the body systems have not been formed (Hathout 2006).

Assisted Reproductive Techniques

Although adoption is not allowed in Islam, there are many verses in the Qur'an that indicate that sponsoring orphans is encouraged and rewarded. In this regard, treating infertility and assisted reproductive techniques are welcomed and encouraged by Muslim religious leaders. From early on, scholars have supported assisted reproductive techniques using different modalities, provided that there is no third party involvement like surrogacy, egg or semen donation, and the technique should be carried out within a valid marriage contract and not with a divorced wife or a widow (Gad El Hak 1992).

Genetic Counseling

Ethical and moral decision-making frameworks are valuable tools that can assist genetic counselors in addressing ethical problems. But the tools should be sensitive to human needs, responsive to contextual considerations, and should emphasize the uniqueness of each situation (Williams and Donahue 2004; Lea *et al.* 2005). In this regard, the following ethical principles, which are in agreement with Islamic teaching, should be considered: autonomy, beneficence, and justice.

Autonomy

Lea *et al.* (2005) argued that the duty to respect the other's autonomy is paramount in virtually all ethical situations. Informed consent, one application of autonomy, includes discussion of the purposes, potential benefits, risks, and limitations of a specific genetic test. Autonomy mandates that decisions be voluntary and free from coercion (Lea *et al.* 2005). The decision to have or not to have a genetic test is widely believed to be a choice persons should make based on their own values and preferences (Lea *et al.* 2005; Grady 1999).

Beneficence and Non-Maleficence

An assessment of risks and benefits is reflected in the principles of beneficence (to do good) and of non-maleficence (to do no harm). These principles apply to the decision to have a test that will reveal genetic information about oneself or one's offspring (Lea *et al.* 2005).

Justice

Justice is the assurance that all people will receive fair and equal treatment (Serour 2000; 1994). In genetic testing, the key elements of justice are equitable access to genetic services to all socioeconomic, ethnic, and geographical groups, and the allocation of scarce resources (Lea *et al.* 2005). Because genetic discrimination and unequal access to genetic services are likely to increase with advances in genetics, the efforts of genetic counselors to adhere to the principle of justice or equity cannot be successful without government and public support, as well as support from researchers and colleagues from health care. Although justice is a valued ethical principle, it is weakened by the absence of universal access to health care in the world, especially in the developing and less developed poor countries.

Ethical and Moral Problems in Genetic Counseling

Ethical problems arise not only from the current state of knowledge about genetic risk factors and the usefulness of genetic tests but also from conflicts that can arise when the needs of the client are in conflict with the interests of others within the family or society (Lea *et al.* 205). In contrast to other medical screening tests, genetic testing in prenatal clients is focused on individual reproductive decision making rather than management of clinical disease (Lea et al. 2005). Genetic counseling might result in difficult choices, including abortion, fetal sex selection, and sterilization.

Families affected by genetic disorders have educational, social, medical, and psychological needs that require attention. Within this context, many ethical dilemmas arise, like the probability of carrying an affected child full term, the choice for abortion, and the right of a couple to have a child regardless of the impact on the offspring. Concerns about the possibility of predicting future health risks for the child need answers (Evans et al. 2004; Lea et al. 2005; WHO 1985).

Genetic Tests Are Probabilistic and Do Not Predict Everything

Part of the problem is that, on the one hand, genetic testing is not conclusive and, on the other, can reveal facts that are beyond the intentions of the tests. Some genetic tests do not identify all the possible genetic mutations that can cause a particular condition; some have only limited predictive value, which can lead to uncertainties for patients and clinicians (Burke 2004). For instance, the cause of birth defects can be determined in only approximately 40% of affected children (Evans et al. 2004). In addition, because some genetic tests are screening tests, some will generate false-positive and false-negative results (Lea et al. 2005). This means that a woman who is screened negatively may have a false-negative result and have a baby affected by a genetic disease (Lea et al. 2005). In addition, a genetic test can only indicate susceptibility to the disease with no certainty of the illness developing. Despite a great deal of research, genetic susceptibility to complex diseases like heart disease, cancer, and obesity has proven difficult to identify, with many poorly reproducible results. Except in a small percentage of cases, genes are poor predictors of future health (Holtzman and Marteau 2000). These issues raise real ethical concerns for a counselor. Many clients need help in understanding the meaning of statistical probability.

The uncertainties in genetic testing lead to problems in counseling and in the choices of the tests that are to be done in particular cases. Tests can reveal conditions that cannot be treated at present (Lea et al. 2005). Therefore, one ethical dilemma that arises is if a newborn should be tested for disorders that cannot be treated at this stage (Lea *et al.* 2005). During the process of genetic testing, there will be other findings like fetal sex (male or female) that might put the counselor in an ethical dilemma if the process was not related to X-linked disorders. The American Society for Reproductive Medicine endorses the use of Prenatal Genetic Diagnosis (PGD) for sex selection to avoid passing on an X-linked disease but discourages use for family planning as "inappropriate use and allocation of medical resources."

The examples of moral dilemmas so far are medical complications. The test results can also have social implications. One example is if the child turns out to have another father: What should the counselor do in this regard? One of the most serious ethical concerns is that it would become possible through extensive genome analysis to gather information on individual sequence variation and unveil someone's predisposition for certain diseases. This would represent a risk of intruding on individual privacy if the genetic information is not scrupulously kept confidential. For instance, there is a risk of discrimination if a third party (insurance companies, employers) has access to this information (Kaplan 2002). Old, outdated information might adversely affect the interests of individuals because medical information always changes over time, leading to revisions in diagnosis, refinements in treatment, improved carrier testing, or prenatal diagnosis (Evans *et al.* 2004).

Costs

A major ethical problem is that overconcentration on research on genes and their health implications could lead to neglect of the effects on human health of other factors, such as the physical, social, and economic environments in which people live (UN 2001; NHMRC 1992). The allocation of resources is a major problem, especially in less developed and developing countries. It is clear that genetic testing has the potential to improve health, but it becomes questionable when it is provided to an entire population that needs many resources (NHMRC 1992). It seems that the genetic approach diverts limited resources (UN 2001). A major ethical problem is the tendency to ignore the underlying socioeconomic or environmental causes of disease in favor of a genetic approach to disease prevention. This can result in using more and more advanced technology—and consequently use limited resources—to study trivial issues more and more while the major population causes of widespread diseases are ignored (UN 2001). Poverty is responsible for most deaths worldwide (Parkin 2001). A poor population is more likely than those with higher incomes to live near polluted areas. In addition, poorer groups/countries are explicitly targeted by those marketing unhealthy products, which in turn leads to more health problems, including genetic diseases.

Discussion and Conclusion

Moral codes among Muslims stem from the Islamic *shari'ah*, which is a comprehensive system of rules and regulations that practically covers all aspects of individual or collective human affairs. *Shari'ah* is not fixed except in the case of worship rituals, basic codes of morality, and some parts of legislation, allowing latitude to adapt to new situations in different times and places. This explains why Islamic teachings can accommodate new scientific discoveries.

Along with other major religions and traditions, Islam has been faced with difficult bioethical questions and has to formulate answers derived from its sources. A few of the new important questions that have been discussed in this chapter are as follows. If genetic research proves that morally objectionable behavior is caused entirely by genetic factors without any meaningful volitional component, what will our moral judgment be? We have argued that genetic material does not cause behavior or most illnesses in such a deterministic way. It indicates a predisposition but seldom a necessity. Due to the comprehensiveness and flexibility of *shari'ah*, Muslim scholars are always at the forefront of those giving their opinions/*fatwas* on new scientific discoveries, especially those that create moral conflicts. *Fatwas* on cloning, gene therapy, and genetic engineering were given in due course after deliberation. Although there are some differences and even some conflicting views and different interprettations, this fact should not undermine these *fatwas*, for there is nothing in Islam that forces anyone to follow a certain school or scholar or specific interpretation. The glory of Islam is that its rulings can be changed to fit different places and different times. Rules in the sense of *fatwas* are not fixed and can be changed to serve the interests (*masaleh*) of the people. Within this context, discoveries in behavioral genetics should not be viewed as irrefutable until there has been substantial scientific evidence. If genetic research proved, with irrefutable evidence, that certain behaviors are imprinted in our genes, Muslim scholars will deliberate on the issue and present the rule that will take into consideration the teachings of Islam, the interests of the people, and the welfare of the community.

Bibliography

Abdel Ati, H. (1975). *Islam in Focus*. American Trust Publications. Kuwait: Mogahwi Press.

Ahmed, H. K. (2000). "New Developments in Biotechnology: An Islamic View." *Splice* V/1 (November/December): 7.

Baherlum, H. (1997). *Human Cloning: Islamic Perspective*. Kuwait: Maarafie Foundation Publications.

Bayaumi, A., and K. Ali. (2001). *Gene Therapy: The State of Art*. Rabat: ISESCO Publications.

Bendall, K. (2001). "Genes, the Genome and Disease." *New Scientist* 169, Special Section: 1.

Bouchard, T. (1998). "Genetic and Environmental Influence on Adult Intelligence and Special Mental Ability." *Human Biology* 70: 281-96.

Burke, W. (2004). "Genetic Testing." In: A.E. Gutmacher, F.S. Collins, and J.M. Drazen (eds.). *Genomic Medicine*. Baltimore: Johns Hopkins University Press. Pp. 14-27.

Clark, W., and M. Grunstein. (2000). "Are we Hardwired? The Role of Genes in Human Behaviour." *BioMedNet* 85 (1 September): 86-88.

Eldadah, Z., J. Grifo, and H. Dietz. (1995). "Marfan Syndrome as a Paradigm for Transcription-Targeted Pre-Implantation Diagnosis of Heterozygous Mutations." *Nature Medicine* 1: 798-803.

El-Hazmi, M. (2004). "Ethics of Genetic Counseling—Basic Concepts and Relevance to Islamic Communities." In: *Annals of Saudi Medicine* 24/2 (March/April): 84-92

Elmert-Dewitt, P. (1994). "The Genetic Revolution." *Times* 3 (17 January). http://www.time.com/time/magazine/article/0,9171,979980,00.html

Evans, M. *et al.* (2004). "Relational Ethics and Genetic Counseling." *Nurse Ethics* 11: 459-71.

Gad El-Hak, A. (1992): "Islam a Religion of Ethics." In: G. I. Serour (ed.). *Proceedings of the First International Conference on Bioethics in Human Reproduction in Research in the Muslim World, 10-13 Dec. 1991.* Cairo: IICPSR. Pp. 37-39.

Grifo, J. *et al.* (1998). "Successful Outcome with Day 4 Embryo Transfer after Pre-implantation Diagnosis for Genetically Transmitted Diseases." *Human Reproduction* XIII: 1656-59.

Hathout, H. (2006). "An Islamic Perspective on Human Genetic and Reproductive Technologies." *Eastern Mediterranean Health Journal* 2 (Supplement): 22-28.

Hawley, R. and C. Mori. (1999). *The Human Genome: A User's Guide.* San Diego: Academic Press.

Holtzman, N.A., and T.M. Marteau. (2000). "Will Genetics Revolutionize Medicine?" *New England Journal of Medicine* 343: 141-44.

Kaplan, J. (2002). "Genomics and Medicine: Hopes and Challenges." *Nature* IX: 658-61.

Lea, D., J. Williams, and M. Donahue. (2005). "Ethical Issues in Genetic Testing." *Journal of Midwifery and Women's Health* 50: 234-40.

Manage, E., and A. Manage. (1999). *Human Genetics.* 2nd ed. Sunderland: Sinauer Associates, Inc.

McLaren, A. (1989). *Can We Diagnose Genetic Disease in Pre-embryos? Report on the Use of Human Fetal Embryonic and Pre-embryonic Material for Diagnostic, Therapeutic, Scientific, Industrial and Commercial Purposes.* Strasbourg: Council of Europe. Pp. 1-6.

National Health and Medical Research Council. (1992). *Ethical Aspects of Human Genetic Testing: An Information Paper.* Issued by NHMRC in accordance with the National Health and Medical Research Act. Act 225. Canberra: Office of Legislative Drafting and Publishing, Attorney-General's Department.

Parkin, D.M. (2001). "Chronic Disease and Disability of the Poor: Tackling the Challenge." *Development* 44: 59-65.

Reik, W., and A. Surani. (1997). *Genomic Imprinting.* Oxford: Oxford University Press.

Reis, M., and R. Straughen. (1996). *Improving Nature? The Science and Ethics of Genetics of Engineering.* Cambridge: Cambridge University Press.

Serour, G. (2001): *Ethical Implications of Human Embryo Research.* Rabat: ISESCO Publications in Arabic and English.

(1994). "Religious Approaches to Bioethics." Paper Presented at the 2nd World Congress of Bioethics, Buenos Aires, Argentina, 24-26 October.

Serour, G., and A. Omran. (1992). "Ethical Guidelines." In: *Proceedings of the First International Conference on Bioethics in Human Reproduction in Research in the Muslim World, 10-13 Dec. 1999.* Cairo: IICPSR. Pp. 1-126.

Singer, S. (1985). *Human Genetics: An Introduction to the Principles of Heredity.* New York: W. H. Freeman and Co.

United Nations. (2001). *Health and Sustainable Development.* New York: UN Economic and Social Council Report E/CN. 1712001/PC/6 2 March.

World Health Organization (1992). *Recent Advances in Medically Assisted Conception: Report of a WHO Scientific Group.* WHO Technical Report Series 820. Geneva: WHO.

World Health Organization Advisory Group (1985). *Community Approaches to the Control of Hereditary Diseases.* Geneva: WHO.

Wilmut, I. *et al.* (1997). "Viable Offspring Derived from Fetal and Adult Mammalian Cells." *Nature* 385 (27 February): 810-13.

CHAPTER V

Genetic Testing and Counseling in the Case of Consanguinity[1]

Facts, Ethical and Legal Consequences

Pascal Borry, Marieke Teeuw,
and Martina C. Cornel

Introduction

The offspring of consanguineous couples have an increased risk of congenital anomalies: first-cousin unions (third-degree relatives) are some 2-3% above the background risk of 2-3% (Hamamy *et al.* 2011). This increase in risk is mainly caused by autosomal recessive disorders and is most evident in rare diseases, which makes the diagnostic process for health care providers often challenging.

A consanguineous marriage is usually defined as a marriage (or "union") between second cousins (fifth-degree relatives) or spouses related more closely. In some regions of Africa and Asia this type of marriage is common (Bittles 1994) but is now uncommon in Western societies and often evokes negative reactions (Modell and Darr 2002). Due to recent migration, consanguinity is appearing more often in Western societies.

Genetic counseling should be aimed at informing couples about their risks and offering them possible genetic testing. With the rapid development of genetic testing options, such as whole-genome sequencing, the possibilities for detecting causative genes for disorders in children of consanguineous marriages will gradually increase.

The ethical principles of genetic counseling were discussed in the third chapter in this volume. Given the controversial status of consanguinity in the West, it seems even more important

---

[1] This chapter is partly based on P. Borry *et al.*, 2009.

to apply ethical principles like respect for autonomy, privacy, and confidentiality when offering genetic testing to consanguineous couples. Despite the perceived importance of these principles among genetic counselors, the increased reproductive risk has also been advanced as a reason to discourage or legally ban consanguineous marriage on medical grounds. There are various arguments, however, that can be advanced to claim that this approach is inconsistent with ethical principles regarding human rights and genetic counseling.

This chapter will provide an introduction into the tradition of consanguinity and its consequences for the birth prevalence of infants with severe recessive disorders as well as an overview of some societal considerations and controversies in relation to consanguinity and consanguineous marriages. First, current knowledge about increased risk to offspring will be presented. We will discuss the ethical principles that have been advanced in the context of genetic counseling and testing and support their use in the context of counseling of consanguineous couples. Next, we will debate the question if the increased risk constitutes a reason for legislation in this domain.

Consanguinity: Facts and Figures

The children of consanguineous couples represent a considerable group, since an estimated 10.4% of all people worldwide are part of a consanguineous union or have consanguineous parents (Bittles and Black 2010). This frequency, however, is very unevenly distributed between countries. In regions such as North and sub-Sahara Africa, the Middle East, and Southeast Asia, the current percentage of consanguineous marriages is high and may even exceed 50%, while most of the marriages in North America, Europe, and Australia are not consanguineous (<1%) (see www.consang.net). In these Western countries, however, there are certain groups that show higher rates of consanguinity. In particular, this can be explained by migration from areas where the rate of consanguinity is high. The available evidence from western Europe, North America, and Australia suggests that the prevalence of consanguineous marriages is decreasing in some countries yet increasing in some migrant groups in these countries (Bittles and Black 2010; Hamamy *et al.* 2011).

Various reasons have been suggested for consanguineous marriages, including the wish to find a partner from within the community and the desire to maintain community traditions. This includes the belief that marriage within the family is the most desirable and reliable marital option (Bittles 2001; Hussain 1999; Hussain and Bittles 1998). Family ties are strengthened in this way, and family members have a strong obligation to assist one another when in need. Also, this custom is viewed as a way for a woman to maintain her status, as opposed to marrying into another family, which implies more uncertainty (Modell and Darr 2002). Contrary to what is often believed, the matching of the present-day distribution pattern of consanguineous marriage to the distribution of Islamic faith is not caused by prescriptions of the Islamic religion. First-cousin marriages are permitted in Judaism, Protestantism, and Buddhism (Bittles and Black 2010). Although first-cousin marriage is subject to approval in the Roman Catholic Church, second-cousin marriage is freely permitted. Marriage between first cousins is proscribed by the Greek and Russian Orthodox Churches.

Prejudices and Misunderstandings concerning Consanguinity

In western societies this type of marriage has been considered controversial, in particular since the 19th century when concerns were raised about the harmful effects on the offspring of such marriages and quickly became widespread among members of the medical and legal professions. Charles Darwin was married to his first cousin. His son George and later epidemiological studies have shown that the increase in risk is only marginal (Bittles and Black 2010).

A common misunderstanding, furthermore, is that cousin marriages (between third-degree relatives) were forbidden in the past in the Netherlands. The law, which was enacted in 1838 and repealed in 1970, applied, among others, to uncle-niece marriages (second-degree relatives) and to marriages between brothers- and sisters-in-law (no genetic relation) (Article 88 Oud Burgerlijk Wetboek).

In western societies, prejudices and misunderstandings are common with regard to consanguinity. Consanguineous marriage is often viewed as causing physical and mental incapacity (Modell and Darr 2002). It has been reported that the general public and many healthcare professionals have a disproportionate view of the genetic disadvantages of consanguineous marriage. Consanguineous couples with a sick child were often told that their child was sick because they were related (Qureshi 1997). A Dutch politician also recently proposed discouraging or legally banning consanguineous marriage.[2]

The Dutch government coalition that was formed in October 2010 intended to prohibit cousin marriages. This ban was included among other measures intended to limit immigration, such as a prohibition of forced marriages and polygamy. No mention was made here about increased medical risks, so the proposed prohibition was probably intended to serve to reduce immigration. Here, as often in such debates, no distinction was made between uncle-niece (second-degree relatives) marriages, cousin marriages (third-degree relatives) and second-cousin marriages (fifth-degree relatives), although medical risks are lower among more distant relatives.

Medical Implications of Consanguinity

Population studies regarding the risk to the offspring of first-cousin unions (third-degree relatives) compared to non-consanguineous unions result in estimations of 1.7%-2.8% extra risk, mostly because of an increased prevalence of autosomal recessive disorders (Bennett *et al.* 2002; Bishop, Metcalfe, and Gaff 2008; Hamamy *et al.* 2011). For second-cousin marriages the additional risk is often estimated at 0.5-1%, a quarter of the additional risk for third-degree relatives. The increased risk in cousin marriages is much lower than what is often perceived. There has been some debate about the lack of adequate control for variables as socioeconomic status, maternal age, maternal education, birth order, and birth intervals in studies on the excess rate of birth defects among first-cousin progeny, and as a consequence this number might even be an overestimate of the real risk figure. Furthermore, studies on the medical implica-

---

[2]   http://www.parool.nl/parool/nl/4/AMSTERDAM/article/detail/238253/2009/04/21/Asscher-verbod-op-neef-nichthuwelijken.dhtml   (accessed 5 July 2010).

tions of consanguinity do not take into account population stratification affecting the expression of genetic disorders, which might be of great influence in communities with a tradition of endogamy and consanguinity (Bittles and Black 2010). The average additional risk in populations may be thus different from the estimated 1.7%-2.8% mentioned above, depending on the gene frequencies of deleterious alleles and the mean coefficients of inbreeding in the (sub)population.

Autosomal recessive disorders will occur if a child inherits a copy of a mutated gene from both parents. If a person only carries one mutated gene, the other gene will function normally and the individual will be healthy with respect to this trait. Without being aware of it, probably every person is a carrier of at least one recessive disorder. If both parents are carriers (mostly without knowing it), they each have a 50% chance of passing the mutated gene on to a specific child, and consequently, for each child, there is a 25% chance that it will be affected. There are numerous autosomal recessive disorders, most of which are extremely rare. Some disorders occur relatively more frequently, like haemoglobinopathies or cystic fibrosis, with carrier frequencies in some populations of up to 1 in 20.

Consanguineous unions provide a higher risk of both partners carrying *the same* recessive gene variants, inherited from a common ancestor. As a consequence, their risk of having children affected with a single gene disorder with a recessive inheritance pattern is increased (Modell and Darr 2002). In communities where consanguineous unions are frequent, there is an increased prevalence of specific rare recessive conditions and an increase in the prevalence of congenital and genetic disorders. The risk figure for first-cousin unions is clearly an *average* number, as it depicts the number of affected children born inside the *group* of first-cousin parents. Keeping in mind the mechanisms through which autosomal recessive disorders segregate, this does not reflect the actual increased risk for an *individual couple*. This is either 25% (or more if they are both carriers for more than one recessive disorder) or 0%.

Increases in reproductive risk can be caused by many different factors, consanguinity being only one of them. Advanced maternal age, for example, increases the risk for Down's syndrome, assisted reproduction in the form of in vitro fertilization

adds an extra risk of birth defects (pooled relative risk estimation 1.37; 95% confidence interval: 1.26-1.48) (Wen *et al.* 2012),
and diabetes mellitus in a mother is said to cause 5-10% of congenital disorders in a child (Evers, de Valk, and Visser 2004).

Genetic Health Care for Consanguineous Couples

This increased risk has been advanced as a reason to systematically include consanguinity as crucial components of accurate
risk assessment in a preconception or prenatal setting. A policy
oriented to allow informed decision making on this genetic reproductive risk should aim to identify and counsel these couples prior to reproduction (Modell and Darr 2002). It has been
recommended that health care professionals (e.g., primary care
services) should ideally look carefully at genetic family history
and identify consanguinity (Bennett *et al.* 2002). Studies show,
however, that the topic of consanguinity is still considered taboo and that various health care professionals do not collect information about consanguinity themselves but rely on their patients to bring up the issue (Bishop, Metcalfe, and Gaff 2008;
Middleton *et al.* 2007). Training health care professionals and
communities is important for learning about genetic risks and
potential pre-reproductive genetic counseling. The designing of
genetic education for professionals and genetic counseling programs for consanguineous couples should pay special attention
to the cultural sensitivity.

At this time, at risk couples are identified only after the
birth of their first affected child. In theory, the extended family
can be contacted as soon as an affected child has been identified
in order to provide genetic counseling or carrier testing.

Genetic testing aims to detect the absence or presence of, or
alteration in, a particular gene, chromosome or a gene product
in relation to a genetic disorder. Genetic testing is often done
for diagnostic purposes to aid in the diagnosis, treatment, and
management of a symptomatic person. Essentially, diagnostic
testing is undertaken to diagnose the underlying cause of a specific medical condition and the ethical imperative for such testing is similar to the testing performed in sorting out the differ-
ential diagnosis of any other medical condition.

Another type of genetic testing is a carrier test. Carriers
tests are intended for healthy people who have no symptoms of

a disease but who are known to be at higher risk because of a family history of the disease, a high gene frequency in their population, or, as we argue in this article, consanguinity. Being a carrier does not usually affect the carrier's health but could have consequences for the offspring. There are two important categories of genetic "carriers": (a) carriers of autosomal recessive disorders and (b) carriers of a sex-linked (X chromosome) disorder or a balanced chromosomal rearrangement. Carrier testing can provide useful information to, for example, couples who are pregnant, couples planning their families, and individuals with a family history of certain genetic conditions. This type of testing is especially applicable in cases where an affected child has been born in the extended family of the couple and a carrier test can be offered before or during a pregnancy. The family history, however, does not often provide clues as to which disease the couple should be tested for.

Furthermore, genetic services can be provided in various contexts, as discussed in the third chapter. Couples intending to have children can consult a genetic counselor before conception in order to examine their family history of genetic disorders (preconception counseling). Prenatal testing can be considered if the future parents have a family genetic history or other grounds raise the suspicion that the fetus may have a genetic disorder for which diagnostic testing is available.

A new type of genetic testing is whole-genome sequencing, a technique that maps the entire genome or exome of the individual to look for mutations. This technique will conceivably be applicable to consanguineous couples as well, either in the preconception phase or after the birth of an affected child. This is already being used in case of unexplained health problems in a child that are suspected as being of monogenetic origin and could also be useful while searching for the carrier status of cousin couples. This development will affect current procedures regarding informing, referring, and counseling these couples.

Principles of Genetic Testing and Counseling

The ethical principles discussed in the third chapter in this volume also apply in the case of consanguinity. Respect for the autonomy of the person has been developed as a main principle that has been translated in operational concepts as informed consent, non-directive counseling, and the right not to know. Second, respect for privacy and confidentiality is another important principle.

The shift away from the right not to know as the duty to inform increases, as described in the third chapter of this volume, is based mainly on the improved availability of highly predictive testing options combined with the availability of effective treatment in autosomal dominant disorders with reduced penetrance. We will therefore not discuss the right (not) to know in this chapter. Non-directiveness based on autonomy as a central ethical value is still the standard in genetic counseling for reproductive issues, due to the very different valuetion of reproductive options (such as terminating a pregnancy, abstaining from having children, use of donor gametes).

Informed Consent

Article 5 of the UNESCO Declaration on the Human Genome and Human Rights (UNESCO 1997) states that "in all cases, the prior, free and informed consent of the person concerned shall be obtained" and that "research, treatment or diagnosis affecting an individual's genome shall be undertaken only after rigorous and prior assessment of the potential risks and benefits pertaining thereto." Also, the European Convention on Human Rights and Biomedicine, an international treaty ratified by the majority of the Member States of the Council of Europe (Council of Europe 1997), stipulates in Article 5:

> An intervention in the health field may only be carried out after the person concerned has given free and informed consent to it. This person shall beforehand be given appropriate information as to the purpose and nature of the intervention as well as on its consequences and risks. The person concerned may freely withdraw consent at any time.

Informed consent can be specified in an information component and a consent component (Beauchamp and Childress 2001). The information component refers to disclosure of information and comprehension of what is disclosed. Without the disclosure of information about the purpose of the test, the chance that it will give a correct prediction, the implications of the test results for the individual and family, the tested person's options and alternatives, the test's potential benefits and risks (including social and psychological), the social risks (and that whatever decision individuals and families make, their care will not be jeopardized) (Wertz, Fletcher, and Berg 2003), patients will have an inadequate basis for decision making. Information should be given in a way that is adequate to the level of understanding of the individual or family. Informed consent can only be considered valid if the individuals have truly understood and assimilated the information. Therefore, genetic counselors should also try to evaluate the understanding of individuals requesting a genetic test and ask them to describe in their own words the aim, benefits, and potential harm of a specific test. This remains a difficult but nonetheless important task. Several empirical studies have shown that persons may encounter difficulties in understanding and assessing genetic risk and understanding patterns of inheritance (Fanos 1997; Denayer *et al.* 1997), and difficulties in processing information about risks (Michie *et al.* 2005). Counselors will always have to look for better procedures for improving the process of understanding.

The consent component refers to both a voluntary decision and an authorization to proceed. This means that somebody wants to undergo genetic testing and is not acting under coercion. This person should provide the authorization to proceed with the genetic testing procedure. It has been suggested that formal informed consent, in the form of a written document, is not necessary for procedures that are part of routine care but should be required for experimental or risky procedures (Wertz, Fletcher, and Berg 2003).

In the context of consanguinity, information on the reproductive risks of consanguinity to the target population is needed. The information needs to be made available to those of secondary school age.

Non-Directiveness

It has been emphasized that the goal of genetic counseling is to provide accurate, full, and unbiased information to individuals and families. Non-directive counseling does not mean just presenting information and letting people make their own decisions without any help or support. The counseling sessions should be oriented to empower individuals and families to make their own decisions. It should guide and help people to work towards making their own decisions, especially with regard to reproductive decisions and if there is not immediately adequate prevention or therapy available. It is linked to the original intent of genetic counseling to respect the profoundly personal nature of decision making (Biesecker 1998). It is clear that the counselor is not completely unbiased, but the counselor should be aware of his personal values and should not attempt to impose them on individuals or families (Elwyn, Gray, and Clarke 2000; Oduncu 2002).

In the case of consanguinity, non-directiveness may pose a challenge to counselors from a Western background. For the other reproductive risks mentioned earlier (increased maternal age, assisted reproduction, maternal diabetes), it may be easier for a counselor to accept any choice a couple makes, since there is no negative connotation in Western societies to having children in the presence of these risk factors.

Respect for Privacy and Confidentiality

The essence of what now is called privacy has for a long time officially and generally been recognized as one of the fundamental rights of the human person. The Hippocratic Oath already mentioned this principle. Traditionally, the duty of confidentiality owed by a health care professional to a patient has provided an appropriate means by which personal health information can be kept safe. The European Convention for the Protection of Human Rights and Dignity of the Human Being stated in Article 10 that "everyone has the right to respect for private life in relation to information about his or her health." In the context of genetic testing, privacy should be understood as the right of someone to determine for himself when, how, and to what extent information about him is communicated to others. The emphasis on privacy aims to prevent that information becoming available to those whose access to the generated data is not wanted. The latter group might include relatives or family members as well as employers or insurers.

Because genetic information has consequences for relatives, the interpretation of privacy might lead to ethical conflicts. Usually, patients make a particular effort to contact family members and distant relatives to inform them about their genetic risk. But conflicts may arise when the patient does not consent to family members being contacted about their genetic risk, and the responsibility of health care professionals to care for other family members. In this context, the question arises if a patient can appeal to a strict interpretation of the right to privacy. Are there exceptional cases that can overrule this confidentiality? Or are genetic data the property of the family and not of a single individual? Various authors state that there should be respect for privacy but also hold that a genetic counselor's duty of confidentiality can be overridden if some conditions are satisfied. If reasonable efforts to elicit voluntary consent to disclosure have failed, if there is a high probability both that harm will occur if the information is withheld and that the disclosed information will actually be used to avert harm, if the harm that identifiable individuals would suffer would be serious, and if appropriate precautions are taken to ensure that only the genetic information needed for diagnosis and/or treatment of the disease in question is disclosed, then the breach of confidentiality might be acceptable. Some authors add as a fifth condition that damage to health has to be something that is expected within a short term.

Genetic testing can generate information that might be of enormous importance for others. If the counselor thinks that the results should be shared with family members, he may invite the patient to assume his responsibility towards his family. But if the patient refuses to inform his family and if the counselor cannot get his consent, it is possible that the counselor has a conflict of conscience. He or she will have to make a proportional weighing of the different values and duties at stake and might have to make the decision to breach confidentiality. The cited conditions might orient the decision making of the counselor.

Privacy and confidentiality may lead to slightly different approaches in the case of consanguinity. As society responds negatively to cousin marriages, couples may not want to discuss the health risks related to consanguinity and physicians may feel uncomfortable. Avoiding providing the information needed and avoiding the issue in training will limit adequate health care.

At the same time, new sequencing techniques are very suitable for diagnostic testing in rare disorders in offspring of consanguineous parents as well as for carrier testing. Thus, opening up the taboo is needed to allow optimal use of genetic knowledge and techniques to the benefit of the individuals in populations with a high prevalence of consanguinity.

Is Legislation Needed?

We have argued that first-cousin marriage increases the risk of autosomal recessive disorders in offspring by some 2-3%. For other reproductive risks, genetic health care professionals consider non-directive counseling essential, based on the ethical principle of autonomy. After informing couples, they should make a choice in line with their values. The only difference between consanguinity and other reproductive risk factors described in this chapter is the fact that it is an uncommon practice nowadays in many Western communities, evoking negative reactions. Proposals for legislation do not mention medical risks but may be mostly intended to limit immigration. Nevertheless, from a medical genetic and ethical point of view we would argue that consanguinity is a reproductive risk like all other reproductive risks and does not need legislation.

Conclusion

For most couples at this time, clinical geneticists and genetic counselors will assist in interpreting the genetic risks, analyzing inheritance patterns, evaluating risks of recurrence of certain conditions, and discussing reproductive options with couples. With the foreseen technological developments, communicating risks is important—also for consanguineous couples without known inherited disorders in the family. Genetic counseling serves in both cases as a process in which couples are advised about the probabilities of having offspring with an inherited disorder, and to provide open choices to them in their reproductive plans. Discussing genetic counseling principles within the context of counseling of consanguineous couples introduces important values and principles. Although these principles are similar for non-consanguineous and consanguineous couples, we have shown that the negative reactions in western societies demand special attention for respect for the autonomy of the person, which includes operational concepts like informed consent and non-directive counseling. Moreover, confidentiality and privacy should be respected with great care, given the prejudices and controversies surrounding the topic of consanguinity.

Bibliography

Allan, D. (1996). "Ethical Boundaries in Genetic Testing." CMAJ 154: 241-44.

Beauchamp T.L., and J.F. Childress. (2001). *Principles of Biomedical Ethics*. 5th ed. New York: Oxford University Press.

Bennett, R.L. *et al.* (2002). "Genetic Counseling and Screening of Consanguineous Couples and their Offspring: Recommendations of the National Society of Genetic Counselors." *Journal of Genetic Counseling* 11: 97-119.

Biesecker, B.B. (1998). "Future Directions in Genetic Counseling: Practical and Ethical Considerations." *Kennedy Institute of Ethics Journal* 8: 145-60.

Bishop, M., S. Metcalfe, and C. Gaff. (2008). "The Missing Element: Consanguinity as a Component of Genetic Risk Assessment." *Genetics in Medicine* 10: 612-20.

Bittles, A.H. (2001). "A Background Summary of Consanguineous Marriage." http://www.consang.net/images/d/dd/01AHBWeb3.pdf.
(1994). "The Role and Significance of Consanguinity as a Demographic Variable." *Population and Development Review* 20 (561): 584.

Bittles, A.H., and M.L. Black (2010). "The Impact of Consanguinity on Neonatal and Infant Health." *Early Human Development*. 86: 737-41.

Borry, P. *et al.* (2009). "Bioethics in Hepatology." In: D. Mamun-Al-Mahtab and S. Rahman (eds.). *Liver: A Complete Book of Hepato-Biliary-Pancreatic Diseases*: Noida: Elsevier Health Sciences. Pp. 30-35.

Council of Europe. (1997). *Convention for the Protection of Human Rights and Dignity of the Human Being with Regard to the Application of Biology and Medicine: Convention on Human Rights and Biomedicine*. Strasbourg: Council of Europe.

Denayer, L, *et al.* (1997). "Risk Perception after CF Carrier Testing and Impact of the Test Result on Reproductive Decision Making." *American Journal Medical Genetics* 69: 422-28.

Elwyn, G, J. Gray, and A. Clarke. (2000). "Shared Decision Making and Non-Directiveness in Genetic Counselling." *Journal of Medical Genetics* 37: 135-38.

Evers, I.M., H.W. de Valk, and G.H. Visser. (2004). "Risk of Complications of Pregnancy in Women with Type 1 Diabetes: Nationwide Prospective Study in the Netherlands." *BMJ* 328: 915.

Fanos, J.H. (1997). "Developmental Tasks of Childhood and Adolescence: Implications for Genetic Testing." *American Journal of Medical Genetics* 71: 22-28.

Hamamy H. *et al.* (2011). "Consanguineous Marriages, Pearls and Perils: Geneva International Consanguinity Workshop Report." *Genetics in Medicine* 13: 841-47.

Harper, P., and A. Clarke. (1997). "Genetics, Society and Clinical Practice." Oxford: Bios.

Hussain, R. (1999). "Community Perceptions of Reasons for Preference for Consanguineous Marriages in Pakistan." *Journal of Biosocial Science* 31: 449-61.

Hussain, R., and A.H. Bittles. (1998). "The Prevalence and Demographic Characteristics of Consanguineous Marriages in Pakistan." *Journal of Biosocial Science* 30: 261-75.

Mahowald, M.B., M.S. Verp, and R.R. Anderson. (1998). "Genetic Counseling: Clinical and Ethical Challenges." *Annual Review of Genetics* 32: 547-59.

Michie, S. *et al.* (2005). "Communicating Risk Information in Genetic Counseling: An Observational Study." *Health Education and Behavior* 32: 589-98.

Middleton, A. *et al.* (2007). "Providing a Transcultural Genetic Counseling Service in the UK." *Journal of Genetic Counseling* 16: 567-82.

Modell, B., and A. Darr (2002). "Science and Society: Genetic Counselling and Customary Consanguineous Marriage." *National Review of Genetics* 3:225-59.

Oduncu, F.S. (2002). "The Role of Non-Directiveness in Genetic Counseling." *Medicine, Health Care and Philosophy* 5: 53-63.

UNESCO. (1997). "The Universal Declaration on the Human Genome and Human Rights." http://www.unesco.org/new/en/social-and-human-sciences/themes/bioethics/human-genome-and-human-rights/.

Wen, J. *et al.* (2012). "Birth Defects in Children Conceived by In Vitro Fertilization and Intracytoplasmic Sperm Injection: A Meta-Analysis." *Fertility and Sterility* (April 3). E-publication before print.

Wertz, D.C., and J.C. Fletcher. (1988). "Attitudes of Genetic Counselors: A Multinational Survey." *American Journal of Human Genetics* 42: 592-600.

Wertz D.C., J.C. Fletcher, and K. Berg. (2003). "Review of Ethical Issues in Medical Genetics." Geneva: WHO.

Wertz, D.C. *et al.* (2002). "In Focus: Has Patient Autonomy Gone Too Far? Geneticists' Views in 36 Nations." *American Journal of Bioethics* 2: W21.

CHAPTER VI

"Notre huile est dans notre farine"

An Exploration into the Meaning of Consanguinity in Northern Morocco against the Backdrop of the Medical Risk of Disabled Offspring

Oka Storms and Edien Bartels

Introduction

A consanguineous union is usually defined as a union between two individuals related as second cousins or closer (Bittles 2001). It is practiced throughout the whole world in varying degrees and has been customary for many generations in North Africa and the Middle East, where parallel first-cousin marriages, i.e. marriages between children of same-sex siblings, are preferred. Consanguineous marriage has been of interest to both clinical geneticists and anthropologists, although for different reasons.[1]

---

[1] Consanguinity is a politically sensitive issue. There is an ongoing political debate in the Netherlands about the permissibility of consanguinity and consanguineous marriages among immigrants. Lodewijk Asscher (2009), a former Amsterdam alderman and now deputy prime minister, recently started a discussion on the prohibition of consanguineous marriages. Later (2009), the former minister of integration and current mayor of Amsterdam (Van der Laan) announced his proposal to restrict immigration with respect to (new) consanguineous marriages in order to prevent the migration of Dutch Moroccans and Turks through forced marriages to the Netherlands. The Dutch government recently (March 2012) proposed a law banning consanguineous marriage. In this debate, consanguinity is related to subjects such as immigration, marriage migration, forced marriages, depriva-

From a clinical genetic perspective, consanguineous couples have an increased risk of offspring with an autosomal recessive disorder. In general, non-related couples have a risk of 2-3% of having children with a congenital/genetic disorder. The risk is double for first-cousin couples, 4-6% (Bennett *et al.* 2006; Stoltenberg *et al.* 1997), and results from the expression of recessive genes inherited from (a) common ancestor(s). This is, however, an average percentage: the risk for most consanguineous couples is comparable to that of non-consanguineous couples, while some (10-12%) have an increased risk of 25% or more.

Marriage and kinship are classical anthropological themes. The anthropological literature on consanguineous unions offers explanations for the practice of consanguineous marriages, especially in terms of group relations and kinship structures in societies where consanguinity is practiced. The argument regarding the social position of women is central in this debate: marriage outside the family can lead to insecurity for women, whereas marriage within the family provides more security. Thus, fear and risk play a central role in kinship marriages. Recently, this anthropological debate was elaborated by a risk approach (Caplan 2000; Shaw 2000), and risk will be our point of entry for analyzing consanguinity in this chapter. The concept of risk is relevant in both clinical genetics and anthropology. Risk has to do with genetic grounds in clinical genetics and in anthropology with people's views on risk related to social, cultural, and religious grounds.

In the Netherlands, it is mostly immigrants from Morocco and Turkey who practice consanguinity. Because of the immigrants' transnational ties and the fact that they are second generation with family in their countries of origin makes partner choice with relatives from this country of origin important (Storms and Bartels 2008), and we should therefore explore the meaning attributed to consanguineous unions in these countries. Thus, we investigated the way in which consanguinity is perceived in northern Morocco (where most Moroccan immi-

tion, and Islam. This debate is only tangentially relevant to the purposes of this chapter and therefore we will not pursue it further.

grants in the Netherlands come from) in order to answer the question: *What meanings do people in northern Morocco attribute to consanguinity against the backdrop of the medical risk of disabled offspring?*

To answer this question, we carried out an exploratory qualitative study in northern Morocco (March and April 2009, November 2010). We conducted 19 interviews with highly and poorly educated women, a few men, and, in one case, a husband and wife. One of these interviews was conducted with the director of a day care center for intellectually disabled children. Moreover, we had the opportunity to have a group discussion with 13 women who had graduated from university. We were later given the opportunity to discuss the subject with students at the university in Fez (not included in the number of respondents because the students came from all over Morocco, not only from the north). In November 2010 we conducted a group discussion with three women in a mountain village in northeastern Morocco. We will not attempt to provide a representative image of the meaning people in northern Morocco attribute to consanguineous unions against the backdrop of the medical risk of having disabled offspring. Nevertheless, we do intend to give an overview of the different discourses we encountered during our research and, in this way, to contribute to the discussion on risk in relation to consanguinity.

In the first section we will describe the main anthropological explanations for consanguinity, and this will be followed by a section on the incidence of consanguinity in Morocco based on the literature. Next, we will describe the theoretical framework, an anthropological perspective on risk. The following section will elaborate on the discourses on consanguinity and the arguments people give in relation to their knowledge on consanguinity and disabled offspring. We will conclude with a discussion and some remarks.

Anthropological Explanations for Consanguineous Endogamy

Who are we allowed to marry? Kinship and marriage rules are seen as the organizing principles of society everywhere. Transgressing marriage rules is seen as incest, and incest is a taboo practically everywhere. What is considered incest differs from society to society. Kottak (2002: 404-06) explains the incest taboo as "instinct" or "biology." Instinct can probably explain a taboo, but it does not explain different boundaries regarding incest. Our ancestors discovered the connection between marriages between close blood relatives on the one hand and disabled children on the other. But this still does not explain different boundaries regarding incest. In northwestern Europe, consanguineous marriages are seen as incest, but such marriages are widespread in other parts of the world. Hence, marriage rules are more culturally determined than biologically. Classic anthropologists like Lévi-Strauss indicated that incest rules signaled the start of humanity's differentiation from animals. *Exogamy*, marriage outside the group, supports the creation of alliances and networks between groups to continue to survive. On the other hand, consanguineous marriage, or *endogamy*, marriage inside the ethnic, religious, or family group, is practiced all over the world too. Cousin marriages especially, i.e. (1) cross-cousin marriages (children of a brother and sister) or (2) parallel-cousin marriages (children of same-sex siblings), are seen as unique types of endogamous marriages in some parts of the world. These types of marriages are discussed by anthropologists within the general frame of cultural rules that are fundamental for the organization of society. The variant *bint 'ammi* (patrilineal parallel-cousin marriages, father's brother's daughter, FBD) is seen in particular as a unique type of endogamous marriage because this form is especially preferred in the Arab world in general.

But why endogamy? In general, the consolidation of a household, offspring, property, or family honor (protection of the chastity of women) is seen as the main reason for endogamous marriages, especially the *bint 'ammi* type. Tillion (1983) gives a feminist explanation for this type: the oppression of women. From a structuralist theory of marriage (Lévi-Strauss 1969), however, in which the exchange of women among family or groups is central to creating alliances, the *bint 'ammi* marriage does not fit because it is more a matter of conserving the family than of creating allies. In endogamous marriages, women and property are kept within the family line instead of moving to another family. Some anthropologists claim that the *bint 'ammi* marriage is not a marriage at all but a remnant of early pre-Islamic rules of inheritance (Fernea and Malarkey 1975). The origin is not important here, but the notion of "pre-

Islamic" plays a role, as we will see below. Murphy and Kasdan (1959) saw this type of marriage as an ideal with the structural implication of creating alliances not with other groups but within a group. They showed how this type counteracts the process of fission, the process of division of a kinship group into smaller groups, which is always a risk in lineal kinship groups because it breaks up the family. Sholkamy (2003) differentiates between the principle and the practice of *bint 'ammi* marriage. The practice removes it from its perceived uniqueness and groups it with other kinship marriages. The justification for choosing either one's *bint 'ammi* or another cousin as a marriage partner is the same in both cases. Individuals can be related to the mother's family as well, but anthropologists probably display a bias because in societies where the preferred parallel-cousin marriage is the ideal, the father's side is the one taken into consideration. Sholkamy shows how students in Egypt and other Arab countries explain that the ideal of parallel cousin marriage does not stem from practice but is an ideal based in the social imagination. Sholkamy (2003) stresses that the practice of parallel cousin marriage is something other than the ideal. The point is to marry close relatives, and the family, even the mother's side, makes that practice possible. But patrilineal parallel marriages keep the women inside the family.

In short, endogamous marriages are a way to consolidate well-being as much as possible in the family, control women, and compete for power between families. Marriage is a route to personal security (Hoodfar 1997) and to the creation of a secure environment for procreation. This is especially the case for patrilineal parallel cousins, from a women's point of view (Sholkamy 2008). Courbage and Todd (2007) show how this system, which, as we have seen, originated in pre-Islamic times, creates a more secure position for women than they have in Russia, India, and in China because endogamy does away with the system of dowry and prevents the infanticide of girls. Sholkamy (2003) indicates how, for Egypt, notions of risk in close kin marriages concerning genetic defects are recognized but marrying a stranger can be even more dangerous for women. In the case of divorce, the woman risk losing control of the children and having to leave her husband's family, thus becoming dependent on her own family again. Mediation on behalf of women is difficult. As Sholkamy (2003) states, keeping women in the family means keeping them safe. Finally, keeping women in the family means more stability with respect to divorce. Consanguineous marriages are embedded in families that prevent divorce among their members through mediation and arbitration (Storms and Bartels 2008).

Hoodfar (1997) describes the preference for kinship marriages as rooted in the desire for security, but he sees how kinship has been replaced by proximity as a criterion for marriage choice among urban citizens. Some authors explain the decline of kinship marriages as a result of modernity but others challenge this relation (Sholkamy 2003). Development in other social and economic sectors may increase or decrease the number of kinship marriages. For instance, the example of increased income of sedentary settles in an Egyptian village, given by Sholkamy (2003), makes clear that it is more important to marry close within the family, to keep wealth for and in the family. As Shaw (2001) shows, the number of kinship marriages among Pakistani immigrants in the UK is higher than the average number in Pakistan. Immigration probably offers another dynamic for taking up this marriage custom again. Charsley (2007: 1119-20) underlines the central importance of women's position in transnational consanguineous marriages among Pakistanis in the UK. Women are vulnerable in an immigrant position. Marriage within the family decreases fear and the risk of being treated badly and gives some guarantee for the welfare of the woman as a spouse rather than as a means to obtain a passport to come to the UK.

The Incidence of Consanguineous Marriages in Morocco

The incidence of consanguineous marriages is difficult to describe. There has been statistical research, but the incidence is not uniformly spread over the country. Benhamadi (1994) counts a general incidence of 33%, and within this 33% first-degree cousins, cross cousins, and parallel cousins dominate two to one (more than 60% of this 33%). He divided Morocco into seven districts, South, Tesitt, Central, Northwest, Central North, East, Central South. The districts South and East have the highest incidence of approximately 40%. The difference in incidence between rural and urban communities is high: 65% in the former over against 38% in the latter. The preference for paternal cousin marriages is clear: rural paternal consanguineous marriages are at 30% in rural areas and maternal at 20%. In urban areas, paternal consanguineous marriages account for 20% and maternal for 15% of the consanguineous marriages. These figures are relatively old. Cherkaoui *et al.* (2005) arrive at 29.9% in the high Atlas region (Benhamadi's South district). The research by Hami *et al.* (2007) in the Rabat-Salé-Zemmour-Zaer region, an urban region (Benhamadi's Central district), shows an incidence of 20%. 70% of this 20% were first-cousin marriages. Sbii *et al.* (2008) give figures of geographical endogamy for the Souss Massa Draa (Benhamadi's South and Central South districts). 77.2 % of the couples studied and 84.9 % of the parents' generation were from the same group origin. 94.7% of the couples studied and 97.6 % of their parents were born in the same place. People stay within their social groups and in their geographical neighborhood for their choice of partner. These regions are characterized as "closed." Tadmouri and others (2009) indicate the percentage of consanguinity in Morocco at 19.9-28 %, based on the literature. So the general estimate of consanguineous unions for Morocco varies per region and location. Jaouad *et al.* (2009: 580) note that the rate of consanguinity in Morocco seems to be decreasing in frequency among the younger generation. Several factors are mentioned in this research: the decrease in the number of offspring, the increase in the level of education of women, the adoption of the nuclear family system, the displacement from rural to urban areas, the increase in the proportion of women in the work force, and an increased recognition of the effects of consanguineous marriages on children's health in families where there are cases of an inherited recessive disease. But the question remains: When people acknowledge the risk of consanguinity for children's health do they calculate a lower risk of security for women who marry an outside partner? How are these risks calculated?

Consanguinity and Risk

Caplan (2000: 8) discusses the anthropological work of Douglas and Wildavsky, who suggest that people fear and this fear has to do with knowledge and the kind of people we are. People see the weight of risks differently, and have to prioritize between them, since, plainly, no one can worry about all potential risks all the time. But in order to rank dangers there must be some agreement on criteria, which is why acceptability of risk is always a political issue.

In sum, for Douglas and Wildavsky, there is always a cultural selection of dangers, and risk perception is determined both by social organization and culture. Inevitably, morality enters the picture through the use of culture, as Caplan deduces from Douglas: "Common values lead to common fears, thus the choice of risks and the choice of how to live are linked and each form of life has its own typical risk portfolio" (Caplan 2000: 9). This leads to the question: Under what conditions will the perception of the risk of consanguinity for the health of children change in a society where consanguineous marriages are linked with social security, especially for women? The answer is that risk selection and perception can be altered only by changing the social organization of society (Caplan 2000: 9). But how do we find this in Morocco?

Consanguinity and Risk: The Discourse of Denial and Acceptance

All those we interviewed in northern Morocco were aware of the notions regarding the risk of genetic defects in close kin marriages. That means all people know about the discussions concerning consanguineous unions and the risk of having disabled offspring. When we asked how people knew about this discussion, most of them indicated television as their source of information. For poorly educated people especially, it is a discussion "at a distance." It is difficult to accept that the ideal of kinship marriages has risks with respect to offspring. As an older women told us: "I don't believe it because I know a couple who are not blood relatives and they have a disabled child." Probably for them, a close kin marriage is not only an ideal but also still self-evident, as it has been for centuries in Arab countries. On the other hand, our research does not show any relation between high and low education and support for or denial of these notions of risk in relation to close kin marriages and disabled children. Highly educated people show both support and denial. As our data shows, there are different reactions to the information on consanguineous unions and the risk of having disabled offspring. We distinguished three discourses in the stories we heard: (1) the discourse of denial, (2) the discourse of acceptance based on education, and (3) the discourse of acceptance based on experience. We will elaborate on these discourses below using our research data to illustrate our points.

The Discourse of Denial: Mounia and Said

Mounia and Said have been married for about four years. Educated and in their early 30s, they gave several reasons why they think consanguineous marriages are still practiced. First are the arguments having to do with name and property: "To stay in the big house," says Mounia. "The big house" means that, generation after generation, people live in the same family house. Said states that the land—and therefore the money—stays within the family. Second, they argue that people who are unknown are not accepted. "An outsider might have different traditions and daily routines, whereas families share these," explains Mounia. Said says that "If you marry an outsider, you can't say everything to each other. The other might not understand you. Within the family you can say anything to another, they won't get angry." The third argument concerns the safety and freedom of the woman. "If a girl marries within the extended family, it means that there won't be any problems between the mother-in-law and the daughter-in-law." "Marrying within the family," Mounia argues, "also means freedom for the woman. During festivities within her own family, a girl doesn't have to wear her headscarf, whereas with outsiders she does." The fourth argument involves conflicts between the partners. Said explains that the role of family is very important when there is a conflict between the spouses. "Our business is our business," says Said. "Within the family a conflict is solved more easily. When there are different families, they both choose their own side."

Said and Mounia chose each other as partners and are not related. "I did think about marrying my cousin, however," Said says. "She lived in our street, we got along very well, but it was based more on friendship." During the conversation neither

Said nor Mounia mention disadvantages on any level regarding consanguineous marriages. Mounia explains a local Arabic expression about consanguinity: "notre huile est dans notre farine," i.e "our oil is in our flour." Mounia explains: "When you bake something with your own products—for example, the boy is the oil and the girl is the flour—it tastes better." In other words, a consanguineous marriage is better. When the topic of risk to offspring is raised, Mounia says: "Do you think my husband is handicapped?!" It turns out that Said's parents are first cousins. The father of Said's mother is the brother of Said's father's mother. Said says: "My mother already had several marriage proposals, but she only wanted to marry my father." Mounia says that, in general, people in Morocco do not believe in any connection between consanguineous unions and the risk of hereditary diseases. "There are many families where people marry within the family, and there are no problems," she explains, "It is not a topic that discussed in Morocco." Said explains:

> It is also because of religion. The Prophet also had family members who married each other. We live according to the Qur'an, those are the rules. Also, the *ulama* [Islamic law scholars] nowadays say that marrying within the family is good; it is not *haram* [forbidden].

Mounia and Said argue:

> Marrying within the family is practiced in North Africa and in the Middle East. If there are disadvantages to it, why is it so widely practiced? This problem doesn't exist in Morocco. People don't believe it. If there were risks, people wouldn't do it. People also say: in that family husband and wife are related and they have healthy children. There is no proof that it isn't good.

They are very aware of the discussion about consanguinity. As their response shows, it is also a topic that is discussed in public. Said and Mounia also said the topic was discussed briefly on television but not very often.

The Discourse of Acceptance (1): Protesting Women

In a small town in the north of Morocco, a group of 13 women sit in front of the city hall protesting. All of them have university degrees, are unemployed, and are in their 30s or older. They want proper jobs, with acceptable wages and insurance. Only 2 of the 13 women are married.

According to these women, family marriage preferences vary. There are families that prefer consanguineous unions. Most of the families of these women have consanguineous unions, their parents, brothers, sisters, or other family members who married cousins. For example, "I have two uncles and they married two sisters. The first couple had a girl, the second a boy. The boy and the girl are married now. They can't have children now because they have the same blood."

These women are very aware of the discussions on consanguinity and the risks to offspring. Contrary to Mounia and Said, they do acknowledge the risks and, like Mounia and Said, these women use their religion to explain their view of consanguinity. They use it, however, to explain why they think it is better to marry *outside* the family.

> Our Qur'an says that it isn't good to marry within the family. Our Prophet says the same. When somebody marries outside the family, the children will be more intelligent than when it is a union within the family.

One of the women says: "Not everybody has studied like we have. They haven't studied the Qur'an properly. We are educated, we understand it."

These women refer to consanguineous unions as unions between "people of the same blood." One woman explains: "When a couple is consanguineous, sometimes there are and sometimes there aren't problems with the children who are born. Marrying outside the family is better." Another woman explains:

> There are two reasons why it's better to marry outside the family. First, the possibility that the children will be sick. And second, if the marriage doesn't work, there will be a dispute within the family. If somebody wants to marry someone within the family they should have their blood tested first.

These unmarried women live with their families and explain that they are in conflict with them because they are pro-

testing in public. Their families are ashamed. "But we have nothing to lose," one of them explains,

> We are all 30 years or older. We want to marry, but we are
> too old. The men don't want us anymore. They all want a
> wife from abroad, so they can emigrate. Girls in their 20s
> would never sit here; they don't understand.

For these women, the only way to start their own lives is either
to marry or to get a proper job so they can support themselves.
But since the unemployment rate is very high, there is no chance
they will be able to find work. Although these women acknowledge the risks of a union with a relative, the question remains:
What will they do if they receive a marriage proposal from a
cousin?

The Discourse of Acceptance (2): The Women in the Mountains

In a small mountain village in northern Morocco, we discussed
the question of choosing a marriage partner with three illiterate
Berber women. The average marrying age for a girl is 16 or 17,
they explain. With the introduction of the new *Mudawwanah*
(Moroccan Family Law) (2004), the marriageable age rose to 18
for both women and men. But parents sue for permission for
their daughters to marry earlier, and that permission is always
granted in this area, one of the women explains. These women
know about the risks for offspring in consanguineous marriages. There was a couple in a neighboring village with six
children, all of whom were severely disabled. The medical practitioner explained that these handicaps resulted from their consanguineous marriage. In a small village north of this village
was another family in the same situation. These women explain
that they are therefore aware of the risks of consanguineous
marriages. One of these women, the mother of a 16-year-old girl
present at the discussion, will look for a husband for her daughter outside the family. Only if they do not succeed in finding
one outside the family will they turn to the family for a suitable
spouse. The daughter says she feels free to accept or refuse any
man who asks for her hand in marriage, as was the case last
summer. Contrary to Mounia and Said and in line with the
protesting women, these women say that Islam requires that its
adherents give their children healthy lives. The woman who

took the lead in the discussion explains that testing is not only allowed by Islam but even recommended by it. We ask her what is to be done if people have a high risk. Her answer is: "Don't marry, or marry but don't have children." This answer causes the other women to remark that she is talking just like an imam explaining the rules of the religion, a remark that leads to laughter among the women.

Discussion and Conclusion

We have seen that consanguineous marriages are a topic in anthropology as well as in clinical genetics. From the anthropological perspective, consanguineous unions, or endogamy, are studied in terms of group relations and kinship structures. Endogamous marriages mean security for women because they stay within their own families instead of moving and belonging to a new kinship group. In clinical genetics, the focus is on the increased risk of consanguineous couples having children with an autosomal recessive disorder.

How risk is perceived and what risk prevails varies with the individual and community, as shown by the three discourses. Mounia and Said argue that there is no medical risk at all. They are aware of the discussion, but they neither acknowledge nor accept the risk. The protesting women in the city, on the other hand, are aware of the discussion on consanguinity and the risk of disabled children and accept both the medical explanation and the fact of medical risks. And the women from the mountain village are aware of the medical risks because of the cases of consanguineous families with disabled children in their immediate surroundings. But they mention the risk of not finding a spouse as a reason to look for one within the family if one cannot be found outside the family. As Jaouad *et al.* (2009: 580) indicate, the rate of consanguinity in Morocco seems to be decreasing among the younger generation. Education plays an important role here but is not decisive, as the case of Mounia and Said on the one hand and that of the illiterate women from the mountain village on the other show. Other factors play a role as well, as Jaouad *et al.* mention.

The question of risk perception for consanguineous marriages is related to the question why people choose to marry non-kin partners. Their decision does not mean that people accept or reject the risk of consanguinity and the possibility of a disabled child. As Hoodfar shows, kin can become less relevant and can be replaced by proximity for choosing a partner in order to ensure security and stability for women. This is more the case in the urban environment than in the rural one. But in urban surroundings, the number of non-kin partners has increased and more non-kin partners are available. At the same time, the social security of women is no longer exclusively related to family and marriage. Education and work are increasingly seen as conditions that bring opportunities for women to gain some security on their own. But, as we can learn from the protesting women, these conditions are not easy to attain. At the same time, we see that it is precisely these women who show a changing perception of risk. Morocco is a changing society.[2] According to Douglas and Wildavsky, as cited by Caplan, risk perception can be altered by changing the organization of society. The changing position of women in Morocco and especially the increasing number of women who have become independent through work and education is probably the basis for the changing ideas on risk perception in connection with consanguineous marriages.

There is a second notable point. All the discourses invoke Islam to sustain the argument, but both religious arguments are incompatible and opposite. On the one hand, Islam offers arguments to sustain and legitimize consanguineous marriages and to deny and reject the risk. But, on the other hand, Islam also offers arguments for rejecting consanguineous marriages. Religion and morality play an important role in risk perception. That is not new. Religion supports perceptions, whatever they are. It is a matter of interpretation. But the question is which interpretation will dominate and carry the most authority for the population in relation to the risk perception of consanguinity. That depends on the position and power of the ones who support the interpretation. Religious scholars can play a role in this debate but even then it is not certain that their interpretation

---

[2] The divorce rate is high, and an increasing number of young people do not marry, which leads to discussion on the "marriage crisis."

will be heard and be followed by ordinary believers, as we know from previous research (Bartels and Loukili 2010).

Bibliography

Asscher L. (2009). "Amsterdam is nog niet eerlijk." *Volkskrant* (11 April). http://www.pvda.nl/opinie/opinie/Amsterdam+is+nog+niet+eerlijk.html.

Bartels, A., and G. Loukili. (2010). *Islam en de legitimiteit van preconceptioneel testen. Verslag van onderzoek ten behoeve van SPIOR (Stichting Platform Islamitische Organisaties Rijnmond)*. Amsterdam: Department of Social and Cultural Anthropology, VU University Amsterdam. http://www. spior.nl/.

Benhamadi, B. (1994). "Les ménages consanguins au Maroc: caractéristiques et déterminants." In: *Ménages, familles, parentèles et solidarités dans les populations méditerranéennes*. Séminaire international d'Aranjuez (27-30 September 1994). www.erudit.org/ livre/ aidelf/1994/001038co.pdf.

Bennett, R.L. *et al.* (2006). "Genetic Counselling and Screening of Consanguineous Couples and their Offspring: Recommendations of the National Society of Genetic Counselors." *Genetic Counseling* 11: 97-119.

Bittles, A.H. (2001). "Consanguinity and its Relevance to Clinical Genetics." *Clinical Genetics* 60: 89-98.

Caplan, P. (2000). *Risk Revisited*. London: Pluto Press.

Charsley, K. (2007). "Risk, Trust, Gender, and Transnational Cousin Marriage among British Pakistanis." *Ethnic and Racial Studies* 30: 6, 1117-31.

Cherkaoui, M. *et al.* (2005). "Consanguinity, Fertility of Couples and Mortality of Children in the High Atlas Population (Commons of Anougal and Azgour, Marakesh, Morocco)." *International Journal of Anthropology* 20: 199-206.

Courbage, Y., and E. Todd. (2007). *Le rendez-vous des civilisations*. Paris: Éditions du Seuils et la République des Idées.

Engels, C. (2010). *Mixing Models: A Research on Moroccan Dutch Mothers with an Intellectually Disabled Child and their Disability Discourse, Explanations and Ideas on Child Care*. Master's Thesis SCA, Faculty of Social Science, VU University Amsterdam.

Fernea, R., and J. Malarkey. (1975). "Anthropology of the Middle East and North Africa: A Critical Assessment." *Annual Review of Anthropology* 4: 183-206.

Jaouad, I.C. *et al.* (2009). "Consanguinious Marriages in Morocco and the Consequence for the Incidence of Autosomal Recessive Disorders." *Journal of Biosocial Science* 41: 575-81.

Lévi-Strauss, C. (1969). *The Elementary Structure of Kinship*. Boston: Beacon.

Hamdi, H., A. Soulaymani, and A. Mokhtari. (2007). "Traditions matrimoniales dans la région de Rabat-Salé-Zemmour-Zaer au Maroc." *Bulletins et mémoires de la Société d'Anthropologie de Paris* 19: 1-2.

Hoodfar, H. (1997). *Between Marriages and the Market: Intimate Politics and Survival in Cairo*. Berkeley: University of California Press.

Kottak, C. (2002). *Anthropology: The Exploration of Human Diversity*. Columbus: McGraw-Hill

Murphy, R.F. and L. Kasdan. (1959). "The Structure of Parallel Cousin Marriage." *American Anthropologists: New Series* 61: 17-29.

Shaw, A. (2001). "Kinship, Cultural Preference and Immigration: Consanguineous Marriages among British Pakistanis." *Journal of the Royal Anthropological Institute* 7: 315-34.

——— (2000). "Conflicting Models of Risk: Clinical Genetics and British Pakistanis." In: P. Caplan. *Risk Revisited*. London: Pluto Press. Pp. 85-108.

Sbii, L. *et al.* (2008). "Endogamie géographique dans la région de Souss Massa Draa au Maroc." *Anthropo* 17: 63-86. http://www.didac.ehu.es/antropo/17/17-7/Sbii.pdf.

Sholkamy, H. (2003). "Rationales for Kin Marriages in Rural Upper Egypt." In: *The New Arab Family*. Ed. Nicholas S. Hopkins, vol 24, number 1-2. Cairo/New York: Cairo Papers in Social Science American University Press.

Stoltenberg, M. *et al.* (1997). "Birth Defects and Parental Consanguinity in Norway." *American Journal of Epidemiology* 145: 439-48.

Storms, O., and E. Bartels. (2008). *De keuze van een huwelijkspartner. Een studie naar partnerkeuze onder groepen Amsterdammers*. Amsterdam: VU University Amsterdam. http://www.fsw.vu.nl/nl/Images/ huwelijkenamsterdam%20Spdf_tcm30-60514.pdf.

Tadmouri, G. *et al.* (2009). "Consanguinity and Reproductive Health among Arabs." In: *Reproductive Health* 6: 17.

Tillion, G. (1983). *The Republic of Cousins: Women's Oppression in Mediterranean Society*. London: Al Saqi Books.

CHAPTER VII

The Treatment of Embryos from an Islamic Perspective

Ayman M. Nassar, Serag El Din Mansour, and Gamal I. Serour

Introduction

The main questions to be discussed in this chapter are: How is the embryo regarded from an Islamic perspective? What is the difference between an embryo and a preembryo? What are the new medical treatments that make use of embryos? What treatment and research are allowed and what is prohibited ethically and religiously?

Since the birth of the first IVF baby, Louise Brown, in England in 1978, medically assisted conception (MAC or IVF) has evoked great interest in the public as well as in the medical profession. For the first time, couples that were not able to conceive naturally were able to conceive now. This new type of treatment for infertility has created a great ethical debate all over the world among different societies and the followers of different religions. The past few years have witnessed marked improvement in preembryo research as well as legislation of such research in some countries. This has evoked the old ethical concerns about techniques and approaches that can alter our inner environment, introduce changes in our very genetic constitutions and structures, and enable us to influence the kinds of people that are born.

What ethical limits should be set on research on preembryos? Should such research be conducted solely for the purpose of improving in vitro fertilization, or can there be other aims, such as the study of the teratogenicity of nicotine, the growth of malignant cells, or the effect of certain medications? How far may research go in the optimization of preembryo development, cloning, hybridization? All these are questions that have been raised over the past few years and have indeed created and continue to create a great deal of ethical debate all over the world.

In this chapter on the Islamic approach to these issues we presuppose Marzouk Aulad Abdellah's introduction to *shari'ah* and *fiqh*. We will concentrate on the status of (pre-)embryos and how we may or may not treat it. This question was unknown at the time of Prophet. In Islam, however, bioethical decision making is carried out within a framework of values derived from revelation and tradition. It is intimately linked to the broad ethical teachings of the Qur'an and the tradition of the Prophet Muhammad (the *Sunnah*), and thus to the interpretation of Islamic law. In this way, Islam has the flexibility to respond to new biomedical technologies. Islamic bioethics emphasizes prevention and teaches that the patient must be treated with respect and compassion and that the physical, mental, and spiritual dimensions of the illness be taken into account. Because Islam shares many foundational values with Judaism and Christianity, anyone acquainted with Islamic ethics will find Islamic bioethics quite familiar.

The medical general practitioners and specialists, on the other hand, are always concerned about the legal basis of their acts that they undertake based on their expertise and ethical prospects. They should always keep the distinctions and potential conflicts between legal and ethical duties in mind. What is legal might not be ethical. Laws rarely establish positive duties such as beneficence. On the contrary, beneficence is a primary obligation in professional medical ethics (Dickens 1992). Research on the human embryo is part of medical research in general, and the ethical requirements and rules of medical research should apply to them. They should be governed by previous international guidelines relevant to this problem such as the Nuremberg and Helsinki Declarations (1964 and 1975), the CIOMS (1982), the Inuyama Declaration (1990), and the Cairo Declaration (1991) for Muslim countries (Bankowski and Capron 1991; Serour and Omran 1992).

In what follows, we will first elaborate on the status of the embryo and its subsequent stages of development from an Islamic perspective. Second, we will present general ethical considerations with regard to the embryo's development. Finally, we will discuss several uses of embryos in both medical treatments and research: Are they allowed, encouraged, or forbidden from an Islamic perspective? In our conclusion, we will summarize our findings by presenting a more general perspective on the use of embryos for medical purposes.

The Status of the Embryo: Distinctions

In order to understand the techniques of embryo manipulation, it is important to understand the early stages of reproduction. In the last part of this chapter we will discuss six sorts of research and treatments in relation to embryos. We first have to describe phases of the development of the embryo and fetus that are ethically relevant.

When the egg and sperm unite to form a zygote, each parent supplies the zygote with one half of the chromosomes necessary for a full set. The zygote, which is a single cell, then begins to reproduce through the cellular division process called mitosis, in which each chromosome is duplicated before separation so that each new cell has a full set of chromosomes. This is called the morula stage; the new cells are called blastomeres. When enough cells have been produced (the number varies from species to species), cell differentiation begins to take place. The first differentiation occurs when the blastocyst is formed, which is an almost hollow sphere with a cluster of cells inside. The differentiation appears to be one between the cells inside, which become the fetus, and the cells outside, which become the fetal membranes and placenta.

Now we can introduce the distinction between an embryo and a preembryo. One way to do this is to refer to the classic Thomistic definition of the person as "an individual substance of a rational nature." The Latin word *individuus* is the translation of the Greek *atomos*, which entails that the "individual" is an "indivisible" entity. Science had shown that the embryo can split into two or more without dying up until the 14th day after fertilization. Therefore, it does not satisfy the definition, and hence the term "preembryo" is used to indicate this period of development (Serour 1993b): before 14 days it is a preembryo, up to 40 days it is an embryo, and then a fetus.

This distinction of phases is very important for the bioethical question of how a preembryo, an embryo, and a fetus may be treated. As we will see in the chapter on abortion in this volume by Moustafa Hegab, this distinction is also central in the Islamic discussions on abortion. The distinction finds support in a text from the Holy Qur'an that speaks about stages in the human's embryonic development:

> We created man from an extract of clay. Then We made him as a drop in a place of settlement, firmly fixed. Then We made the drop into an *alaqah* [leech, suspended thing, and blood clot], then We made the *alaqah* into a *mudghah* [chewed substance; fetus], then We made out of that lump bones and clothed the bones with flesh; then We developed out of it another creature. So blessed be God, The Best to create. (Al-Mu'minun (23):12-14)

The Prophet Mohamed later explained that each phase of this development lasts for forty days (*Hadith* Shareef in: Ibn Rajab al-Hanbali 2001: 153). The Arabic word *alaqah* has three meanings: (1) leech, (2) suspended thing, and (3) blood clot. In comparing a leech to an embryo in the *alaqah* stage, we find a similarity between the two (Moore and Persaud 1997: 8). Also, the embryo at this stage obtains nourishment from the blood of the mother, similar to the leech, which feeds on the blood of others. The second meaning of the word *alaqah* is "suspended thing," the suspension of the embryo, during the *alaqah* stage, in the womb of the mother.

The third meaning of the word *alaqah* is "blood clot." We find that the external appearance of the embryo and its sacs during the *alaqah* stage is similar to that of a blood clot. This is due to the presence of relatively large amounts of blood present in the embryo during this stage (Moore, Johnson, and Persaud 1997: 8). Also during this stage, the blood in the embryo does not circulate until the end of the third week (Moore and Persaud 1997: 36). Thus, the embryo at this stage is like a clot of blood.[1]

So the three meanings of the word *alaqah* correspond accurately to the descriptions of the embryo at the *alaqah* stage. The next stage mentioned in the verse is the *mudghah* stage. The Arabic word *mudghah* means "chewed substance"; if we were to

---

[1] For illustrations see: www.islam-guide.com.

chew a piece of gum and then compare it with an embryo in the *mudghah* stage, we would conclude that the embryo at the *mudghah* stage has the appearance of a chewed substance. This is because of the marks on the back of the embryo that "somewhat resemble teeth marks in a chewed substance (Moore and Persaud 1997: 8). From a Muslim perspective, excess preembryos in an IVF program can be used for genetic research purposes provided informed consent is obtained from the couple.

Ethical Considerations

The main ethical concern in embryo research has been the alleged immorality of using embryos for research purposes. Embryo research denigrates the importance of human life by treating embryos as means rather than ends. Embryo research could cause harm to children if the embryos used in research are then placed in the uterus of a woman.

One should not forget, however, that embryo research has non-procreative interests as well, including:

1) improvement of knowledge in "the treatment of infertility";
2) improvement of contraception;
3) treatment and prevention of cancer;
4) treatment and prevention of birth defects.

Population-based embryo research is allowed if it abides by the following principles:

1) it must be in the interest of humanity;
2) it must not cause any harm to the individual, fetus, humankind, or society;
3) it must respect the autonomy of competent persons and protect those incapable of autonomy;
4) it should observe justice, both distributive and corrective;
5) it should insure academic integrity.

The ethical concerns that surround embryo research include the creation of embryos solely for research purposes, limits on the purposes of embryo research, transfer to the uterus after research, and keeping embryos alive in vitro for more than 14 days.

Research could be done only on spare embryos created as by-products of IVF treatment of infertility. Cryopreservation of excess embryos, however, has limited the number of embryos donated for research. The other source of embryos for research can be the creation of embryos solely for research purposes. This leads to the *question if creating embryos solely for research purposes is a reproductive freedom?* Some think we do not have the freedom to create embryos for research purposes only. But one also has to ask if there is a significant moral difference between research on embryos created solely for research purposes and research on spare, discarded embryos. Although most ethical commissions now accept a generous degree of embryo research, controversy continues to surround the production of embryos solely for research purposes. Do the ethical benefits of protecting embryos from being created solely for research purposes justify this loss?

Only a few European nations and the state of Victoria in Australia have legislation prohibiting the production of embryos solely for research purposes. Embryo research was discussed in depth at the first International Conference on Bioethics in Human Reproduction Research in the Muslim world, held in Cairo, 10-13 December 1991. The participants endorsed the following statements on this issue guided by previous recommendations and recent developments in this rapidly developing scientific field (Serour and Omran 1992):

1) Cryptopreserved preembryos may be used for research purposes with the free informed consent of the couple.

2) Research conducted on preembryos should be limited to therapeutic research. The treated embryos will only be transferred to the uterus of the wife who is the owner of the ova and only within a valid marriage contract. This should be applicable to research involving microsurgical techniques as sperm pronuclear extraction to correct polyspermy (Malter and Cohen 1989), and genetic diagnosis of a portion of the embryo, one blastomere, or its nucleus for a specific genetic defect (Gandner and Edwards 1968).

3) Research aimed at changing the inherited characteristics of preembryos, including sex selection is forbidden.

4) The free informed consent of the couple should be obtained before preembryos are subjected to non-therapeutic research. These preembryos are not to be transferred to the uterus of the wife or that of any other women. Research of a commercial nature or not related to the health of mother or child is not allowed.

5) Research should be conducted in research institutes of sound reputation such as specialized research institutes. The researchers should have medical justification and should be skilled at their jobs.

These were the statements issued by the First International Conference on Bioethics in Human Reproduction Research in the Muslim world.

Embryo Research

Judgments about research and treatment in the early stages of human life should be related to the distinctions mentioned. We first have to consider various types of research into the human embryo:

1) research on surplus embryos in in vitro fertilization programs (IVF);
2) preimplantation genetic diagnosis (PGD) for diagnosing various diseases;
3) sex determination for fetal selection;
4) gene therapy;
5) human cloning;
6) research on fetal tissue after abortion.

Research on Surplus Human Embryos in IVF Programs

In IVF programs excess preembryos can be and are used for embryo research in some centers all over the world. This raises an important ethical question concerning the ethical implications of such research.

Science tells us that the human embryo, which is a little clump of cells, is the beginning of human life. It can be shown to be human by the nature of its genetic material, DNA, and the structure of its chromosomes. These components contain the information in chemical code for the development of the embryo into a human person. But one must not forget that it is not only the human embryo that is genetically unique, but every sperm and ovum is also genetically unique. They have all arisen from meiosis, the cell division in the gonads. One must not forget, however, that not every sperm cell and ovum or even an embryo will develop into a human person. There is an enormous natural prenatal loss that is known to occur. Indeed, if everything is favorable, then a human being gradually emerges from only about 20% of embryos. It is, therefore, not surprising that some ethicists and scientists do not consider a human embryo a human person and may, therefore, allow experiments on it that involve killing it (Seller 1993: 135). But these scientists admit the potentiality of human embryos to develop into a human person. This means that great respect must always be accorded to it. Experiments that may harm the embryo, while still allowing it to subsequently realize its potential and become a person, should not be permitted.

The existence of the higher brain is necessary for any form of human rationality. As science has shown that the higher brain only develops several weeks after fertilization, the embryo, therefore, is not a person. This is far from the view voiced by Iglesias and Serra who consider the embryo a person from fertilization (Iglesias 1990: 87; Serra 1990: 78). Surveys of bioethical literature on personhood showed the great difficulty of arriving at an agreed upon set of criteria for personhood (Macklin 1984).

Preimplantation Genetic Diagnosis (PGD)

Following IVF/ICSI preimplantation, genetic diagnosis (PGD) became possible by taking a blastomere from the embryo and performing genetic analysis. Fluorescent in situ hybridization (FISH) with sex and autosomal chromosome probe combinations are used to diagnose the sex of the embryo and aneuploidies. A polymerase chain reaction (PCR) has enormous potential for genetic diagnosis since it amplifies DNA from as few as one or two embryonic cells. A variety of diseases can be identified within a few hours. Sensitivity can be improved by using highly sensitive PCR.

Recent advances in preimplantation genetic diagnosis have significantly increased the possibility of genetic selection at a very early stage. It is now possible to detect these genetic defects before the actual occurrence of pregnancy. Consequently, this will save the couples and the treating physicians from facing the dilemma of late prenatal genetic diagnosis with the difficult decision of whether to terminate the pregnancy or not. If a serious genetic disorder is detected before implantation, the couple may choose to discard transfer of embryos produced in the IVF laboratory. The decisions taken before the occurrence of pregnancy should prevent the birth of a severely handicapped child without the need to induce abortion. A model of this pre-implantation screening is the detection of Down's syndrome, Trisomy 13 and 17, cystic fibrosis, hemophilia, Marfan's syndrome, Bloch-sulzemberg Syndrome (incontinentia pigmentosa), or X-chromosome linked immune deficiency, retinitis pigmentosa, and FG Syndrome (mental retardation and hypotonia), muscular dystrophy, and Lesch-Nyhan disease.

Diagnostic aids should be provided for people in high risk categories for genetic disease. Should the embryo be found genetically defective, the decision not to transfer should be left up to the individuals after proper counseling by their physician.

An ethical controversy on fetal anomalies and viability is raised in reference to the role of newborn intensive nurseries who are sustaining the life in severely deformed babies for the purpose of organ donation (Omran 1992).

Islam has given great importance to the prevention of congenital malformation. Seeking to protect the well-being of children, it advised men to choose wives with great care. The Prophet said: "Select your spouse carefully in the interest of your offspring because lineage is a crucial issue" (*Hadith* Sharif). He also said: "Do not marry your close relatives because you will beget weak offspring" (*Hadith* Sharif). Omar Ibn El-Khattab, one of the Prophet's Companions, after noting that the Saib tribe intermarried too frequently, told them: "You have weakened your descendants. You should marry strangers." Islam has also determined the rights of the fetus in that the mother should not harm or expose the fetus to harm (Gad El-Hak 1992). From a Muslim perspective, if the decision not to transfer is made to protect the mother's life or health or because of a fetal anomaly incompatible with life, it is acceptable (Serour and Omran 1992).

Fetal Sex Selection

Prenatal genetic diagnosis (PGD) on a single blastomere from the embryo in IVF laboratories made it possible for very early selection of the sex of the embryo in IVF programs. This poses the ethical question of the right of the mother or the couple to choose the sex of the baby. It opens up a wide and conflicting debate around non-ethical discrimination against female fetuses in favor of males. Non-therapeutic fetal sex identification and selection and its implications on reproductive self-determination and women's or couple's choices is likely to be a topic of debate in international forums. Sex selection was practiced by the Arabs before Islam when female babies would be buried after their birth. Islam has forbidden such selection since this constitutes a challenge to the will of God (Serour and Omran 1992; Gad El-Hak 1992; Surah Al-Takwir (81):8-9).

There has been a debate in the Muslim world on the possibility of sex selection for non-therapeutic reasons at such an early stage of development (Serour 1997c; Kilani 1999). Social and family balance concerning the number of either sex in the family is one consideration for supporting such an argument. But there is no unanimous agreement among Muslim religious leaders on this issue. Most are agreed that research aiming at changing the inherited characteristics of preembryos, including sex selection, are forbidden since it constitutes a challenge to the will of God. Research of a commercial nature or not related to the health of mother and child are not allowed (Serour and Omran 1992; Gad El Hak 1992).

Gene Therapy

Genetic research on human embryos is part of medical research in general and the ethical requirements and rules of medical research should apply. These rules are governed by agreed international guidelines such as the Nuremberg and Helsinki Declarations (1963 and 1975), the CIOMS (1982) guidelines, the Inuyama Declaration (1990), and the Cairo Declaration (1991) for Muslim Countries.

There are four well-known categories of human gene therapy that help delineate the ethical gene therapy discussion. These include somatic cell gene therapy, germ line gene therapy, enhancement genetic engineering, whether somatic cell enhancement or germ line enhancement, and eugenic genetic engineering.

Genetic manipulation may be desirable to remedy genetic defects. Serious ethical questions begin to arise in those borderline cases where the aim of genetic manipulation shifts from therapy to the creation of a new human type.

From a Muslim perspective, human gene therapy should be restricted to therapeutic indications. Somatic cell gene therapy is encouraged since it should lead to the remedy and alleviation of human suffering. But enhancement genetic engineering or eugenic genetic engineering would involve changing God's creation, which may lead to an imbalance of the whole universe and must therefore be prohibited. Gene therapy to manipulate hereditary traits such as intelligence, stupidity, stature, beauty, or ugliness may unbalance the life of man (Serour 2010).

If any germ line gene therapy is practiced, it should be restricted solely to therapeutic purposes. A prerequisite for this application is that scientists should be absolutely certain that such manipulation will not affect the descendants of patients in an unforeseen pattern, which, given the present state of the art, is almost impossible (Serour 1997a; 1998b).

Cloning

A review on the bioethics of human embryo research would not be compete without a brief reference to the most exciting scientific achievement of the past few years, namely mammalian cloning. The announcement by Wilmut and his colleagues in February 1997 that a lamb had been produced (not created because creation is only for God) by transferring the nucleus of an adult mammary cell from a sheep into an emptied-out egg cell and implanting it, took most people by surprise (Wilmut *et al.* 1997). This largely unanticipated development demonstrates that asexual reproduction of mammals can be brought about with the possibility it may also work in humans.

This development has many implications that need to be thought through so that a sensible and ethical policy can be put in place. Several statements had been issued on this important subject by many scientific bodies and scientific and non-scientific organizations. Most of these early statements, however, did not clearly define what is meant by human cloning, distinguish between embryo splitting and somatic nuclear transfer, or distinguish between cloning for producing a human being and cloning of human embryos for research and therapeutic purposes only (Serour 2006).

a) Embryo Splitting

Embryo splitting naturally occurs in identical twins. Manmade embryo splitting was used for the first time on human embryos in 1992, when researchers divided 17 chromosomally abnormal human embryos (which they therefore would not have implanted in a woman, so they would not have survived). From these embryos, they obtained a total of 48 developing embryos in vitro (Hall et al. 1993). There is no evidence that embryo splitting in the human has ever been used or that it would be effective if it were so used to increase the success rate of IVF because of the pattern of early development of the human embryo.

b) Nuclear Transplantation from Somatic Cells

The second kind of cloning to produce an animal is the one that made headlines with the birth of Dolly, which was done quite differently. A genetic copy of an adult animal was made, bypassing the usual reproductive process. An egg cell from one sheep was emptied of its nucleus and then fused with a body cell containing the nucleus of another adult sheep. This was then implanted in the uterus of yet another ewe. Dolly does not have two genetic parents; rather her genomic DNA is a copy of the DNA in the nucleus of an adult animal. In other words, she is a clone of that adult (Wilmut et al. 1997: 810).

c) Non-Reproductive Cloning

The third type of cloning is non-reproductive cloning. Non-reproductive cloning is not aimed at producing an animal or a person and is limited only to the in vitro phase. Consequently, the resulting embryo is not transferred to the uterus of another woman or animal. It may be stimulated to grow a certain tissue or an organ but not a replicate of the donor of the nucleus (Serour 1998a).

d) Therapeutic Implications of Cloning

Human nuclear transfer could have important therapeutic implications, such as development of appropriate stem cell cultures for repairing human tissues and development of organs for transplantation. It could also provide insight into how to induce the regeneration of damaged human tissues. It may also be used to overcome transfer of mitochondrial diseases and help in the treatment of very severe cases of infertility.

e) Ethical Issues in Cloning
In human beings, a distinction must be made between reproductive cloning aimed at the birth of identical individuals, which has never been performed in humans, and non-reproductive cloning limited to the in vitro phase. Also, a distinction must be made between cloning by embryo splitting and cloning by nuclear replacement.

Human reproductive cloning has been totally banned by almost all organizations and even by Wilmut himself (Wilmut 1997). The reasons for this total ban were basically religious and ethical. For Muslims, procreation is restricted to within the bounds of the marriage contract between a wife and a husband within the framework of the family. No third party participates in the process of procreation by providing an egg, sperm, an embryo, or even a uterus (Serour at al. 1995; 2006). The genetic material of the offspring has to be inherited from both parents. It was felt that if cloning is allowed and widely practiced in its limited concept of producing a human being, it would break family ties, the genetic links between the offspring and both parents, would allow procreation in single women and would create a chaos in the family structure. Furthermore, there are also other risks with cloning. The cloned individuals may have a shorter life span, may suffer from early ageing, and a greater susceptibility to cancer. There were also concerns about whether they would be fertile or not and, if so, whether they or their offspring would suffer from an abnormal rate of genetic abnormalities. Another worry was the cost of the procedure, and it is likely to be immensely expensive since such an attempt would require several eggs and an available uterus. Also, many attempts would have to be done before success could be achieved. The issue of human responsibility and instrumentalization of human beings were other reasons for the prohibition of such techniques (Serour 1998a).

The World Medical Association issued a statement on cloning, calling upon doctors engaged in research and other researchers to abstain voluntarily from participating in the cloning of human beings until the scientific, ethical, and legal issues had been fully considered and any necessary controls put in place (World Medical Association 1998).

The general opinion in the Muslim world today is that research on cloning in laboratory animals, which would add to our understanding of biological processes and contribute to human well-being, is encouraged. After enough experiments on animals ensure its safety, the technique may be applied in the human for alleviation of human sufferings and treatment of diseases such as correction of mitochondrial defects. But under no circumstances whatsoever should it be applied to produce a genetically identical human individual by nuclear substitution from a human adult or child cell (Serour 1998a).

Human cloning may be performed in absolutely infertile married couples to overcome their infertility problem. Nuclear transfer from the husband's somatic cell to the enucleated ovum of the wife may be performed within a valid marriage contract. This scenario should be restricted only to a very few cases that are not amenable to treatment by other simpler methods. This line of treatment should not be implemented except after enough animal data shows its efficacy, safety, and that no serious genetic alternations are likely to occur in such situation. It should not be ignored, however, that there is no consensus among the various religious bodies on this issue. Some see it as farfetched and not likely to happen in the near future and should not be done (Serour 1998a).

Research on Fetal Tissue Obtained through Abortion

Is research performed on fetuses or fetal tissue obtained through abortion permissible? An example of such is research connected with the transplantation of fetal tissue into patients suffering from Parkinson's disease. From a Muslim perspective, such research is permitted, provided the informed consent of the couple, the owners of the fetal tissue, has first been obtained.

Fetal ovarian tissue transfer could enable the provision of eggs for use and research in artificial reproduction. This includes the possibility of creating children who will have a fetus as their genetic mother. The genetic grandparents of these children will be the contemporaries of their birth parents. Though research on fetal ovarian tissue for the improvement of the results of artificial reproduction and other therapeutic purposes is ethically acceptable in the Muslim world, its use for creation of children is unacceptable since those children would not be related to their genetic parents (Serour 2010).

Conclusion

In this chapter we investigated the treatment of embryos from an Islamic perspective. First, we discussed how the stages of embryonic development are approached in Islam. Subsequently, we presented some general ethical considerations with regard to the distinctions made in the embryo's development. Finally, we discussed the use of embryos in both medical treatments and research: What treatment and research is allowed and what is prohibited ethically and religiously? For each specific use, we formulated an ethical position from an Islamic perspective. In this last section, we will now present a concluding overview of our consideration of the treatment of embryos from an Islamic perspective.

Those to whom religion is important, which it is to Muslims, need to distinguish between medical ethics and humanitarian considerations on the one hand and religious teachings and national laws on the other. MAC-IVF was not mentioned in the primary sources of *shari'ah*, but these same sources have affirmed the importance of marriage, family formation, and procreation. In Islam adoption is not acceptable as a solution to the problem of infertility. The treatment of infertility is allowed and encouraged in Islam as long as the treatment remains within the legal relations of marriage. It is essential if it involves the preservation of procreation and treatment of infertility in one or both spouses. This applies to MAC which is one way of treating infertility. The modern techniques of MAC, including micromanipulation of the oocyte (the immature female reproductive cell) to facilitate fertilization, are no exceptions. The prevention and treatment of infertility are of particular significance in the Muslim world. The social status of the Muslim woman, her dignity, her self-esteem and her place in the family and society as a whole are closely related to her procreation. Childbirth and child rearing are regarded as family commitments and not just biological and social functions. MAC-IVF is therefore a sensitive area, both with concern to scientific research and medical treatment.

First and foremost, in Muslim societies, account should be taken of the provisions and spirit of Islamic *shari'ah* in formulating rules and guidelines, taking into account local and social conditions of the society where research is conducted. In Islam, however, since it is a religion of mercy and compassion, one should not inflict any harm on human beings or animals in conducting or applying the results of such research (Gad El-Hak 1992).

Central to the Islamic ethical argumentation is the division of three stages in the earliest development of human life. We have seen that the preembryos should be treated carefully and with respect but are not considered human persons. Research can help understand human life and improved treatments. Nevertheless, gene therapy for improvement of the genetic codes of humankind is very debatable. With concern to fertility procedures, the foremost restriction for help in fertilization is that only the egg and seed of the married couple will be used—for the reason that the lineage in the family, on which family law is based, would otherwise be broken.

Bibliography

Bankowski, Z. and A.M. Capron. (1991). *Genetics, Ethics and Human Values: Genome Mapping, Genetic Screening and Gene Therapy. Ethical Issues*. XXVIth CIOMS: The Tokyo and Inuyama Conference. Geneva: CIOMS.

Dickens, B. (1992). "Guidelines on the Use of Human Subjects in Medical Research." In: G.I. Serour (ed.). *Proceedings of the First International Conference on Bioethics in Human Reproduction Research in the Muslim World, 10-13 December 1991*. Vol. I. Cairo: IICPSR, Pp. 190-201.

Eldadah, Z.A.; J.A. Grifo, and H.C. Dietz (1995). "Marfan Syndrome as a Paradigm for Transcription-targeted Preimplantation Diagnosis of Heterozygous Mutations." *Nature Medicine* 1: 798-803.

Fathalla, M. (1992). "Ethics in Medical Research." In: G.I. Serour (ed.). *Proceedings of the First International Conference on Bioethics in Human Reproduction in Research in the Muslim World, 10-13 December 1991*. Cairo: IICPSR. Pp. 173-182.

Gad El-Hak, Ali. (1992). "Islam a Religion of Ethics." In: G.I. Serour (ed.). *Proceedings of The First International Conference on Bioethics in*

Human Reproduction in Research in the Muslim World, 10-13 December 1991. Cairo: IICPSR. Pp. 37-39.

Gardner, R.L., and R.G. Edwards. (1968). "Control of Sex Ratio at Full Term in the Rabbit by Transferring Sexed Blastocysts." *Nature* 218: 346-48.

Gibbons, W.E., S.A. Gitlin, and S.E. Lanzendorf. (1995). "Pre-implantation Genetic Diagnosis for Tay Sachs Disease: Successful Pregnancy after Pre-embryo Biopsy and Amplifications by Polymerase Chain Reaction." *Fertility and Sterility* 63: 623-28.

Grifo, J.A. *et al.* (1998). "Successful Outcome with Day 4 Embryo Transfer after Preimplantation Diagnosis for Genetically Transmitted Diseases." *Human Reproduction* 13: 1656-59.

Hall, J.L. *et al.* (1993). "Experimental Cloning of Human Polypoid Embryos Using an Artificial Zone." *The American Fertility Society cojointly with the Canadian Fertility and Andrology Society, Program Supplement*, 1993. Abstract of the Scientific Oral and Poster Sessions, Abstract 0.001, S1.

Harper, J.C. (1994). "Preimplantation Diagnosis of Inherited Disease by Embryo Biopsy: An Update of the World Figures." *Journal of Assisted Reproduction and Genetics* 13: 90-95.

Ibn Rajab al-Hanbali. (2001). *Jami Al-Uloem Wa-Al-Hikam*. Vol. I. Beirut: Moasasat Al-Risalh.

Iglesias, T. (1990). *What Kind of Being to the Human Embryo? IVF and Justice*. London: The Linacre Center for Health Care Ethics.

Kamali M.H. Urf. (1991). "Custom." In: *Principles of Islamic Jurisprudence*. Cambridge: Islamic Texts Society. Pp. 283-96.

Kilani, Z. (1999). "Pre-implantation Genetic Diagnosis for Family Balance and Sex Chromosome Aneuploidies." Paper submitted to the 5th International Conference of the Egyptian Fertility and Sterility Society, Cairo, 23-24 September.

Lagay, Faith (2003). "Pre-implantation Genetic Diagnosis." *American Medical Association*. http://www.ama-assn.org/pub/category5717.html. (Accessed 1 May 2003).

Macklin, R. (1984). "Personhood and the Abortion Debate." In: J.L. Garfield and P. Hennessey (eds.). *Abortion: Moral and Legal Perspectives*. Amherst: University of Massachusetts Press. Pp. 81-102.

Malter, H.E., and J. Cohen. (1989). "Embryonic Development after Microsurgical Repair of Polyspermic Human Zygotes Fertil." *Sterility* 52: 373-80.

McLaren, A. (1989). *Can We Diagnose Genetic Disease in Pre-embryos? Report on the Use of Human Foetal Embryonic and Pre-embryonic Material for Diagnostic, Therapeutic, Scientific, Industrial and Commercial Purposes.* Strasbourg: Council of Europe.

Moore, Keith L., and T.V.N. Persaud. (1997). *The Developing Human: Clinically Oriented Embryology.* 5th ed. Houston: Darussalam.

Moore, Keith L., E.M. Johnson, and T.V.N. Persaud (eds.). (1997). *Human Development as Described in the Qur'an and Sunnah.* Houston: Islamic Academy for Research.

Omran, A. (1990). "UN Data on Demography of the Islamic World." Paper presented at the International Conference on Islam and Population Policy, Jakarta and Lhokseumawe, Indonesia.

Omran, K. (1992). "Women's Perspectives on Bioethics in Human Reproduction Research: Women's Viewpoint." In: G.I. Serour (ed.). *Proceedings of the First International Conference on Bioethics in Human Reproduction in Research in the Muslim World, 10-13 December 1991.* Cairo: IICPSR. Pp. 163-69.

Rahman F. (1979). "Legacy and Prospects." In: *Islam.* 2nd ed. Chicago: University of Chicago Press. Pp. 235-54.

Robertson, J. (1994). *Freedom and the New Reproductive Technologies in Children of Choice.* Princeton: Princeton University Press.

Seller, M.J. (1993). "The Human Embryo: A Scientist's Point of View." *Bioethics* 7: 135-40.

Serour, G.I. (2010). "Bioethics in infertility Management in the Muslim World": http://Islamic-World.Net/sister/h12.htm.

(2006), "Human Cloning." *International Journal of Gynaecology and Obstetrics* 93: 282.

(2005). "Religious Perspectives of Ethical Issues in ART. 1. Islamic Perspectives of Ethical Issues in ART." *Middle East Fertility Society Journal* X. http://www.bioline.org.br/pdf?mf05030.

(1998a). "Human Cloning: Its Applications and Ethical Guidelines." Paper presented at the Conference on the "Cloning Dilemma." Dubai, UAE, 4-5 April.

(1998b). "Islamic Perspectives on Genetic Technology and Information Use." In: J. Kegley (ed). *Genetic Knowledge: Human Values and Responsibility.* Lexington: ICUS. Pp. 197-214.

(1997a). "Islamic Developments in Bioethics." In: B.A. Lustig (ed.). *Bioethics Yearbook.* Vol. 5. Dordrecht: Kluwer Academic Publishers. Pp. 171-88.

(1997b). Paper in the Scientific WHO Ethical Review Group. Human Cloning, The Global Response, Geneva, 24 October.

(ed.). (1997c). *Proceedings of ISESCO Al-Azhar International Workshop on Assisted Reproductive Technology, 25-27 August 1997*. Cairo: ISESCO.

(1995). "Bioethics in Medically Assisted Conception in the Muslim World." *Journal of Assisted Reproduction and Genetics* 12: 559-65.

(1993a). "Bioethics in Artificial Reproduction in the Muslim World." *Bioethics Special Issue*. Inaugural Congress of the International Association of Bioethics, Amsterdam. 7: 207-17.

(1993b). "Ethical Issues in Population Based Genetic Research." In: *Proceedings of the International Seminar on Bioethics, 22-26 November*. Knox College, Dunedin, New Zealand, Bioethics Research Center, University of Otago.

(1992). "Bioethics in Medically Assisted Conception Research: Dilemma of Practice and research: Islamic Views." In: *Proceedings of the First International Conference on Bioethics in Human Reproduction Research in the Muslim World, 10-13 December 1991*. Cairo: IICPSR. Pp. 234-42.

Serour, G.I., M.A. Aboulghar, and R.T. Mansour (1995). "Bioethics in Medically Assisted Conception in the Muslim World." *Journal of Assisted Reproduction and Genetics* 12: 559-65.

Serour, G. I., M.A. Aboulghar, and R.T. Mansour. (1990). "In Vitro Fertilization and Embryo Transfer: Ethical Aspects in Techniques in the Muslim World." *Population Sciences* 9: 45-53.

Serour, G.I., and A. Omran. (1992). "Ethical Guidelines." In: *Proceedings of the First International Conference on Bioethics in Human Reproduction Research in the Muslim World, 10-13 December 1991*. Cairo: IICPSR. Pp. 37-39.

Serra, A. (1990). "Dalle Nuove Frontiere Della Biologia et Della Medicina Nuovi Interrogativi alla Filosifa al Diritto alla Teologia in Embriopoiesi Umana." In: A. Serra, E. Sgreccia, and M.L. Di Pietro (eds.). *Nuovo Genetica ed embriopoiesi umana*. Milan: Vita et Pensiero.

Sharif. "El Moghny 'an Haml El Asfaar." In: *El-Eraqi ma'a El Ahyaa* 2/41. El Rayan-El Torath.

WHO Technical Report Series 820. (1992). *Recent Advances in Medically Assisted Conception*. Report of a WHO Scientific Group. Geneva: WHO.

Wilmut, I. (1997). "Cloning Never on Humans." Paper on the FIGO World Congress of Gynecology and Obstetrics- Copenhagen, 3-8 August.

Wilmut, I. *et al.* (1997). "Viable Offspring Derived from Foetal and Adult Mammalian Cells." *Nature* 385: 810-13.

World Medical Association (1998). "Resolution on Cloning." *The Egyptian Journal of Fertility and Sterility* II: 67.

CHAPTER VIII

The Moral Status
of the Human Embryo

Christian Perspectives
and the Impact of New Technologies

Egbert Schroten

Introduction

Let me start my contribution to this volume by making two introductory remarks. In the first place, I would like to thank Ayman Nassar and his colleagues for their clear and informative chapter on the approaches regarding the status of human embryos from the perspective of Islamic ethics. He offers relevant and fundamental information on human embryology, fertilization, and reproductive technologies. That is why I can refer to his chapter for embryological data as well as for an overview of the various types of embryo research. It gives me the opportunity to concentrate on ethical issues from a Christian perspective. This brings me to my second remark, however: I would like to stress that there is no such thing as "the" Christian position concerning the moral status of the human embryo. In Christian tradition we can find a variety of views.[1] But, as far as I can see, this is the case in the Islamic context as well. What I want to do, then, is to make some remarks on the main lines of thought in Christian tradition, followed by facing a problem raised by new technologies in the context of reproduction, like IVF and cryopreservation (preservation through deep-freezing).

---

[1] There is much literature on this theme, but personally I think that the books by J.T. Noonan Jr. are very informative. Cf. Noonan 1972 and 1986. For the Netherlands I can refer to the PhD thesis of Jan te Lindert; cf. Te Lindert 1998.

The aim of my chapter is to show that science and technology lead us here into new problem areas where we have to reconsider traditional moral positions.

Roots and Context

The roots of Christian thinking about the human embryo can be found in Greek philosophy and in the Bible. In Greek philosophy, it is, in particular, Aristotelian embryology that has been very influential. Aristotle teaches that a human embryo, after conception, develops into a living being (*zoon*). A crucial phase in this development is the formation of the heart, the seat of sensitive life. When the heart is formed the embryo can have sensations. So there are, at least, two phases in the development of an embryo: a vegetative phase and a sensitive phase. And an embryo is a living being as soon as it acquires human similarity in form. It would be interesting to elaborate in this context on what Aristotle teaches about "ensoulment" during pregnancy, but here the important thing to know is that it is the "soul" that makes an embryo a living being. He distinguishes between a vegetative "soul" (which is present right from the beginning), the "soul" that makes an embryo a living being, and a rational "soul." According to Aristotle, this last phase of ensoulment takes place after birth, which means that for him, quite unlike many thinkers after him, it does not play a role in the evaluation of the moral status of the embryo (cf. Te Lindert 1998: 43ff., 110f.).

As to the second root, the Bible, its influence cannot of course be reduced to one text, but it is nevertheless clear that Exodus 21:22 (in the *Septuagint*, the Greek translation of the Old Testament) plays an important role in Christian thinking about the status of the embryo. In this text, in the second book of the Bible, a distinction is made between an "unformed" (*mè exeikonismenon*) and a "formed" (*exeikonismenon*) fetus: if a woman is hit when men are fighting and consequently suffers a miscarriage, a fine must be paid if the fetus is "unformed." But if the fetus is "formed" then it is a question of giving a life for a life. In other words, the moral status of a "formed" fetus appears to be higher than that of an "unformed" fetus. This was, in any case, the opinion of Philo of Alexandria (first half of the first century C.E.), a Jewish thinker who influenced many thinkers in early Christianity. He teaches, in the wake of Aristotle and the Septuagint translation of Exodus 21:22, that the "formed" fetus is to be seen as a "person" (Te Lindert 1998: 111).

A third relevant point here is the social context in the Hellenistic world in which early Christianity developed. In this society abortion, infanticide, and certain forms of contraception were present, perhaps not everywhere but in any case so often and so widespread that they were mentioned and rejected already in early Christian writings. So we can read in the *Didachè* (i.e. *The Teaching of the Apostles*, probably written at the beginning of the second century): "…. thou shalt not kill a child by abortion, nor take the life of what is born …" (II, 2; see also the *Epistle of Barnabas* 20). In the context of this presentation it is not feasible to elaborate on the many documents that are available in the ages that follow. They all show the rejection of abortion, infanticide, and (often also) contraception. It was Tertullian (second half of the second century) who formulated one of the main arguments against these practices: *Homo est et qui est futurus* ("A future human being is a human being as well") (Tertullian, *Apologeticum* IX, 8). This "slogan" clearly indicates the (moral) status of the human embryo: an embryo is a future human being and should be treated as such, which means in practice that it should be protected. It is also interesting to read at the same place that Tertullian thought that the *fructus* (= embryo) was present in the sperm. This view must be the reason why, in those days, contraception and masturbation were often rejected.

Lines of Thought

One could thus say that, in early Christianity, the trend (and tone) was set already at the end of the first century. As to the moral status of the human embryo, however, it may be clear that it was of vital importance to know when a human embryo could be seen or treated as a "person." In the language of that time, the answer to this question depended on the answer to the question of when the human soul came into the body. In theory, two lines of thought can be distinguished in Christian tradition: traducianism and creationism. In traducianism, in the wake of Aristotelian embryology, the soul is present in the embryo from conception onward, which presupposes a kind of growth process in the developing embryo or an "ensoulment" in phases. In creationism, the soul is created immediately by God (at conception). In practice, there is much discussion between representatives of these two lines of thought and sometimes both may even be found in the writings of one thinker, for instance, in Augustine. A combination or compromise also became very influential: life is "traduced" by the parents, but the (rational) soul is created by God after the embryo has been "formed" in the womb, for boys after forty days and for girls after ninety. Killing an "ensouled" embryo could therefore be seen as homicide (Te Lindert 1998: 93ff.; Noonan 1986: 86ff.).

Let me repeat that, in Christian tradition, there are many viewpoints and nuances as to the status of the human embryo. But if one tried to summarize the discussion, one could say that these viewpoints and nuances are somewhere in between the two lines of thought: (1) the embryo is a human being right from the beginning because the soul is created by God immediately after conception, and (2) the embryo is a human being after it is "formed" because the human soul is created by God after the embryo has been "formed." If the language of "ensoulment" is left behind one could "translate" these positions into one that stresses the continuity of development from conception onward and another that holds that some conditions must be met before one can speak of (an embryo as) a human being or person.

A modern example of the first approach can be found in the Roman Catholic Instruction *Donum Vitae* (1987). This official document of the Congregation for the Doctrine of the Faith takes its starting point in the conviction that God entrusted the gift of life to humans and demands that they be aware of its priceless value and accept responsibility for it. Against this background three norms are mentioned for science and technology in the context of (the beginning of) human life: (1) respect, defense, and the development of human life; (2) the first and fundamental right to life; and (3) the dignity of the human person with a spiritual soul, moral responsibility, and called into communion with God (Introduction, § 1). In the light of these norms *Donum Vitae* teaches that the human embryo must be respected as a person from conception onwards because a human being is the only creature created by God for its own sake, his soul is created directly by God, he is created in the image of God, and he (therefore) has a special relation to God. In other words, the human embryo from conception on is a bearer of human dignity and must be protected as such (Introduction, § 5).

An Anglican report called *Personal Origins* (1985, revised in 1996) may be seen as a modern example of the combination of the approaches that were mentioned above. In the light of recent developments in science related to human fertilization and embryology, both approaches are accepted as valid interpretations of the status of the early embryo, because they (1) are based on the same scientific evidence but interpret this evidence differently, (2) both appeal to biblical and theological arguments, (3) have their roots in Christian tradition, and (4) agree that the status of the embryo depends on (aspects of) the embryo itself (ch. 3, §§ 91ff.). The divergence between the two lines of thought in Christian tradition

> lies in the different ways in which the two schools of thought have framed the question about the human subject, the one concentrating upon its individual continuity, the other on its generic dignity as the subject of consciousness. (ch. 3, § 101)

This difference in assessment of the status of the (early) embryo means in practice that part of the working party that wrote *Personal Origins* showed more openness for technological interventions and embryo research than the other part, albeit under strict conditions (ch. 5, §§ 119ff.).

That there are various trends in modern Christianity as to the status of the human embryo is also clear in some documents issued by the Conference of European Churches (CEC).[2] One of them contains a nice summary of the various positions:

---

[2] The CEC is the regional ecumenical organization for the whole of Europe, comprising 126 churches from all traditions (Protestant, Orthodox, Anglican, Old Catholic) except the Roman Catholic Church. The documents were prepared by a working group on bioethics and biotechnology. Like the Anglican report *Personal Origins*, they do not have the status of an official instruction, like the Roman Catholic *Donum Vitae*, but they can be seen as documents to stimulate reflection

Among our member churches there are many for whom all research on embryos which causes their destruction is completely unacceptable, as a matter of fundamental principle. Human life is seen as a continuum from conception to death. To destroy an embryo by using it for research is tantamount to the willful destruction of a human life. For those holding this view, the ethical case is clear and straightforward. The position is "under no circumstances".... Many of our churches do not, however, share this view and consider that the status of the human embryo increases with development, and would allow embryo research under particular circumstances ... providing that no other means are possible and that embryos are not used beyond 14 days. This is a "yes, provided ..." position. Others argue, on the contrary, that to use embryos merely as a source of cells is too instrumental, negating any sense that the human embryo has a special status. To the extent that embryo research is allowed for limited purposes, a measure of instrumentality is accepted, but this does not mean that all uses are thereby permitted. Many .... might reluctantly agree to the use of surplus embryos from IVF treatment, given that these would normally be destroyed. This position is "No unless ...." (CEC 2006: 1-2)

In a report, *Mensen in wording,*[3] written on behalf of the two Protestant churches that now form, together with the Evangelical Lutheran Church, the Protestant Church in the Netherlands, one can also find the two approaches we have met above: the underlining of the continuity of embryonic life from conception on one hand, and the underlining of the growth process of the embryo as ethically relevant on the other. The report argues for keeping these two approaches closely together and speaking of an "increasing worthiness of the human embryo of protection" (p. 20).

---

and discussion on certain themes in the member churches. In *Personal Origins* it is expressly stated that "This report has only the authority of the Board by which it was prepared" (p. ii).

[3] See especially pp. 16-20.

New Technologies and the Status of the Human Embryo[4]

It should be possible to make a provisional conclusion by now, namely, that, from a Christian perspective, killing human embryos is either not allowed or morally very problematic because embryos are (future) human beings. Precisely for that reason they deserve a high level of protection. In the light of Christian tradition one could perhaps defend this position, but at present some additional remarks should be made. The two lines of thought on the status of the human embryo, and therefore this provisional conclusion as well, are about embryos in the womb, since until recently there were no other embryos. But since about the 1970s, new technologies have been developed in the field of reproduction, such as in vitro fertilization (IVF) and embryo cryopreservation (preservation of embryos by deep-freezing). This new situation has an important consequence, namely, that there are now two categories of embryos, one inside the womb, *in utero*, and one outside the womb, in vitro or in the freezer. This consequence of new technologies is far reaching, for it gives us the possibility, for the first time in human history, to make decisions about the destination of these embryos. In a parental context we could transfer them into the womb of the mother *in spe*, but we could also use them for other purposes, such as (stem cell) research. And it is even possible to create and culture embryos, not for a possible pregnancy but merely for other aims.

It goes without saying that the impact of these new technologies is not restricted to Christian ethics alone. Science and technology are of global importance, and my plea is that we discuss it together in (religious) ethics. So I appreciate it that the issue of the moral status of the human embryo was on the agenda of this dialogue conference. One of the crucial questions here is, of course, if the distinction between the two categories of embryos (*in utero* and in vitro/the freezer) is morally relevant—in other words, if these two categories of embryos have different moral statuses. In my view they have: if we decide to use human embryos for other aims than a possible pregnancy, they

---

[4] Part of what follows here is taken from Schroten 2008.

are not future human beings though they are human embryos. Consequently, it is not necessary to treat them like that. It means that we may change the earlier formulated provisional conclusion so that the use of spare embryos or cultured embryos for research is allowed under strict conditions (including, for instance, the importance of the aim of research and the lack of alternatives), to be assessed by an independent ethics committee.

But this, perhaps, may sound as if we are jumping to conclusions. One could think of counterarguments. One that is often used could be labeled "the ontological status argument." The attempt to make a distinction regarding the moral status of the human embryo, falling back on the destination of the embryos, does not take into account the ontological status of the embryo, in other words, its essence or nature. Because of its genetic makeup, every human embryo is essentially a potential human being, an embryo in vitro or in the freezer as well. This is undeniably so,[5] but I do not think that it is a strong argument against my position that the destination of embryos is morally relevant and, thus, should be taken into account in ethics and in policy making. Let me explain this as follows: the potentiality of a human embryo to become a human being is certainly there but it is, if I may say so, a very weak potentiality because its actualization is heavily dependent on external factors. In other words, the actualization depends on conditions that do *not* belong to the potentiality or the "ontological status" of the embryo itself. This is already the case for an embryo in the womb but even more so for an embryo in vitro: In order to become a future human being, such an embryo must be transferred into the womb and it must nestle there so that (hopefully) a healthy

---

[5] This is the very reason why I underlined, at the end of the previous section, that the use of human embryos in research has to meet strict conditions. Because of their genetic makeup, because of their potentiality, their moral status must, for instance, be distinguished from that of laboratory animals. How this moral status should be worked out in practical rules and guidelines is an important and interesting issue on its own.

pregnancy may begin. If these conditions are not met and the embryo is left to its own inherent potentiality, it will die. In other words, the genetic makeup of a spare embryo is certainly a necessary but not a sufficient condition for becoming a future human being. It means, in my view, that the ontological status argument is not convincing.[6]

Or is it nonetheless convincing, if combined with another argument, the "right to life" argument? This argument purports that every (any?) human embryo (thus a spare embryo as well) has the right to life. I do not want to elaborate on the difficulties of "rights language" in the context of unborn (future) human beings, let alone fertilized eggs. In practice, the argument means in this context that every spare embryo must be brought into the situation that it has a chance to become a future human being. Every spare embryo (fertilized ovum) must be transferred into a womb. But the question here is: Why? And how? It may, for instance, be very difficult to find enough future (surrogate) mothers. Moreover, many spare embryos may have biological/genetic deficiencies or may be damaged when they are thawed, which would make it immoral to transfer them into a womb because of the risk of spontaneous abortion or (severe) congenital defects. In short, the questions "why" and "how" are open moral questions. It may be clear that they cannot be answered by falling back on the ontological status argument, for that would be a *petitio principii* (circular argument, begging the question). As has already been said above, the genetic makeup of embryos is a necessary but not sufficient condition to become a future human being. In my view, it is indeed an open moral question as to what we are allowed to do with this category of human embryos.

---

[6] In my opinion, the same way of arguing can be used when "ontological status" is replaced by "entelechy." The concept "entelechy" was originally coined by Aristotle, and means, roughly, the realization or actualization of what is potentially present in a being, more specifically in an organism. The point I want to make is that this actualization, at least in the case of a human embryo, depends on conditions that do *not* belong to what is potentially present in the organism.

But there is more. We know that, in natural procreation, probably more than 60% of human embryos will never become future human beings because they "disappear" at an early stage, probably partly because of problems in cell division, in short by natural selection. This, of course, does not mean that we can use human embryos for whatever purpose we want. What it does mean, however, is that it is not a law of nature that every human embryo becomes a future human being. In the light of all this, the "right to life" argument, then, could be rejected through *reductio ad absurdum* (refutation of an argument because of its absurd consequences), mainly because it will lead to irresponsible and thus to morally objectionable behavior.

From a Christian (and Muslim) perspective, however, we have to mention a religious argument as well: the human embryo is God's creation. In this chapter I will limit myself to two remarks regarding this argument. The first is a theological question: We may very well believe that the human embryo is God's creation, but what does that mean in practice? The concept of creation is not restricted to human embryos. It is a very wide concept, and it is difficult to make it operational in ethics, partly because it is not clear, partly because it is applied in various ways (at least in Christian tradition). It cannot be interpreted as a sort of taboo, for we do not treat creation as such. If it is supposed to mean that we should respect human embryos, it is not of great help, for the next question would be: How? In what way? It looks as if this argument is not of much help in this context.

Nonetheless, and that is my second remark, in Christian tradition—and, as far as I know in Muslim and Jewish tradition as well—special attention is paid to the creation of the soul. We have already seen that there are roughly two lines of thought here: first, the (rational) soul is created during pregnancy, and, second, it is created at conception. Let me be clear: this is not an attempt to return to the embryology of the old days—it is an attempt to read the creation argument in a certain way. We should respect the human embryo because it is a *human* embryo, because it has human dignity. Let us, for the sake of argument, leave out the line of thought that the (rational) soul is created during pregnancy, which means that the human embryo does not possess human dignity immediately after conception. If we follow the line of thought that attributes human dignity to embryos immediately after conception, we find ourselves back with a religious version of the ontological status argument and/or the "right to life" argument. But in that case, the creation argument would meet the same difficulties as these two arguments, including the *reductio ad absurdum* problem, for it would mean that more than 60% of created souls never become human beings. Theologically, the absurdity would be underlined by the implication that the Holy One would create futile "things." It goes without saying that Christians and Muslims have much more to say about their belief in creation, but the point I want to make here is that the counterarguments just mentioned are not convincing.

Conclusion

In this chapter I have tried to briefly clarify the roots and context of Christian thinking on the moral status of the human embryo. Two main lines of thought have been distinguished, based on the idea that a human embryo has to be seen and treated as a future human being. Some examples have been put forward to show how these two approaches play a role in recent documents in some Christian churches. Then I argued that new technologies in the field of reproduction, like IVF and cryopreservation, force us to make a distinction between two categories of (human) embryos, (1) inside the womb and (2) outside the womb. Moreover, this distinction is morally relevant because an embryo outside the womb is not necessarily a future human being. Some counterarguments have been analyzed and found unconvincing. The practical consequence of my position is that the use of spare embryos or embryos especially created for research is allowed under strict conditions.

This means that I want to stick to my claim, made at the end of my introduction, that science and technology, whether we like it or not, lead us into new situations where we have to rethink traditional moral principles and values, and where we have to make new distinctions and choices. Needless to say, this goes for Christian and Muslim ethics as well. Ethics (and faith in general!) is a dynamic undertaking, and new situations cannot always be met by old answers.

In a volume on dialogue between Muslims and Christians we find ourselves confronted with the same questions in changing societies and in the development of sciences and (new) technologies. What do they mean for our communities of believers? How could we help them? What is the function of our holy books, the Qur'an and the Bible, in this context? How should we make use of the treasury of our traditions? In short, it will not suffice to discuss interesting topics. Rather, discussing interesting topics should take place in the perspective of what our rich traditions could mean for modern society. It is a problem we have to deal with, both as Muslims and Christians. So, in this respect, the dialogue could not only be fruitful for understanding each other but also for helping each other to solve moral problems in modern society.

Bibliography

Barnaba Epistolè. In: Joseph A. Fischer *et al. Schriften des Urchristentums.* Vol. 2. Darmstadt: Wissenschafliche Buchgesellschaft, 1993/2004. Pp. 101-202.

Conference of European Churches (CEC). (2006). *New Issues in Stem Cells and Regenerative Medicine.* csc@cec-kek.com.

Congregation for the Doctrine of the Faith. (1987). *Donum Vitae: Instruction on Respect for Human Life in Its Origin and on the Dignity of Procreation.* http://www.vatican.va/roman_curia/congregations/cfaith/documents/rc_con_cfaith_doc_19870222_respect-for-human-life_en.html.

Didachè toon apostoloon. In: Joseph A. Fischer *et al. Schriften des Urchristentums.* Vol. 2. Darmstadt: Wissenschafliche Buchgesellschaft, 1993/2004. Pp. 1-100.

Lindert, Jan te. (1998). *Over de status van het menselijk embryo in de joodse en de christelijke ethiek.* Ph.D. Dissertation. Utrecht University.

Mensen in wording. Theologische, ethische en pastorale overwegingen bij nieuwe voortplantingstechnieken en prenataal onderzoek. Een verkenning. Report submitted to the General Synods of the Netherlands Reformed Church and the Reformed Churches in the Netherlands. 1992.

Noonan, J.T. Jr. (1972). *The Morality of Abortion.* London: Oxford University Press.

(1986). *Contraception: A History of its Treatment by the Catholic Theologians and Canonists.* Cambridge, MA/London: The Belknap Press of Harvard University Press.

Personal Origins: The Report of a Working Party on Human Fertilisation and Embryology of the Board for Social Responsibility. 2nd rev. ed. London: Church House. (Originally published 1985).

Schroten, E. (2008). "Human Embryo Research: The European Perspective." In: Lars Ostnor (ed.). *Stem Cells, Human Embryos and Ethics: Interdisciplinary Perspectives.* Heidelberg: Springer. Pp. 111-20.

Tertullianus Apologeticum: Verdediging der Christenen. Transl. and explained by P.C. IJsseling. Amsterdam: Uitg. Holland, 1947.

CHAPTER IX

Reflections on Termination of Pregnancy for Genetic or Non-Genetic Congenital Disorders

Leo P. ten Kate

Introduction

When I started my career in genetics in the late 1960s I opposed induced abortion, except where the mother's life was in danger. A few years later, when prenatal diagnosis for Down syndrome and other chromosomal anomalies became possible, I had already changed my mind. I had, in the meantime, seen enough patients and parents suffering from genetic disorders that I could now justify the choice of couples to terminate a pregnancy when confronted with a genetic or non-genetic congenital disorder in the couple's expected child. That does not mean that my wife and I would have made the same decision when personally confronted with an increased chance of Down syndrome in our child. We discussed this and were of the opinion that we would not opt for prenatal diagnosis for advanced maternal age. We were never challenged, however, to show the credibility of our intention, as our children were born before we reached that age.

Many years later, in the early 1990s, when I became full professor of clinical genetics at the VU University, I devoted my inaugural lecture to arguing against the position of the leading confessional political party in this country, the Christian Democratic Appeal, which had produced a report called *Genen en Grenzen* (Genes and Boundaries), that advanced a conservative view based on the notion of stewardship (CDA 1992; Ten Kate 1994). Stewardship, in my opinion, puts a one-sided emphasis on protection and conservation, tacitly implying that nature is ideal and perfect. I made the case that nature, the result of creation, was too merciless not to act. I referred to the notion of co-creation as a mission for us. Co-creation assumes that God's creation is unfinished and should be complemented by human beings (Sölle and Cloyes 1984).

My indignation about the unfairness of nature has remained (Ten Kate 2003), but I no longer emphasize the mission of co-creation, since co-creation can be easily misunderstood as an excuse for eugenic approaches. Moreover, the term co-creation has at present been secularized to mean a market or business strategy that emphasizes the collaboration between firms and active consumers to enhance each other's capabilities. Also, there was a symposium at VU University Amsterdam some time ago on co-creation in rehabilitation medicine, suggesting that doctors and patients should work together to create recovery of health and well-being through shared values.

In this chapter I will show that clinical genetics, community genetics, prenatal diagnosis and screening, as well as the Dutch Termination of Pregnancy Act, are characterized by respect for the autonomy of the client or patient and that their success should be judged, not by counting prevented births, but by a measure of informed choice. In addition, three cases will be presented that illustrate some difficult ethical or emotional aspects of decisions about termination of pregnancy for genetic disorders.

Clinical Genetics

Clinical genetics is a medical specialism devoted to informing individuals and families about genetic aspects of the disorder or the risk of a disorder in them, their children, or elsewhere in the family. To be able to deliver correct information a precise diagnosis is necessary, as well as an evaluation of the pedigree and family medical history. The end product of the clinical genetic work-up is genetic counseling. Genetic counseling was defined by the American Society of Human Genetics as follows:

> Genetic counseling is a communication process which deals with the human problems associated with the occurrence, or the risk of occurrence, of a genetic disorder in a family.
>
> This process involves an attempt by one or more appropriately trained persons to help the individual or family to

(1) comprehend the medical facts, including the diagnosis, probable course of the disorder, and the available management;

(2) appreciate the way heredity contributes to the disorder, and the risk of recurrence in specified relatives;

(3) understand the alternatives for dealing with the risk of recurrence;

(4) choose the course of action which seems to them appropriate in view of their risk, their family goals, and their ethical and religious standards, and to act in accordance with that decision; and

(5) to make the best possible adjustment to the disorder in an affected family member and/or to the risk of recurrence of that disorder. (Ad Hoc Committee 1975)

Although this definition was published in 1975, it still holds and is endorsed by clinical geneticists worldwide. Central to the discussion today is the attempt to help the individual or family "choose the course of action which seems to them appropriate in view of their risk, their family goals, and their ethical and religious standards, and act in accordance with that decision." If a couple is at increased risk of a genetic disorder in their child, the course of action may include prenatal diagnosis and termination of pregnancy when the fetus is affected. The definition emphasizes that it is not the counselor who decides what is appropriate for them but the counselee. Respect for autonomy is the leading principle in this definition. The counselor helps the counselee achieve the course of action chosen by the counselee.

Autonomy, of course, is not without boundaries. We respect autonomy in decisions about disorders in the fetus—mostly serious disorders—but we do not consent to the wishes of those who want to have their fetus tested for so-called normal variation or for traits that are subject to non-discrimination acts, such as skin color or homosexuality. We do not agree with prenatal diagnosis for sex selection, unless there is an increased risk for disorders that are clearly sex-limited and cannot be diagnosed directly. Sex-limited disorders are diseases affecting only one sex.

The Dutch Termination of Pregnancy Act

Termination of pregnancy is allowed in the Netherlands, but it is subject to the Termination of Pregnancy Act (Wet Afbreking Zwangerschap) and accompanying governmental measures. The act came into effect in 1984. A central paragraph in this act stipulates requirements with regard to assistance and decision making meant to ensure that every decision to terminate a pregnancy is made with care and the termination is carried out only if the emergency situation of the woman makes it inevitable. Termination of pregnancy can only be done by a medical doctor in a hospital or clinic that is licensed by the minister of health. The act of termination is not to be carried out for six days after the woman has expressed her intention to terminate the pregnancy and discussed this with her doctor (this period is meant to guarantee time for reflection). Alternative courses of action to end the emergency situation of the woman are to have been discussed (mainly carry to term and give away for adoption). The doctor must be convinced that the woman has come to her decision voluntarily, after careful deliberation and full appreciation of her responsibility toward the unborn life and if aftercare has been secured. Termination of pregnancy is allowed only within the first 24 weeks. Although the act does not refer to a legal position of the father of the fetus, in practice fathers may be deeply involved in the decision process as shown in the examples at the end of this paper.

The act does not define what an emergency situation is because an exact description of the emergency situation cannot be given as it is a subjective emotional state of the woman that cannot be objectified. The emergency situation is caused by what the woman has experienced and it results in her refusal to complete her pregnancy. We respect the autonomy of the woman in these situations.

Community Genetics

Clinical genetics is a reactive specialism: we sit in our offices and see the individuals and couples who come to us with their questions and problems. If they do not come or come too late in pregnancy, they may be confronted with a genetic or non-genetic disease in their child. In my experience from clinical practice and as a former leader of a registry of congenital disorders, this situation is frequent. So a more proactive role for genetic services is required. We are now entering the field of medical community genetics. Medical community genetics is defined as

> the art and science of the responsible and realistic application of health and disease-related genetics and genomics knowledge and technologies in human populations and communities to the benefit of individuals therein. Community genetics is multi-, inter- and transdisciplinary and aims to maximize benefits while minimizing the risk of harm, respecting the autonomy of individuals and ensuring equity. (Ten Kate *et al.* 2010)

Typical activities in medical community genetics are genetic screening, genetic education, genetics in primary care, genetic services for underprivileged people, including low and middle income countries. Again, along with other ethical principles, respect for autonomy is emphasized in the definition of medical community genetics.

Prevention

How should we evaluate genetic testing and screening? One possibility is to measure how successful we are in preventing disease. The problem with prevention, however, is that termination of pregnancy is not prevention of disease but prevention of the existence of a person with the disease. That is a perversion of the term prevention.

Informed Choice

Marteau and colleagues have developed a measure of informed decision making, called the measure of informed choice. The measure is based on the following definition of an informed choice: "one that is based on relevant knowledge, consistent with the decision-maker's values and behaviorally implemented" (Marteau *et al.* 2001). Others have proposed also including in the measure the question if the decision was taken after deliberation (Van den Berg *et al.* 2006). Whatever version is used, it is clear that the measure agrees with the above definitions of genetic counseling and medical community genetics.

No one would argue that termination of pregnancy is not a very serious matter. It is ethically serious, as well as emotionally so. If there are other means to prevent suffering of a wanted child they should be considered first.

Reproductive Options

What options are available for couples with an increased risk of a genetic disease in their offspring? If the risk is based on the genetic make-up of one or both partners, a complete list of options would include the following:

1) If pregnant:
   i.   accept the risk, wait until the birth, and then see;
   ii.   opt for prenatal diagnosis; if the fetus turns out to be affected, the choices are:
   a.   termination of pregnancy
   b.   accept the diagnosis and prepare for the birth of an affected child;
2) Before pregnancy:
   i.   accept the risk and become pregnant the natural way;
   ii.   make use of donor gametes (sperm or egg cells);
   iii. make use of IVF with embryo selection after preimplantation genetic diagnosis;
   iv.   adopt;
3) Other options:
   i.   find another partner;
   ii.   since risk increases with the number of children, limitation of the number of children may be helpful as well.

Preconception consultation may identify genetic risk before pregnancy and identify courses of action mentioned above. Promoting reproduction at an earlier age may result in the prevention of chromosomal anomalies, such as Down syndrome. Periconceptional folic acid supplementation will prevent many cases of spina bifida. The list goes on.

Three Cases

The following three cases illustrate some ethical and emotional aspects of decisions concerning termination of pregnancy for genetic disorders.

Case I

This case concerns a woman who embraced me when I told her that prenatal diagnosis would be possible.

Cystic fibrosis (CF) is a serious genetic disease. Children with this disease have unaffected parents, who both carry a mutation in the CF gene. If both parents pass the mutation on to a child, this child has two mutated copies of the gene and will develop the disease. Each child of parents who are both carriers has a 25% chance of being affected. When I wrote my dissertation in 1975 on the prevalence of this disease in the Netherlands, the projected median age of death of CF patients was between 10 and 15. The median age of death is the age at which half of the patients have already died. Due to progress in treatment, most patients now survive into adult life, but they will need a lung transplant at some point in time and run the risk of dying while on the waiting list.

In the second half of the 1980s prenatal diagnosis for CF became possible in selected families. For technical reasons, it was not yet possible in all families, but only when the inherited DNA markers close to the CF gene were informative and could be followed in the family. Therefore, the decision if prenatal diagnosis would be possible had to be made on a case-by-case basis. So, when a couple with a child with cystic fibrosis consulted us and asked if prenatal diagnosis would be possible in a subsequent pregnancy, we had to take blood samples from both parents and their affected child, send these samples to the lab, and wait for several weeks to receive the results. In the case described here, it turned out that the markers were informative so that prenatal diagnosis would be possible. When I informed the couple of this, the woman rose and embraced me. Apparently, people can be made very happy when new technology allows them to have more children, even if termination of pregnancy may be the result. This case shows how stressed parents can become by the prospect of having to fear another child will be affected by a serious disease.

Case II

This case is about a couple who asked if prenatal diagnosis would be possible for PKU.

PKU is a genetic disease with the same inheritance pattern as cystic fibrosis. It is one of the diseases newborns are screened for at present. Children with PKU cannot handle one of the components in their food and become severally mentally challenged unless the component is omitted in their food. Following a restricted diet prevents mental retardation. The couple who asked if prenatal diagnosis would be possible for PKU already had a child with PKU, and the chance for PKU in subsequent children was 25% for each child. The possibility of preventing mental retardation in a PKU patient is generally regarded as successful. So requests for prenatal diagnosis are unusual. The couple, however, was determined, since they felt that the burden of following this strict diet, while other children in the child's environment did not have these restrictions, should be avoided. I asked the lab that was able to do the necessary test if they were willing to do the test for prenatal diagnosis. They were. I also asked the gynecologist if he was willing to obtain a sample from a fetus of this couple and to terminate the pregnancy if it was affected. He was willing to do so. The couple was also seen by our psychosocial worker, who concluded that the couple was indeed well informed and knew what they were up to. I even discussed with the couple what would happen if the media found out that we had performed prenatal diagnosis for PKU. A comparable situation of prenatal diagnosis for blindness had caused a great upheaval recently. But the couple remained determined, and we agreed that we would help them realize their chosen course of action.

Case III

This is a case involving hereditary breast and ovary cancer. It is hypothetical: contrary to cases 1 and 2, I have no professional experience with it involving real patients. Some families have a dominant gene mutation that entails a 60-80% risk of breast or ovary cancer in females. If one of the parents carries such a mutation each child has a 50% chance of inheriting this mutation. Carriers who develop these cancers do so at a much earlier age, on average, than people who do not have the mutation. Moreover, there is a chance of having not just one cancer but several—for instance, breast and ovary cancer—or independent cancers in both breasts. Being a female in such a family is scary, especially when genetic testing has revealed that a woman carries the same mutation that killed her mother, sister and/or one or two other female family members. Before there were any requests for prenatal diagnosis for this disease, the Dutch Society of Clinical Genetics declared that there was no a priori reason for a negative response to such a request. Of course, the requirements for termination of pregnancy when such a request would come, still apply. Although, in general, finding that a fetus is affected by a genetic disease that manifests itself at birth or early in life does not imply that the pregnancy should be terminated, we here have the additional complication that finding a mutation for a disease that manifests itself later in life and not deciding to terminate the pregnancy denies the right of the resulting child to live without the knowledge that she has this high probability of developing cancer (Cobben *et al.* 2002)

Conclusion

Looking back at these cases, it becomes clear that the personal experience and emotions of parents are a stronger determinant for experiencing a pregnancy as an emergency situation than the average severity of a given disorder. It is also clear that we should restrain from judging from the outside if there is an emergency situation. Only the woman can tell us. We may have our own thoughts about the decisions of some of our patients, but what we need most is empathy and a drive to help our patients achieve the course of action that is most appropriate for them. Respect for autonomy and informed choice are keywords here.

Empathy and compassion are components of charity: "Though I speak with the tongues of men and of angels, and have not charity, I am become as sounding brass, or a tinkling cymbal" (New Testament; 1 Corinthians 13:1 [KJV])

Bibliography

Ad Hoc Committee on Genetic Counseling. (1975). "Genetic Counseling." *American Journal of Human Genetics* 27: 240-42.

Berg, M. van den *et al.* (2006). "Informed Decision Making in the Context of Prenatal Screening." *Patient Education Counselings* 63: 110-17.

Christian Democratic Appeal. (1992). *Genen en Grenzen. Een christendemocratische bijdrage aan de discussie over de gentechnologie. Rapport van een Commissie van het Wetenschappelijk Instituut voor CDA.* The Hague: Wetenschappelijk Instituut voor het CDA.

Cobben J.M., A.H.J.T. Bröcker-Vriends, and N.J. Leschot. (2002). "Prenatal Testing for Hereditary Predisposition to Mammary and Ovarian Carcinoma—Defining a Position." *Nederlands Tijdschrift voor Geneeskunde* 146: 1461-65.

Kate, L.P. ten. (2003). "Victims of Nature Cry Out." In: W. Drees (ed.). *Is Nature Ever Evil? Religion, Science and Value.* London/New York: Routledge.

——— (1994). *Genen, grenzen en co-creatie.* Inaugural lecture. VU University Amsterdam. Amsterdam: VU Boekhandel/Uitgeverij.

Kate, L.P. ten *et al.* (2010). "Community Genetics: Its Definition." *Journal of Community Genetics* 1: 19-22.

Marteau, T.M., E. Dormandy, and S. Michie. (2001). "A Measure of Informed Choice." *Health Expectations* 4: 99-108.

Sölle, D., and S.A. Cloyes. (1984). *To Work and to Love: A Theology of Creation.* Philadelphia: Fortress Press.

CHAPTER X

Treatment of the Embryo

Facts and Moral Questions

Guido de Wert

Introduction

"The treatment of the embryo" is regularly front-page news. This is hardly surprising as it is one of the most controversial topics in modern medicine and scientific research. While some consider developments in the field to be fascinating and promising, for others these developments are startling and deeply problematic.

But what precisely are we talking about? This is by no means evident: the concepts of both the "embryo" and "treatment" are not unequivocal. The embryo is usually defined as the product of fertilization in the first 8 weeks of development. It seems to have many faces, however—in fact, the concept of the embryo is contested: what some consider to be embryos are non-embryos according to others.

The concept of "treatment" is just as equivocal. In this context, treatment in the strict sense would refer to medical treatment of affected embryos. "Treatment" in a wider sense, however, refers to all the ways people deal with or handle embryos, to many different practices involving the use, for example, of intrauterine devices (IUDs), preimplantation genetic diagnosis (PGD) and the prospective parents' lifestyle insofar as this may harm an embryo intended to develop into a child.

The aim of this chapter is, first, to briefly illustrate the conceptual puzzles (the variety of meanings) inherent in some of the central terms used and the variety of relevant practices. In addition, this chapter will also clarify that these practices raise many moral questions that are partly related to the concept and the moral value ("status") of the embryo and at the same time urge us to take a broader perspective that incorporates other parties' interests and other values, thereby avoiding "embryo-centered ethical one-dimensionality." My underlying aim is to contribute to agenda-setting for further normative reflection.

Conceptual Puzzles, Highly Diverse Practices

What Is a Human Embryo?

Let me simply presume that what is meant in current societal debates on the "embryo" is the *human* embryo. This specification is, obviously, not unimportant but may be less clear than is often assumed: the qualification "human" may be as puzzling as the concept of the embryo.

Let us first look at the concept of the embryo. Traditionally, the embryo means the conceptus from fertilization (the *terminus a quo*) until the end of week eight of development (the *terminus ad quem*). This definition is imprecise, however, as fertilization is not a "moment" but a process that takes approximately 24 hours (Jones, 1987). This process starts with the penetration of the oocyte by the sperm and comes to an end when the chromosomes are mixed together (so-called "syngamy"). What, then, is the nature of the entity in between the start and the end of this process, this entity *in statu fertilisandi* (de Wert 1999)? Is it already an embryo or just a "half-fertilized" oocyte?

Apart from this, some consider this definition too broad — it includes too much. A first qualification suggested is that the "product of fertilization" should have the potential to develop into a child (a baby) to qualify as an embryo. If "viability" (or: potentiality) is indeed a defining characteristic of embryos, non-viable embryos are not, strictly speaking, embryos at all. Critics may argue, of course, that, since non-viable babies are still babies, non-viable embryos are truly embryos.

Some commentators suggest a second qualification, which is especially relevant for *in vitro* embryos, namely intention: what are currently regarded as embryos would be more accurately described as *potential* embryos that only become *"bona fide"* embryos in the face of efforts to realize that potential. In the absence of a reproductive intent, potential embryos are no different from any other tissue (De Sousa 2010). One might reply, of course, that to *have* the potential and to *get* the possibility to realize this potential should be clearly discerned—an embryo that does not get this possibility is still an embryo.

Others consider the definition mentioned to be too narrow: it excludes too much. They point out that embryos may be generated by a blastomere biopsy (for example) in the context of PGD. If the blastomere in question is totipotent, i.e. has the capacity to develop into a child, the blastomere is in fact a "secondary" embryo—a view that has been incorporated into, for example, the German Law on the Protection of Embryos (Embryonenschützgesetz, 1990).

The question as to precisely what entities qualify as embryos was given additional relevance by the discussion on a variety of *constructed* "embryo-like entities" artificially generated by laboratory procedures that do not involve fertilization at all. These entities were suggested primarily in the context of searching for "embryo-saving" alternatives for the derivation of human embryonic stem cells (hESC), alternatives that, so it is assumed, do not involve the destruction of human embryos (de Wert and Mummery 2003; President's Council on Bioethics 2005; Dondorp and de Wert 2005). Examples include the following.

1) Clonotes, "embryos" generated by somatic cell nuclear transfer (SCNT), which involves transferring the nucleus of a cell taken from a patient's body into an enucleated donor oocyte. In principle, the embryo-like entity thus constructed could be used as a source of hESC for autologous cell therapy. This procedure is better known as "therapeutic cloning," a misnomer as therapeutic applications are not yet on the horizon—and may in fact never become available (see below).

2) Embryo-like artifacts produced by *altered* SCNT (aSCNT). This variant of SCNT entails the deliberate introduction of a mutation into the somatic cell's nucleus transferred in order to guarantee that the artifact is not able to implant and is non-viable (Hurlbut 2005).

3) Parthenotes, generated by parthenogenesis, which involves the chemical stimulation of an oocyte to transform into a diploid cell with two identical sets of maternal chromosomes (De Sousa 2010).

Second, what about the qualification "human"? This be-came a public issue in the context of *interspecies* SCNT, which involves transplanting a human somatic cell nucleus into an e-nucleated animal oocyte; the oocyte would thus no longer have its *nuclear* DNA (DNA in the cell nucleus), which is related to the whole phenotype of the future organism but still entail its *mitochondrial* DNA (extra-nuclear DNA in the mitochondria, the organelles in the oocyte's cytoplasm), which is considered to be involved in energy production. There are two reasons for devel-oping this procedure. First, this would circumvent the scarcity of human oocytes for SCNT. Second, it is argued that hybrids (or cybrids) thus created are not human embryos—so this pro-cedure would be "embryo-saving." Obviously, the presumed *non*-human status of these hybrids is contested; after all, the nu-clear DNA is completely human (de Wert and Mummery 2003).

There is an ongoing discussion about the nature of these constructs; some commentators argue that (at least some of) these constructs are truly embryos—even though parthenotes and "artifacts" constructed by aSCNT are definitely unable to develop beyond the (early) embryonic stage (Dondorp and de Wert 2005). But clearly, the interest in developing such con-structs has almost completely disappeared since it proved to be possible to get human pluripotent stem cells by directly re-programming adult cells (Takahashi *et al.* 2007). The potential of such "induced pluripotent stem cells" (iPSC) for research and future therapy has been studied since then by many expert centers worldwide (Robinton and Daley 2012).

Treatments—in Plural

Treatment in the strict sense refers to the medical treatment of a diseased embryo. A—still hypothetical—example is germ line gene therapy (GLGT), i.e. intervening in the germ line for thera-peutic purposes. Regarding embryo "treatment" in the wider sense of dealing with or handling embryos, it may be helpful to make a double distinction between a) *in vivo* and *in vitro* embry-os and b) *pre*implantation and *post*-implantation embryos. As-suming that the *in vitro* culture of *post*-implantation (human) embryos may become technically possible in the future, there are four different contexts of "treatment" (the following does not claim to present an exhaustive overview).

a) The Preimplantation Embryo *in Vivo*

In the context of natural reproduction, for every successful pregnancy that results in a live birth, perhaps as many as five early embryos will be lost or "miscarry"—we now know and accept this (Harris 2004). (These may not be true miscarriages, of course, as the loss will often take place before pregnancy.) Many of these embryos will be lost because of genetic abnormalities, but some could have been viable. The "sacrifice" of embryos seems to be an inescapable and inevitable part of the process of reproduction.

Second are intrauterine devices (IUDs). The mechanisms of action of IUDs have been disputed for many years. At the heart of the discussion is the distinction between *pre*fertilization and *post*-fertilization mechanisms/effects. The former concerns all contraceptive effects that reduce the probability of fertilization. The latter are those effects that operate after fertilization to reduce the probability of implantation. A review study concludes that although prefertilization mechanisms of action are (far) more prominent for the copper IUD, both types of mechanisms contribute significantly to the effectiveness of all types of IUDs (Stanford and Mikolajczyk 2002).

b) The Preimplantation Embryo *in Vitro*

In this category we can discern at least four relevant practices.

First is fertility treatment by means of regular *in vitro* fertilization (IVF) or intracytoplasmic sperm injection (ICSI). IVF as usually practiced generates more embryos than can be safely transferred in the cycle at hand. Some of the additional embryos may be cryopreserved for a possible later transfer. The major advantage of this approach is that it increases the success rate of IVF and decreases the burdens for women involved. As cryopreserved embryos may become "spare" ("leftover embryos") later on, the loss of embryos is inherent in IVF thus practiced. Some countries impose a different policy: to avoid (or at least minimize) embryo loss, they require cryopreservation at the pronuclear stage, *in statu fertilisandi* (see above). Obviously, others will deny that this is truly an "embryo-saving" strategy. This illustrates that the underlying dissent regarding the definition of the embryo does not just reflect theoretical interest (is not just an academic game) but may have major implications for clinical practice.

Furthermore, in at least some countries it seems to be common practice for new clinicians to learn how to do ICSI by fertilizing so-called "IVF-failures," i.e. oocytes that were not successfully fertilized in the context of IVF. This is considered to be just a matter of good clinical practice (or quality control).

Second is the use of embryos in research. A crucial distinction is between embryo research followed by transfer and embryo research where no transfer will occur (Robertson 1986). The introduction of new assisted reproductive technologies is closely related to pre-clinical research with human preimplantation embryos aimed at adequately investigating the safety, reliability, and effectiveness of the respective experimental techniques. Obviously, the status of the embryo is a central issue here. The embryos involved may be spare embryos (see above), but for some preclinical research projects embryos need to be specifically created (Dondorp and de Wert 2011). Again, the definition of the embryo is highly relevant for adequate guidance (cf. section "Embryo Research," below, pp. 157ff.).

Research involving embryos *to be transferred* raises altogether different concerns as such research may risk health damage to future children.

The third practice is the selection of embryos by means of PGD or preimplantation genetic screening (PGS). PGD was introduced in the context of IVF some 20 years ago as an alternative for regular prenatal diagnosis aimed at preventing the birth of a child with a serious disability or disease. It may be an option for both fertile and infertile people at high risk of having an affected child. In the future, a *non-reproductive* application of PGD might be introduced, so-called PGD/HLA testing type 2. This strategy, at the interface of IVF and stem cell research/ therapy, would involve IVF/PGD-HLA typing in order to select HLA-matched embryos from which hESC could be derived to produce hematopoietic stem cells for cell therapy (de Wert *et al.* 2007).

PGS, i.e. the routine (offering of) genetic testing of IVF embryos, may be performed in at least three different ways:
1) regular screening for triploidy (PGS-PN) aimed at excluding zygotes with three pronuclei (3PN zygotes) which have 69 instead of 46 chromosomes and are in principle non-viable;

2) experimental aneuploidy screening (PGS-A) aimed at eliminating aneuploid, mostly non-viable, embryos, mainly in order to increase the success rate of IVF (Geraedts *et al.*, 2010; Treff *et al.*, 2011);

3) future "comprehensive" screening, using "genome-wide" approaches, aimed, perhaps, at conceiving the "best possible," or even "perfect," child (de Wert 2009).

A possible fourth practice is germ line genetic modification (GLGM). There are in theory two types of GLGM: therapeutic (=GLGT) and non-therapeutic. With regard to GLGT, one may make a distinction between two types, depending on the type of DNA that is modified: *nuclear* DNA (DNA in the cell nucleus), which is related to our whole phenotype (including personality traits), and *mitochondrial* DNA (DNA in the mitochondria, the organelles in the cytoplasm), which is considered to be primarily involved in energy production/metabolism. GLGT is mostly considered to be futuristic as the experimental procedures involved are presently considered to be too risky for the health of the future child. Nevertheless, there is considerable interest in preclinical research aimed at the development of GLGT regarding *mt*DNA. This may be a relevant option for the prevention of mitochondrial disorders caused by defects in mtDNA. The procedure involves either pronuclear transfer (PNT) or maternal spindle transfer (MST): basically, a donated oocyte, with non-mutated "healthy" mtDNA, is enucleated, and its nuclear DNA is replaced with the nuclear DNA of a zygote or an oocyte of a woman carrying a mtDNA mutation (Nuffield Council 2012). The new embryo will then have the nuclear DNA of the prospective parents and the healthy mtDNA of the oocyte donor. *Non-therapeutic* GLGM mostly refers to enhancement-like applications, like designing a highly intelligent or "athletic" child. This, however, seems to be especially futuristic.

c) The Post-Implantation Embryo *in Vivo*

Let me focus on just two relevant "practices." I will first look at unhealthy lifestyles that may have adverse consequences for the development of the embryo/fetus and, as a consequence, for the condition of the future child. There is increasing evidence that women's unhealthy behavior early in pregnancy (when organogenesis takes place) may have adverse health effects for (the embryo and) the future child. In some cases, the future child may even be seriously harmed. One can think of fetal alcohol syndrome (FAS), caused by the woman's (excessive) drinking during (early) pregnancy. In view of this, the question arises as to whether prospective parents (and maybe other stakeholders as well) have any moral (and legal) duties to protect the health of the fetus/future child, and if so, when these duties emerge and what their weight is. As will be illustrated below, future children may also be harmed by other (medical, laboratory) interventions at the early embryonic stage: for example, by research involving IVF-embryos to be transferred.

The second practice here is non-invasive prenatal testing (NIPT). Since the discovery of cell-free fetal DNA/RNA (cffDNA/RNA) in maternal plasma in 1997, the possibility to use this for NIPT has been investigated. Currently, cffDNA/RNA can be reliably obtained from a maternal blood sample as early as seven weeks of gestation (i.e. five weeks after fertilization). This development holds the promise of large-scale NIPT early in pregnancy and without the risk of fetal loss (miscarriage) inherent in invasive chorionic villi sampling (CVS) and amniocentesis. NIPT for sex selection for medical reasons (X-linked disorders) and for Down syndrome is now being translated into clinical practice (Bianchi *et al.* 2012). Research and discussion on possible broader applications (like NIPT for other chromosomal aberrations, for maternally inherited Mendelian disorders, and maybe even whole-genome testing) take place in various countries.

d) The Post-Implantation Embryo *in Vitro*
Until now, it was simply not possible to culture human embryos *in vitro* for longer than around a week. Still, some researchers hinted already in the early days of the debate about the acceptability of human embryo research at the theoretical importance of culturing human embryos for more than two weeks, thinking of embryological studies of (disturbed) organogenesis in the third and fourth weeks of development, eventually aimed at contributing to primary prevention of developmental or congenital disorders. Recent scientific developments may refuel the debate about such extended human embryo research. Researchers at Cambridge have developed a new *in vitro* culture system that for the first time allows the study of mouse embryonic de-

velopment in stages that normally occur after implantation (Morris *et al.* 2012). Similar systems may become available for studying later human embryonic development.

Selective Overview of Relevant Practices

	In vivo	*In vitro*
Pre-implantation embryo	IUD	IVF/ICSI treatment, embryo research, PGD/PGS, GLGT
Post-implantation embryo	NIPT, lifestyle of pregnant women	embryo research

Moral Questions

For adequate agenda-setting, the challenge is to present an overview of general and more specific moral questions regarding the various types of "treatment" of the embryo, taking account of the various definitions of the embryo. Obviously, I have to confine myself to a more modest aim in the present chapter: only giving an initial impetus.

First, allow me to tick off two overarching issues, each of which is relevant for various practices mentioned in the previous section: the status of the embryo and the responsibility to avoid (risk of) harm to the future child at the embryonic stage. Second, I will consecutively briefly sketch the moral landscape regarding 1) embryo loss, both *in vivo* and *in vitro*, 2) embryo research, *with* and *without* transfer, 3) embryo selection, by means of both PGD/PGS and NIPT, 4) embryo therapy, particularly GLGT, and 5) the unhealthy lifestyle of pregnant women that possibly harm the future child.

Overarching Issues

a) The Status of the Embryo
Are embryos worthy of respect and protection, and if so, to what degree? Roughly, there are three different views on the "status" of the embryo (de Wert 1999; Health Council 1998). The first view holds that the moral status of human persons accrues also, and to the same degree, to human embryos: the embryo is no less worthy of respect than a child or an adult human being and should be treated and protected accordingly: the embryo has equal moral value. Whereas, for example, the Ro-

man Catholic Church argues that the embryo is entitled to e-
qual respect from fertilization onwards, others think that the
embryo is worthy of equal respect from "developmental individuation" onwards, when the so-called primitive streak emerges (Ford 1988; McCormick 1991): until the embryonic cells are
differentiated and organized to become the primitive streak,
there *is* no individual in any sense of the word—biologically,
legally, or morally.

The second view holds that embryos have no *independent*
moral status that makes them worthy of respect and protection;
embryos are only *potential* persons. The capability of developing into a human being is just a possibility. Having no independent status does not mean that human embryos may be subjected to every treatment. What matters first and foremost is the
reproductive intent of the providers of the gametes; if they want
the embryo to develop into a child, the embryo gets *indirect* protectability. Furthermore, if they want to have a child, the future
child's interests should be taken into account in the way embryos are treated (see below). Apart from this, embryos have a
symbolic status—yet another reason for granting them indirect
protectability at least to some extent: it is then not for the sake
of the embryo itself that it should be treated with (some) respect
but for the sake of the community in which it has acquired social significance.

A characteristic of the third (group of) view(s) is that moral
relevance is attached to both the difference (the embryo is not
yet a human being) and the continuity (a human being could
develop from the embryo). This represents a view between the
positions just sketched. Because of its human origin and its potential to develop into a human being the embryo has an intrinsic value, but the embryo's status is not equal to that of human beings.

Most ethical theories and religious views hold—albeit for
different reasons—that embryos need not to be respected as
persons and have a relatively "low" moral status (Hursthouse,
1987). This is an example of a so-called "overlapping consensus."

Obviously, the picture becomes even more complicated because of the conceptual embryo puzzle briefly sketched above
(cf. section "Conceptual Puzzles," pp. 146ff., above): people

who agree on the status of the embryo may use different concepts of the embryo and *vice versa*. This makes the proclaimed "end of the embryo war" rather unlikely (Caplan 2009).

b) Harm to the Future Child in its Embryonic Stage

Traditionally, ethical quandaries regarding the embryo (and fetus) are about its contested moral status and originate in the context of the abortion debate: (When) is the embryo (or the fetus) a human person with a right to life? This is not the issue at hand here. We need to make a clear and simple distinction between embryos intended to become babies and other embryos who are not, i.e. embryos that will not be brought to birth as they are not part of a "parental project" (Murray 1987). It is the former category that is relevant here.

Most people will, generally speaking, accept that there are moral obligations to the fetus intended to be born and that it is primarily the prospective parents who carry this responsibility. They should, in principle, not inflict harm on the "not-yet-born" child. In view of the fact that the fetus is fully dependent on the pregnant woman, her responsibility is even more direct than the father's. But obviously, this view, even though convincing, raises quite a few other questions.

A crucial issue regards the *timing* of harm and the timing of the current responsibility: Does it start at viability, developmental individuation, fertilization, or even before fertilization — at the preconception stage? Murray invites us to imagine two different cases (Murray, 1987): In the first, a man assaults a woman with the intention of inflicting grave harm on her fetus. He succeeds, causing permanent, irreparable — but not fatal — damage to the fetus's spinal cord, resulting in paralysis. In the second case, all the circumstances are identical, except that the man attacks an infant rather than a fetus, with the same result. Was the first act any less wrong than the second? In both cases, lifelong harm was done to a human who, whatever one's beliefs about when personhood begins, would eventually cross that line and attain moral status. Murray rightly asserts that the timing of the harm is irrelevant.

But what *types of harm* are we talking about? The paradigm case regards harms (including disabilities) caused by the dangerous lifestyle of the pregnant woman, but harm may also be caused by (research in) assisted reproductive technologies. As we will see, harm may also be of a psychosocial nature, related to predictive information about the child's future health, so-called "informational harm." In any event, various parties, other than the prospective parents, appear to be responsible (to share responsibility) for harm avoidance.

Specific Ethical Questions and Debates

a) Embryo Loss

Let me focus on three relevant practices: contraception, assisted reproduction, and natural reproduction.

Let us first look at IUDs. These devices are usually classified as contraceptives—but this qualification is contested since IUDs, even though they first and foremost prevent fertilization, have a small but significant post-fertilization effect. Some people may argue that this latter effect of IUDs regards just "possible" embryos (not true embryos) as there is no reproductive intent (cf. above). It seems to make more sense, however, to admit that IUDs may well involve embryo loss. If one takes the view that the embryo has equal moral value right from fertilization onwards, the use of IUDs seems difficult to justify. But what if one takes the dominant view? It may be surprising that there is hardly any moral discussion on IUDs among people who take this view. After all, in view of the principle of subsidiarity, one may well argue that people should in principle opt for one of the truly contraceptive alternatives that do not involve embryo loss. Still, women may have good reason to choose an IUD: safety, effectiveness, reversibility, and convenience. The authors of the above-mentioned review conclude that "our ... estimates could be used for counselling women who may object to postfertilization effects" (Stanford and Mikolajczyk 2002: 1705). Obviously, the principle of respect for autonomy and the related prerequisite of informed consent suggest that women *should* be informed about possible embryo loss inherent in the use of UIDs and be counseled adequately.

The second practice is IVF. For adherents to the "equal protection from fertilization onwards" view, IVF as commonly practiced entails a deeply problematic structural spoiling of embryos and in fact amounts to (or at least comes close to) infanticide. To avoid this critique, clinics in some countries engage in freezing at the pronuclear stage (*in statu fertilisandi*) instead of freezing embryos at day 3 after fertilization. One may doubt, however, if this alternative is truly "embryo-saving"—is this "solution" not hypocritical?

If one accepts the dominant view (taking account of the overlapping consensus mentioned before) that the embryo has a relatively low moral status, IVF as usually practiced is, no doubt, morally acceptable. That said, it remains a challenge to find alternatives that are both "female-friendly" and embryo-saving. The cryopreservation of oocytes (instead of embryos) may be such an alternative: it may both benefit women (increase the IVF success rate per treatment cycle and minimize the number of hormonal stimulations) and at the same time minimize embryo loss. But what about the possible health risks for children thus conceived? Follow-up data seem to be reassuring so far. Still, one may seriously doubt if the clinical introduction of oocyte cryopreservation some years ago was preceded by adequate preclinical research to study and minimize possible risks (cf. section "Embryo Research," below, pp. 157ff.).

Natural reproduction is the third practice. Harris challenges us to address the question of how to think morally about the decision to reproduce in view of the fact that (even) natural reproduction entails large-scale embryo loss (Harris 2004). The sacrifice of embryos is part of reproduction: even though it may not be intentional, it is a conscious and deliberate sacrifice. If this sacrifice is morally acceptable, so he asks, then why not accept the sacrifice of embryos in embryo research?

b) Embryo Research

Although it is important to make a distinction between research with IVF embryos to be transferred and IVF embryos not to be transferred, the international discussion on embryo research focuses almost exclusively on the latter. In this particular context, the fundamental controversy is whether (preimplantation) embryos have the same moral status as children or adults who are to be protected from "destructive" research (cf. The Declaration of Helsinki, etc.).

If one accepts the "equal moral value right from the start" view, such research, obviously, is abhorrent and totally unacceptable. According to the dominant view that embryos have only a relatively low moral status, however, research with (preimplantation) embryos can be justified—with some constraints of course.

   Procedural conditions are the informed consent of the providers of the gametes, and the approval of a (national) ethics committee. Widely accepted *material* conditions include:

1) The principle of proportionality. It is generally accepted that the aim of such research should be "important." But there may, of course, be differences of opinion regarding the way in which this principle should be made operational. In a number of countries, embryo research was originally restricted to research related to human reproduction. Internationally, this limitation has been increasingly disputed. The isolation of human embryonic stem cells for research into cell (replacement) therapy operated as a catalyst in this regard.

2) The principle of subsidiarity. Embryo research may be justified only if there are no good alternatives. Again, there may be differences of opinion regarding the way in which this principle should be made operational: restrictively or permissively (de Wert and Mummery 2003)?

3) The time limit to be respected. Most committees and regulations set a time limit of 14 days after fertilization —often without clear arguments. Typically, the Health Council of the Netherlands pointed at the pragmatic nature of the emerging international consensus with respect to the 14-day limit (Health Council 1998). While research with (human) embryos *in vitro* "older" than two weeks was a rather academic issue up till now, extended embryo culture may become feasible in the future (Morris *et al.* 2012). Does the phenomenon of "developmental individuation" dictate a strict time limit of two weeks? Or could longer culture be morally justified on the condition that such research could generate substantial scientific progress and clinical benefits? But what alternative *terminus ad quem* should then be imposed? Would criteria related to early brain development be acceptable, extending the research period to, say, four to six weeks after fertilization (Lockwood 1988; Tauer 1985)? And what if embryogenesis *in vitro* is slow-

er than *in vivo*, delaying developmental individuation and/or neural development?

A major point of controversy remains the origin or source of the preimplantation embryos to be used in research. The "Convention on Human Rights and Biomedicine" of the Council of Europe accepts the use of spare embryos in research but prohibits the creation of embryos solely for research purposes (Council of Europe 1997). This prohibition has been enacted in many countries. But one may doubt if there is a fundamental moral difference between using spare embryos in research on the one hand and the generation of embryos for research purposes on the other. After all, embryos are used instrumentally in *both* cases, and their moral status is *identical* (Health Council 1998). Some commentators stress that the intention at the moment of fertilization is fundamentally different. But is this difference not merely relative? It is a misunderstanding to think that in the context of regular IVF each and every embryo is created as a "goal in itself." After all, the goal of IVF is the solution of involuntary childlessness—the loss of some spare embryos is generally calculated beforehand (cf. section "Embryo Loss," pp. 156f.).

Some feminist critics question the acceptability of creating embryos for research out of concern for the autonomy and the interests of women donating oocytes for research. After all, women have to undergo hormone stimulation and a biopsy of the ovaries, which carry some medical risks. Furthermore, there is a risk of their being exploited (Gerrand 1993). Do these concerns justify an absolute ban of creating embryos for research purposes? The interests of donors may be protected by imposing the material condition that medical risks should be minimized by, for instance, limiting the numbers of hormone treatments as well as the dosage of hormones given to candidate donors and by excluding women at high risk of developing ovarian hyperstimulation syndrome (OHSS) (de Wert 1999; Pennings *et al.* 2007). Of course, a valid informed consent presumes adequate information about potential residual risks. Finally, the creation of embryos for research purposes does not necessarily involve hormonal treatments and/or invasive interventions specifically to gain (access to) the oocytes needed for research. Oocyte cryopreservation in the context of both fertility preservation and regular IVF treatment may well solve (or lessen) the scarcity of oocytes for research (Mertes and Pennings 2011).

Critics often disregard the fact that a complete prohibition against making embryos for research purposes would hamper an adequate *pre-clinical risk assessment* of some new, potentially valuable, techniques, like the *in vitro* maturation (IVM) of oocytes—which could make burdensome hormonal stimulations of IVF patients obsolete—and pronuclear transfer (PNT) or maternal spindle transfer (MST) to prevent mitochondrial disorders (cf. above, section "The Preimplantation Embryo *in Vitro*," pp. 149f.). Spare embryos are useless for this type of research; it would be necessary to create embryos from oocytes having undergone the relevant manipulations. A categorical prohibition against creating embryos for research purposes then means that, if centers want to do the relevant type of safety studies in embryos, they are legally not allowed to do so. As a consequence, risky reproductive procedures may be prematurely introduced in the clinic, which means in fact that embryos *to be transferred* are involved in research. How does this fit with the responsibility to avoid harm to the future child (cf. section "Harm to the Future Child in its Embryonic Stage," pp. 155f.)? Is it indeed not ironic that society gives so much protection to human preimplantation embryos *in vitro* that, as a consequence, future children (and their parents) may be put at greater, avoidable health risk (Health Council 1998; de Wert 1999)? Perhaps the responsibility of scientists and reproductive physicians involved in ART to take account of the health interests of possible future children thus conceived means that society should be more permissive regarding research with embryos *not to be transferred* and more critical/restrictive when it comes to research with embryos *to be transferred* (Dondorp and de Wert 2011)?

It is obviously inconsistent to allow the creation of embryos for "instrumental use" in the context of quality control regarding ICSI (cf. section "The Preimplantation Embryo *in Vitro*," pp. 149f.) and at the same time categorically object to the creation of embryos for research purposes. The latter may likewise contribute to quality control, especially if it regards pre-clinical safety studies for new reproductive technologies.

The former focuses on the research use of IVF/ICSI embryos. The use of embryos as a source of hESC to be used in research (which is not embryo research in the strict sense) may be justified under the same conditions. Some commentators and committees argue that the latter holds true for IVF/ICSI embryos—embryos created by means of fertilization—but not for creating and using (at least some types of) *constructed* embryos; because these entities, so they argue, do not qualify as embryos, guidelines for embryo research simply do not apply here. The view that these entities do not qualify as (human) embryos is, however, questionable. Is it not undesirable to "resolve" the debate on the moral status of non-standard or non-viable embryos on the level of the definition (Dondorp and de Wert, 2005)?

c) Embryo Selection
The major rationale of embryo selection is to prevent the conception or birth of a child affected with a particularly serious disease or disability. Three types of embryo selection should be discerned: PGD, PGS, and NIPT.

Let us first look at the ethics of PGD (de Wert 2009). Are there any overriding *a priori* ethical objections? According to critics, objections include the following.

To begin with, selecting embryos is inherently wrong. A first argument is the "equal value right from the start" view—which is highly contested. By the way, one might argue that even if one accepts this view, selecting against *non-viable* embryos may be justified (assuming that not transferring an embryo does not amount to active killing).

A second argument is the so-called "disability rights" critique (Wasserman *et al.* 2005). Generally, the objection holds that PGD (like regular prenatal diagnosis etc.) is at odds with the rights and interests of people with the disabilities/disorders "selection against." But is this necessarily the case? Obviously, one can allow prospective parents to avoid the conception of a child with a particular disease or disability without denying the equal worth of people affected with this condition. And it is very possible to combine the provision of reproductive genetic services like PGD with the provision of adequate care for people with disabilities (and their families). Interestingly, some commentators use the "disability rights" critique, not as an objection to PGD (and similar technologies) but as an argument to get rid of the so-called "medical model" used to regulate PGD: they argue in favor of allowing prospective parents to select for *non*-medical traits as well (Gavaghan 2007). Should we accept this argument?

A second objection regards the preceding biopsy: it is argued that in view of the totipotency of individual blastomeres, this biopsy *de facto* entails the creation of a second embryo, to be destroyed in the diagnostic procedures (cf. section "Conceptual Puzzles," pp. 146ff., above). Obviously, even if we would agree that the isolated totipotent blastomere should be considered as an embryo, the moral status of the early embryo is relevant for the moral evaluation of the biopsy: according to the dominant view, its status is relatively low, so the possible embryo loss inherent in the biopsy may well be justified. By the way, when PGD (or PGS) makes use of cells of the trophoblast at the blastocyst stage, cells that are definitely no longer totipotent, the present objection becomes obsolete. A recent study even suggests that embryonic DNA may be obtained from the blastocoel (the fluid-filled cavity in blastocysts), thus avoiding any (cell) biopsy of the embryo (Palini *et al.* 2013).

A third objection is that IVF/PGD is disproportionally burdensome for women. But clearly, the weighing of the possible benefits and burdens of PGD and alternatives like regular prenatal diagnosis and selective abortion is deeply personal. Why not allow women to decide for themselves then? By the way, for infertile people at high genetic risk of having a disabled child who need IVF anyway to conceive a child, PGD is far less burdensome than IVF combined with a non-selective embryo transfer, followed by regular prenatal diagnosis.

There is a strong consensus, at least in Western countries, that "selective reproduction" aimed at the prevention of the birth of a seriously disabled/affected child is morally justified and that respect for people's reproductive autonomy includes their choice to engage in PGD as a means to reach this aim. But where is the line to be drawn? Some consider PGD for dominant midlife or late-onset disorders, like Huntington's disease (HD), to be unjustified because the child will be healthy for at least several decades. Most people, however, argue that this application is fully acceptable given the fact the Huntington mutation involved has a complete penetrance, HD is lethal, and members of affected families often lack reproductive confidence. Somewhat more controversial is PGD for carriers of so-called reduced penetrance alleles (RPA) for HD and PGD exclusion testing for people at 50% risk of being a HD carrier who claim a right not to know their carrier status but want to avoid the conception of a child carrying the HD mutation. These applications may, however, be morally justified as well, taking account of applicants' significant reproductive risk and/or their right not to know (de Die-Smulders *et al.* 2013). The concern that applicants at high risk of contracting a late-onset disorder like Huntington's disease will lose parental competence, with adverse consequences for the welfare of their possible children, should be handled on a case-by-case basis, taking account of possible protective factors like adequate coping mechanisms of the partner and the availability of a strong social network.

Generally more controversial is PGD for disorders caused by mutations with an *incomplete* penetrance and/or disorders that may be preventable/treatable. A good example is hereditary breast and ovarian cancer (HBOC). In view of the fact that the penetrance is (incomplete but) still high and the relevant preventive measures (including prophylactic bilateral mastectomy) are highly invasive and burdensome, PGD is widely considered to be justified in these cases. The same may hold true for some cardiogenetic disorders (Kuliev *et al.* 2012).

What about PGD for so-called *intermediate* (or indirect medical) cases? These regard applications that do not fit into the medical model in the strict sense as part of the testing is not linked to possible disease in the future child, whereas there is still a link to the medical model in the *wider* sense in that the testing may be relevant for the health of a *third party* (de Wert 2005). A well-known example is PGD/HLA testing aimed at the so-called "savior baby." While critics argue (among other things) that the future child is being instrumentalized, proponents argue that this procedure may be perfectly acceptable on condition that the parents will also love the child for itself. A practical problem of this procedure remains the low "take-home baby rate" (Fiorentino *et al.* 2005). It remains to be seen if PGD/HLA testing type 2, which aims at stem cell therapy on the basis of hESC obtained from HLA-matched embryos, could be a useful alternative strategy. This approach is controversial as it entails the creation of embryos for "instrumental use"—but this is not an overriding objection if one takes the dominant view that preimplantation embryos have a relatively low independent moral status (de Wert *et al.* 2007).

Most controversial are *non*-medical applications of PGD. This is not a uniform category but includes highly different applications. First here is sex selection for non-medical reasons. Objections are both deontological ("this practice is discriminatory") and consequentialist ("this practice distorts the sex ratio"). These objections may, however, not apply to sex selection for so-called "family balancing" (Pennings 1996). Second is the "*dys*genic" use of PGD to select, for example, a deaf embryo. This is rather controversial as it seems to disregard the interests of the future children. The premise that deafness is "just a variant on the spectrum of normalcy" is difficult to accept. And third is PGD aimed at the selection of "super-embryos," i.e. embryos genetically predisposed to become highly talented children. As stated above, the latter application is highly theoretical at this moment. If it would become possible, a timely ethical reflection would, obviously, be required (see below).

Let us now turn to the ethics of PGS. PGS-PN, which aims at the non-transfer of zygotes with an incorrect number of pronuclei, seems to be self-evident as these embryos hardly ever develop into a child and, if they do, the child will be seriously disabled and non-viable. PGS-PN may well be acceptable even to proponents of the "equal status right from the start" view. They may even agree that it would be problematic *not* to screen IVF embryos for triploidy.

For the moment, PGS for aneuploidy (PGS-A) is still experimental (Geraedts *et al.* 2010; Harper *et al.* 2013)—and IVF patients should be informed accordingly. It is of utmost importance that the effectiveness and efficiency of PGS-A is proven before it is routinely offered in the clinic. That said, if PGS-A would aim exclusively at the exclusion of *non*-viable embryos from transfer, it would probably—like PGS-PN—get (almost) universal support. As viable aneuploid embryos are excluded from transfer as well, PGS-A is somewhat more controversial. But is PGS-A not at least as acceptable as present prenatal screening for Down syndrome, in view of both the lower status of the preimplantation embryo and the avoidance of traumatic miscarriages and terminations of pregnancy?

In the future, "comprehensive" preimplantation genetic screening may be introduced, aimed at transfer of "the best embryo." A more moderate approach would be "genome-wide" screening that focuses on a selected number of genetic characteristics. Vexing issues to be analyzed further are, among others, the feasibility of informed consent and the implications of the future child's right not to know. If this type of PGS would include risk factors for late-onset disorders, it could involve an interference with the future child's right to later decide for himself whether or not to be predictively tested for genetic susceptibilities. In principle, this intrusion could be prevented by not transferring embryos carrying susceptibility, but then there will often be no suitable embryo for transfer as we are all "fellow mutants." This illustrates the fact that harm to the future child caused by interventions at the embryonic stage may not only include health damages but also psychosocial harms generated by knowledge of genetic risk factors for dreadful disorders and breaches of their future autonomy, especially their right not to know (cf. section "Harm to the Future Child in its Embryonic Stage," pp. 155f.). The offer of preconception carrier screening (PCS), possibly followed by targeted PGD, may avoid some of the problems inherent in comprehensive PGS (de Wert 2009; Hens et al. 2012). Obviously, the ethics of PCS needs further scrutiny (de Wert et al. 2012).

A largely disregarded moral issue that concerns decision-making authority in the context of PGD and PGS is as follows. In the context of regular prenatal diagnosis and screening, the principle of respect for autonomy is of utmost importance. This means, first, that doctors should not put pressure on pregnant women to opt for testing. Second, in the case of a positive result of prenatal diagnosis, women should be free to decide whether or not to terminate the pregnancy: the doctor should support them, whatever decision they make. Does the same moral framework apply to IVF/PGD?

If an infertile couple is at high risk of having an affected child, some centers will only offer fertility treatment/IVF if the couple intends to make use of PGD offered for "avoidance." Critics hold that such a "coercive offer" of PGD clashes with the principle of respect for the applicants' reproductive autonomy. They ignore, however, that doctors offering ART—being actively and causally involved in conceiving children—have their *own* responsibility to avoid serious harm to future children (de Wert 1999; Harper *et al.* 2013). The real issue, then, is not *whether* it is acceptable to "coercively" offer PGD to infertile couples at high genetic risk, who apply for ART but *when* it is acceptable. Is the "high risk of serious harm" standard the criterion to be preferred and, if so, how can it be made operational? The second issue concerns "post-PGD" decision-making authority. When there are no other "definitely healthy" embryos available for transfer, couples may insist that embryos be transferred in case of an inconclusive result of PGD and/or when they consider the (residual) genetic risk for the future child to be acceptable. Again, the question arises: What standard should be used in over-ruling the preferences and autonomy of the couple and in insisting the couple engage in another IVF/PGD cycle, and how can this standard be made operational?

We will now look at the ethics of NIPT. Let me focus primarily on the use of NIPT in the context of prenatal screening for chromosomal abnormalities, such as trisomy 21 (offered to all pregnant women, at least many Western countries). In the discussion so far, it is expected that NIPT (as a one-step approach) may in the future replace the present two-step approach of risk assessment (maternal serum screening and nuchal translucency screening) and invasive diagnosis. What about the ethics (de Jong *et al.* 2010)? Concerns and objections include the view that offering NIPT on a wide scale would undermine informed consent: it is supposed that a one-step approach will make it more difficult to provide all pregnant women with adequate information and pre-test counseling. But will the challenge of informed consent indeed be greater? Another concern is that the introduction of NIPT as a risk-free (non-invasive) procedure may lead to the "normalization" of prenatal testing—but obviously, this should be avoided by sticking to the prerequisite of adequate pre-test counseling. Furthermore, early and safe NIPT might lead to an increase in the number of affected fetuses aborted. But, one may reply, cannot the lower moral status of the embryo and the possibly less traumatic psychological implications of early abortion justify a somewhat higher number of terminations after NIPT?

The question as to "where to draw the line?" will again be among the major issues. Concerns presently have to do with two non-medical applications in particular: sex selection for non-medical reasons and paternity testing. Could sex selection for "family balancing" be morally justified (see above)? In any event, in the context of NIPT, this practice will be difficult to regulate and monitor. Does this provide an (additional) argument to allow controlled preconception sex selection and perhaps even PGD for family balancing? With regard to prenatal paternity testing, it has been suggested to counsel women involved about the only relative significance of biological kinship. One might, however, suspect that reluctance to provide paternity testing may be prompted by a condemnation of a promiscuous life. But is this not moralistic and unprofessional— taking account of the fact that applicants of paternity testing may be in an emergency situation?

Obviously, NIPT may well become a good alternative to IVF/PGD for at least a number of fertile patients at high genetic risk. What would a comparative ethical analysis of these options look like? Should the indications for PGD and NIPT be the same in principle? Taking account of the scarcity of resources, would collective funding of PGD for fertile people become less evident if NIPT is a much cheaper alternative? Or should we (continue to) be willing to collectively fund PGD as preimplantation selection of the "early" embryo is, in principle, to be ethically preferred to post-implantation selection involving further developed embryos or fetuses, and because some women may experience even an early abortion as far more traumatic then PGD?

A large future expansion of the scope of NIPT has been brought up several times. If it becomes possible to perform prenatal comprehensive screening by means of whole genome (or whole exome) sequencing and analysis, such screening will include not only chromosomal and monogenetic disorders but also risk factors for (late-onset) complex disorders. This would lead to various ethical challenges, partly similar to comprehensive PGS (see above): Would informed consent be feasible, then? What about the ethics of generic consent? Would such screening be proportional, i.e. would the possible benefits clearly outweigh the possible disadvantages? And how is the future child's right not to know to be protected (Dondorp and de Wert 2010)? The concern that comprehensive screening would present a "roadblock for life" (Shuster 2007), in that no embryo would ever be allowed to develop into a baby, seems to be rather exaggerated as many, if not most, women are reluctant to terminate *wanted* pregnancies and seem willing to accept genetic susceptibilities for complex disorders and minor disabilities.

d) Embryo Therapy
In theory, GLGT is an embryo-saving alternative for PGD and PD—and as such to be valued positively. Furthermore, PGD and PD for *mitochondrial* disorders carry some technical limitations that may be circumvented by means of GLGT. The ethical debate, however, is intense and includes the following issues (Rasko *et al.* 2006).

First is the instrumental use of embryos. GLGT is risky for children thus conceived (and, possibly, further generations) and can be developed only via pre-clinical embryo research, particularly via the creation of embryos specifically for such pre-clinical safety studies. Furthermore, embryos may be lost in future clinical applications. Obviously, the morality of these implications is codetermined by one's view of the status of the embryo (cf. sections "The Status of the Embryo" and "Embryo Research,"pp. 153f. and 157ff.).

Second, would it be acceptable to take the (residual) health risk involved (cf. section "Harm to the Future Child in its Embryonic Stage," pp. 155f.)? As preclinical studies can only give an indication of possible health risks for children thus conceived, it will not be possible to completely eliminate risk. A related question is if (and if so, under what conditions) the introduction of a potentially risky technique is justified when safe reproductive alternatives, like oocyte donation, are at hand. This requires a determination of the weight assigned to genetic parenthood (Peters 2004).

A third, deontological, objection holds that GLGT is at odds with human dignity (United Nations 1997). This objection is contested, however: Why would therapy that aims at preventing a potentially dreadful disease in future children be against dignity?

Would the type of DNA to be modified make a moral difference? The traditional normative debate on GLGT focuses exclusively on modifying *nuclear* DNA—but what about recent discussions to engage in modification of *mt*DNA that aims at the prevention of mitochondrial disorders? There seems to be a strong consensus among experts that mtDNA does not influence our "character" or identity. GLGT involving mtDNA may, therefore, be more easily justified than GLGT involving *nuclear* DNA (Nuffield Council 2012). But obviously, one may also argue that the moral difference between germ line therapeutic interventions in either nuclear DNA or mtDNA is only relative —and that both types of interventions may be morally justified if they are proven to be acceptably safe and effective (Bredenoord *et al.* 2008; Bredenoord *et al.* 2011).

A specific objection regarding GLGT to prevent mitochondrial disorders concerns the fact that the future child thus conceived would have "three genetic parents": the (genetic) father, the woman providing the enucleated oocyte (which still contains her mtDNA), and the woman providing the nuclear DNA. Would this be more or less morally problematic, taking account of the child's perspective, than gamete donation, which is widely accepted, at least in Western countries (Robertson 1994)? The Nuffield Council on Bioethics recently concluded that mitochondrial donation does not indicate, either biologically or legally, any notion of the child having either a "third parent" or "second mother" (Nuffield Council 2012).

Finally, critics point to the slippery slope: future GLGM for non-therapeutic applications ("designer" babies). If this scenario is not to be altogether unrealistic, a proactive ethical reflection is needed. Relevant questions include the goals of medicine, the moral quality and weight of the couple's reproductive interests, the proportionality of destroying embryos for designing purposes, and, last but not least, possible adverse effects (harm) on the child and society at large (President's Council on Bioethics 2003). With regard to the latter, views differ: is "designing" future children (reproductive enhancement) categorically wrong? Should we accept, for instance, Habermas' view (2003) that we should categorically oppose genetic reproductive designing as this would transform our (children's) self-understanding: they could no longer see themselves as the authors of their own life histories and recognize one another as autonomous persons. Or is a differentiated view appropriate, as Glover (2006) asserted: "For a richer life or for greater power to shape ourselves some loss of independence may be a price worth paying"? He argues that it may be morally justified to cross the medical boundary (i.e. leave the medical model) and eliminate (both medical and) *non-medical obstacles to human flourishing*. But how do we then define (children's) flourishing and identify the non-medical obstacles to flourishing? Are our intellectual limits among these, as Glover seems to suggest? Or should we worry about parents who may be so obsessively interested in the child having a specific excellence that they may prevent it from living its own life and developing its own identity—thereby *causing* an obstacle to flourishing? In any event, this again suggests that how we select IVF embryos *to be transferred* may be problematic from the perspective of the future child—even if the procedure would be safe from a medical point of view.

e) Embryo Damage by Unhealthy Lifestyles during Pregnancy
What, finally, can be said about the *weight and scope* of the responsibility of pregnant women to avoid harm to the future child? Should they completely refrain from drinking alcohol during pregnancy? Is it completely morally unacceptable to smoke a few cigarettes on the weekend or a joint occasionally? Should they stop working because of the stress involved, etc.? A preliminary question concerns the evidence of risk and the harm/probability ratio. Although scientific knowledge has increased substantially, many questions remain: What about the relevance of the timing of prenatal exposure, the dosage of relevant substances, the combined effects of exposure to various substances, the (ir)reversibility of adverse health effects, etc.? And apart from these scientific questions, the ethical question of how to balance any possible health risks to the embryo or, more precisely, the future child and the interests and autonomy of the pregnant woman, needs further scrutiny. Obviously, a "zero tolerance" policy regarding health risks would be disproportional and reduce pregnant women to "fetal containers."

The case of alcohol abuse seems to be most clear-cut. But even then, questions are manifold: How should prospective parents be informed about the risks involved? How is uncertainty about the effects of low-level alcohol intake during pregnancy to be handled? When is directive (including motivational) counseling justified? How is the risk of "advice fatigue" (Gavaghan 2009) to be weighed?

Unfortunately, some pregnant women drink far too much, thereby imposing serious health risks on the future child, such as FAS. Should physicians and/or society then intervene—and if so: how? Is this a case of prenatal child abuse, which should be treated accordingly and would even justify legal pressure or compulsory seclusion in a hospital? Obviously, this scenario raises difficult questions regarding effectiveness, proportionality, and subsidiarity. In some countries, there seems to be a trend to accept the view that the harm principle, particularly the prevention of harm to the future child, may justify the enforced seclusion of alcoholic pregnant women *from viability onwards.* But is the viability of the fetus relevant in this context (cf. section "Harm to the Future Child in its Embryonic Stage," pp. 155f.)? One should acknowledge that alcohol abuse may harm the future child already early in pregnancy, at the *embryonic and early fetal* stage. If compulsory seclusion after viability comes too late (and is, as a consequence, ineffective), it seems to be *a fortiori* disproportional. Should we then accept compulsory seclusion *early* in pregnancy and, if so, under what conditions?

Related questions concern the capacity/competence of alcoholic pregnant women. If they truly lack capacity, early compulsory seclusion may be (much) easier to justify—taking account of the fact that this measure could simultaneously protect the embryo or, more precisely, the future child from irreversible harm, restore the addicted woman's autonomy and serve her best interests. But when do addicted people really meet the criteria for incompetence?

Conclusions and Recommendations

First, any analysis of moral questions regarding "the treatment of embryos" should pay due attention to the concept of the embryo. A further reflection on the necessary and sufficient conditions for being qualified as an embryo is of utmost importance. What seem to be "embryological facts" are often covert and contestable value judgments.

Second, the proclaimed "end of the embryo war" is as unlikely as the proclaimed "end of history."

Third, no doubt many practices at "the beginning of life" raise questions about the moral status of the embryo. Still, an exclusive focus on the status of the embryo amounts to ethical one-dimensionality; patient/client-centered and (future) child-related perspectives and concerns are at least as important.

Fourth, assuming that the embryo has a relatively low independent moral status (an assumption in line with the overlapping consensus in ethics), embryo loss *in vivo* and *in vitro*, research with embryos not to be transferred and embryo selection are morally acceptable. A further discussion on the conditions to be imposed on embryo research and embryo selection is urgently needed. The ethical debate on embryo selection wrongly concentrates on PGD and disregards PGS.

Fifth, safe and effective germ line gene therapy (GLGT) to prevent mitochondrial disorders by means of PNT or MST may well be morally justified. A presumed categorical, morally overriding difference between modifying nuclear DNA on the one hand and mtDNA on the other seems to be debatable. Further analysis is required.

Sixth, experimental procedures involving both gametes to be used in medically assisted reproduction and *in vitro* embryos to be transferred should be preceded by adequate preclinical safety research. This may well include the creation of human embryos specifically for such research. A categorical prohibition of the latter hinders good clinical practice in medically assisted reproduction. A critical evaluation of relevant European regulations is needed.

Seventh, while the responsibility to avoid harm to the future child is widely accepted, its precise implications for the "treatment" of the embryo *in vivo* and the allocation of related responsibilities need further ethical analysis. How is the proportionality of (strong) pressure by professionals or even compulsion regarding pregnant women with unhealthy lifestyles to be defined? Harm that is to be prevented includes "informational harm": the question how to protect future children's right not to know should be timely addressed in view of the rapid introduction of whole genome prenatal testing and, possibly, PGS.

Bibliography

Bredenoord, A.L., G. Pennings, and G. de Wert. (2008). "Ooplasm and Nuclear Transfer to Prevent Mitochondrial DNA Disorders: Conceptual and Normative Issues." *Human Reproduction Update* 14: 669-78.

Bredenoord, A.L. *et al.* (2011). "Ethics of Modifying the Mitochondrial Genome." *Journal of Medical Ethics* 37: 97-100.

Bianchi, D. *et al.* (2012). "Genome-Wide Fetal Aneuploidy Detection by Maternal Plasma DNA Sequencing." *Obstetrics & Gynecology* 119: 890-901.

Caplan, A.L. (2009). "The Beginning of the End of the Embryo Wars." *The Lancet* 373: 1074-77.

Council of Europe. (1997). *European Convention on Human Rights and Biomedicine.*

De Sousa, P. (2012). "Parthenogenesis and Other Strategies to Create Human Embryos for Stem Cell Research and Regenerative Medicine." In: J. Nisker *et al.* (eds.). *The "Healthy" Embyo: Social, Biomedical, Legal and Philosophical Perspectives.* Cambridge, etc.: Cambridge University Press. Pp.70-83.

Die-Smulders, C.E.M. de *et al.* (2013). "Reproductive Options for Prospective Parents from Families with Huntington's Disease." *Human Reproduction Update* 19: 304-15.

Dondorp, W., and G. de Wert. (2012). *The "Thousand-Dollar Genome": An Ethical Exploration.* The Hague: Health Council of the Netherlands.

Dondorp, W., and G. de Wert. (2011). "Innovative Reproductive Technologies: Risks and Responsibilities." *Human Reproduction* 26: 1604-08.

Dondorp, W.J., and G. de Wert. (2005). *Embryonic Stem Cells without Moral Pain? Health Council of the Netherlands.* The Hague: Health Council of the Netherlands.

Fiorentino, F. *et al.* (2005). "Short Tandem Repeats Haplotyping of the HLA Region in Preimplantation Matching." *European Journal of Human Genetics* 13: 953-58.

Ford, N. (1988). *When Did I Begin? Conception of the Human Individual in History, Philosophy and Science.* Cambridge: Cambridge University Press.

Gavaghan, Colin. (2009). "'You Can't Handle the Truth'; Medical Paternalism and Prenatal Alcohol Use." *Journal of Medical Ethics* 35: 300-03.

(2007). *Defending the Genetic Supermarket*. Abingdon: Routledge.

Geraedts, J.P.M. *et al*. (2010). "What Next for Preimplantation Genetic Screening? A Polar Body Approach!" *Human Reproduction* 25: 575-77.

Gerrand, N. (1993). "Creating Embryos for Research." *Journal of Applied Philosophy* 10: 175-87.

Gesetz zum Schutz von Embryonen ("Embryonenschutzgesetz"). 1990.

Glover, J. (2006). *Choosing Children: The Ethical Dilemmas of Genetic Intervention*. Oxford: Clarendon Press.

Habermas, J. (2001). *Die Zukunft der menschlichen Natur. Auf dem Weg zu einer liberalen Eugenik?* Frankfurt am Main: Suhrkamp.

Harper, J. *et al.*, on behalf of ESHG, ESHRE and EuroGentest. (2013). "Current Issues in Medically Assisted Reproduction and Genetics in Europe: Research, Clinical Practice, Ethics, Legal Issues and Policy." *Human Reproduction* 28 (at press).

Harris, J. (2004). *On Cloning*. London/New York: Routledge.

Health Council of the Netherlands. (1998). *IVF-Related Research*. The Hague: Health Council of the Netherlands.

Hens, K. *et al*. (2012). "Comprehensive Preimplantation Genetic Screening: Ethical Reflection Urgently Needed." *National Review of Genetics* 13: 676-77.

Hurlbut, W. (2005). "Altered Nuclear Transfer." *New England Journal of Medicine* 352: 1153.

Hursthouse, R. (1987). *Beginning Lives*. Oxford: Blackwell.

Jones, H.W. (1987). "The Process of Human Fertilization: Implications for Moral Status." *Fertility and Sterility* 48: 189-92.

Jong, A. de *et al*. (2010). "Non-Invasive Prenatal Testing: Ethical Issues Explored." *European Journal of Human Genetics* 18: 272-77.

Kuliev, A. *et al*. (2012). "PGD for Inherited Cardiac Diseases." *Reproductive BioMedicine Online* 24: 443-53.

Lockwood, M. (1988). "Warnock versus Powell (and Harradine): When does Potentiality Count?" *Bioethics* 2: 187-213.

McCormick, R. (1991). "Who or What is the Preembryo?" *Kennedy Institute of Ethics Journal* 1: 1-15.

Mertes, H., and G. Pennings. (2011). "Ethical Concerns Eliminated: Safer Stimulation Protocols and Egg Banking." *American Journal of Bioethics* 11: 33-35.

Morris, S. *et al*. (2012). "Dynamics of Anterior-Posterior Axis Formation in the Developing Mouse Embryo." http://www.nature.com/ncomms/journal/v3/n2/full/ncomms1671.html.

Murray, T.H. (1987). "Moral Obligations to the Not-Yet Born: The Fetus as Patient." *Clinics in Perinatology* 14: 329-43.

Nuffield Council on Bioethics. (2012). *Novel Techniques for the Prevention of Mitochondrial DNA Disorders: An Ethical Review.* London: NCoB.

Palini, S. *et al.* (2013). "Genomic DNA in Human Blastocoele Fluid." *Reproductive BioMedicine Online* (at press; DOI: 10.1016/j.rbmo. 2013.02.012).

Pennings, G. (1996). "Ethics of Sex Selection for Family Balancing." *Human Reproduction* 11: 2339-45.

Pennings, G., *et al.* (2007). "ESHRE Task Force on Ethics and Law: Oocyte Donation for Non-Reproductive Purposes." *Human Reproduction* 22: 1210-13.

President's Council on Bioethics, The. (2005). *Alternative Sources of Human Pluripotent Stem Cells: A White Paper.* Washington D.C.

(2003). *Beyond Therapy.* New York: HarperCollins.

Rasko, J. *et al.* (eds.). (2006). *The Ethics of Inheritable Genetic Modification.* Cambridge: Cambridge University Press.

Robertson, J.A. (1999). "Reconstituting Eggs: The Ethics of Cytoplasm Donation." *Fertility and Sterility* 71: 219-21.

(1986). "Embryo Research." *Western Ontario Law Review* 24: 15-37.

Robinton, D.A., and G.Q. Daley. (2012). "The Promise of Induced Pluripotent Stem Cells in Research and Therapy." *Nature* 481: 295-305.

Shuster, E. (2007). "Microarray Genetic Screening: A Prenatal Roadblock for Life?" *Lancet* 369: 526-29.

Stanford, J.B., and R.T. Mikolajczyk. (2002). "Mechanisms of Action of Intrauterine Devices: Update and Estimation of Postfertilization Effects." *American Journal of Obstetrics and Gynecology* 187: 1699-1708.

Takahashi, K. *et al.* (2007). "Induction of Pluripotent Stem Cells from Adult Human Fibroblasts by Defined Factors." *Cell* 131: 861-72.

Tauer, C.A. (1985). "Personhood and Human Embryos and Foetuses." *Journal of Medical Philosophy* 10: 253-66.

Treff, N.R. *et al.* (2011). "Cleavage Stage Embryo Biopsy Significantly Impairs Embryonic Reproductive Potential while Blastocyst Biopsy Does Not." *Fertility and Sterility* 96: 2.

United Nations. (1997). *United Nations Universal Declaration on the Human Genome and Human Rights.*

Wasserman, D., J. Bickenbach, and R. Wachbroit (eds.). (2005). "Quality of Life and Human Differences: Genetic Testing, Health Care, and Disabilities." Cambridge: Cambridge University Press.

Wert, G. de. (2009). "Preimplantation Genetic Testing: Normative Reflections." In: J. Harper (ed.). *Preimplantation Genetic Diagnosis*. 2nd ed. Cambridge: Cambridge University Press. Pp. 259-73.

(2005). "Preimplantation Genetic Diagnosis: The Ethics of Intermediate Cases." *Human Reproduction* 20: 3261-66.

(1999). *Met het oog op de toekomst. Voortplantingstechnologie, erfelijkheidsonderzoek en ethiek*. Amsterdam: Thela Thesis.

Wert, G. de, and C. Mummery. (2003). "Human Embryonic Stem Cells: Research, Ethics and Policy." *Human Reproduction* 18: 672-82.

Wert, G. de, I. Liebaers, and H. van de Velde. (2007). "The Future (R)evolution of PGD/HLA Testing: Ethical Reflections." *Stem Cells* 25: 2167-72.

Wert, G.M.W.R. de, W.J. Dondorp, and B.M. Knoppers. (2012). "Preconception Care and Genetic Risk: Ethical Issues." *Journal of Community Genetics* 3: 221-28.

CHAPTER XI

Abortion

Medical and Moral Aspects
in Islamic Perspectives

Moustafa H. Hegab

Introduction

In this contribution I will describe the Islamic ideas and the rules concerning abortion in Islam. Although Islamic religion opposes abortion in the case of unwanted or unplanned pregnancies, it does allow it if the pregnancy endangers the mother's life. Islam teaches that abortion is a sin that increases in seriousness as the pregnancy progresses; nonetheless, it does permit abortion to save the life or protect the health of the mother and in some other circumstances.

I will start with a short introduction to abortion and then deal with abortion in Islam. We will see that Islamic law distinguishes three phases in the growth of the fetus into a human being with a soul. On this basis I can mention the rules on abortion according to various schools of Islamic law. Although Egypt and Iran are Islamic countries, they completely prohibit abortion despite the exceptions that Islam makes to preserve a woman's life or health.

The official teaching of a religion is not always reflected in the way its members actually live their lives: many people feel that they must make decisions based on their own conscience and circumstances even when they do not fit with the official teachings of their religion. Abortion is a good example of this since it takes place in every culture and every country in the world, often in opposition to the community's culture, religion, or law. According to the safe motherhood initiative organization, over a third of all pregnancies across the world are unplanned.[1] This comes down to about 75 million of 200 million pregnancies. The discovery of an unplanned pregnancy affects all women differently. Each woman's circumstances are unique, and there are sometimes reasons why she may not feel able to continue with a pregnancy. The World Health Organization states that an estimated 70,000 women die each year through illegal abortions, demonstrating that prohibiting abortion does not prevent it from happening but makes it unsafe by removing access to doctors and sanitary medical facilities (Grimes 2006).

Pregnancy occurs when the fertilized ovum implants in the endometrium of normal uterine cavity. Implantation in the fallopian tube or rudimentary horn of the uterus is considered an abnormal pregnancy. The termination of the latter is mandatory to avoid maternal complications that might end in death, and such termination is not considered abortion (Haseeb 2007).

Abortion (miscarriage) means the expulsion or removal of the products of conception from the uterus before the 20th week of pregnancy, i.e. before viability. The latter means that when the fetus is expelled from the uterus it can survive under favorable conditions (Haseeb 2007).

Abortion may be spontaneous or induced; the latter means termination of an intact healthy pregnancy either for medical reasons or because of an unwanted pregnancy, i.e. abortion on demand. There is another type of abortion called missed abortion, a condition where the embryo or fetus has died but remains inside the uterus. In such case, termination of pregnancy is a must to avoid complications for the mother (Haseeb 2007).

Advancements in medicine with the use of ultrasonic imaging enabled physicians to detect fetal abnormalities (structural) as early as the 10th-12th week of pregnancy. The use of ultrasonography and fetoscopy also allowed physicians to correct some fetal malformations *in utero* before birth.

In this chapter I describe the *fiqh* tradition. Islam is a code for living; consequently, Islamic law is very comprehensive and does not deal exclusively with questions of faith and worship. It also regulates moral behavior, social interaction, husband-wife relationships—including sexuality, family formation, family

---

[1] www.safemotherhood.org.

planning, and abortion. Islamic law is "evolutionary" in the sense that its full growth took centuries and passed through various phases (Mussalaam 1978). It began with general principles stated in the basic sources of Islam. At first, it dealt with simple, practical problems of everyday life, but as time passed it grew complex and inclusive. The Islamic views on abortion are important for our planet since one out of every six people on this earth is a Muslim.

The central question of this chapter is whether *shari'ah* allows or prohibits abortion. If it is not prohibited under all circumstances, a list of sub-questions arises: At what stage in the pregnancy does the fetus become a human being? What are the circumstances in which Islamic law permits abortion? And under what circumstances is abortion prohibited? I will attempt to answer these questions in what follows. Islamic law on abortion depends on distinctions between the phases of the growth of the fertilized egg and the fetus. These phases approximate phases that medical theory distinguishes worldwide, but the Qur'an already makes important distinctions that indicate if the abortion is legitimate.

Stages of Fetal Growth as Described by Theologians

The *Sunnah*

Qur'anic references leave no doubt that the fetus undergoes a series of transformations before becoming human. The main Qur'anic verses referring to fetal growth are as follows:

> O mankind: If you are in doubt as to resurrection, consider that We have created you of earth, then of a blood like clot then of a lump of flesh (which is) formed and not formed so that We may demonstrate to you [our power], and We establish in the wombs what We will till a stated term; then We bring you out as infant. (Surah al-Haddj (22):4)

> We created man of a quintessence of clay. Then We placed him as semen in a firm receptacle. Then We formed the semen into a blood like clot; Then We formed the clot into a lump of flesh; then We formed out of that lump bones and clotted the bones with flesh. Then We made him another creation. So blessed be God the best creator. (Surah al-Muminun (23):13)

There are at least two significant *hadiths* that make direct reference to fetal development:

> Each of you is constituted in your mother's womb for forty days as a *nutfa*; then it becomes an *alaqa* for an equal period, then a *mudgha*; then an angel is sent .... (Imam Muslim, *Sahih* Book 33, no. 6390)[2]

> When forty nights pass after the semen gets into the womb, Allah sends the angel and gives him the shape. Then he creates his sense of hearing, sense of sight, his skin, his flesh, his bones, and then says: My Lord, would he be male or female? And your Lord decides as He desires and the angel then puts down that also. (Imam Muslim, *Sahih* Book 33, no. 6393)

In the Qur'an and hadith literature this terminology has been explained as follows: a) *nutpha* literally means "a drop of fluid," which refers to the semen; b) *alaqa* literally means something that clings and adheres to the uterus (womb)—clearly it refers to the implantation stage (blastocyst); c) *mudghah* literally means "a piece of flesh that has been chewed; this could refer to the stage of the embryo.

In the first *hadith* above, direct reference is made to the ensoulment of the fetus after 120 days from the time of fertilization. At the same time, some of the commentators on the Qur'anic texts, hold that the words *khalqan akher* (i.e. another act of creation) at the end of the first Qur'anic verses above signify the ensoulment of the fetus and that the stage of *mudghat ghayer* (i.e., the lump not yet completely created) in the second Qur'anic verse denotes the stages when no soul has yet been breathed into it. It is noteworthy that the second *hadith* states that organ differentiation occurs forty-two nights after fertilization (Madkour 1974). In sum, the three tiers of time that figure in the

---

2 On the authority of Abdullah Bin Mas'ud. For a word index in four collections of hadiths, see: http://www.searchtruth.com/search Hadith.php?keyword=womb&translator=2&search=1&book=&start=0& records_display=50&search_word=all. See also the description of these stages in the chapter by Nassar, Mansour, and Serour in this volume (chapter VII).

Islamic scholars' consideration of abortion are: before 40 days, before 120 days, after 120 days. We will return to that below.

As was mentioned above, the fundamental question for Islamic law is: At what point of the process of development does a fetus become a human being? Mussallam indicates that Muslims believed that point to be at the end of the fourth month of pregnancy, when the fetus was ensouled. There is also another view that indicates that point to be at the end of 42 days, when organ differentiation starts (Omran 1992; Mussallam 1978; Madkour 1974).

Scholars' Opinions Regarding Abortion

There is a consensus among theologians that abortion is categorically prohibited after 120 days except to save the mother's life. The 120-day limit is based on the tradition of the "forties" in which the Prophet relates that the fetus is a *nutfa* for 40 days, an *alaqa* for another 40, and a *mudgha* for an additional 40. Then ensoulment takes place at about 120 days.

In contrast to abortion after 120 days, when scholars agree it is prohibited, there are different views regarding abortion before that time.[3] We can summarize the points of view of the various schools in relation to abortion as follows.

1) *The Hanafi School* generally allows abortion before 120 days, before ensoulment (Omran 1992; Madkour 1974). Some feel it to be disfavored without reasonable justification, because once conceived, the fetus has the potentiality of life (Omran 1992). One of the most commonly cited indications of justified abortion in the school is the case in which a woman becomes pregnant while lactating and her milk stops and the father does not have the resources to provide milk. This is justified as a means of preserving the life of the baby who is nursing. Another indication is the mother's ill health or if there is the risk of a difficult labor, especially if such has occurred previously. The underlying rule is that a greater danger or harm is warded off by a lesser risk,

---

[3] For the schools and their authority see Aulad Abdellah's contribution on *shari'ah* in this volume (chapter II).

and the mother's life takes precedence over that of the fetus because she is the origin;

2) *The Maliki School* does not allow abortion, not even in the first 40-day period (only one Maliki scholar al-Lakhim, allows it during that period);

3) *The Shafe'i School* is divided on abortion before 120 days. Some scholars, like Ibn al Imad, prohibit it while others, like Muhammed Ibn Abi Sad, allow it in the *nutfa* and *alaqa* periods (80 days), and still others allow it before 120 days;

4) *The Hanbali School* allows it before 40 days, otherwise it is prohibited;

5) *The Zaydi School* permits abortion before 120 days by analogy with *al-azl* (coitus interruptus);

6) The *Imami Shi'ites* do not allow abortion at any time;

7) The *Zahiri School* permits abortion before 120 days but is not equated with killing; after 120 days it is considered to be killing;

8) The *Ibbadis School* does not allow abortion at any time.

Special Circumstances

There are some aspects of abortion that need special emphasis, among them abortion for pregnancies resulting from relations outside of marriage, rape, and fetal deformities. The following are the opinions of theologians regarding these issues.

Islam and Abortion Because of Pregnancy Outside of Marriage

Islamic law does not condone the termination of pregnancies resulting from illegitimate sex (any sexual relation outside valid marital relations) (Ebrahim 1989). Islam not only condemns illegitimate sex but dictates that persons guilty of such a crime should be publicly punished. An incident in the life of the Prophet sheds light on the Islamic stand against abortion as an option in the event of pregnancy resulting from illegitimate sex:

> There came to Him a woman from Ghamid and said "Allah's Messenger, I have committed adultery, so purify me."
> He turned away. On the following day she said, "Allah's Messenger why do you turn me away? Perhaps you turn me away as you turned Ma'iz. By Allah, I have become pregnant." He said: "Well, if you insist upon it, then go away

until you give birth to (the child)." When she delivered she came with the child (wrapped) in rags and said, "Here is the child whom I have given birth to." He said: "Go away and suckle him until you wean him." When she had weaned her child she came to Him with the child, who was holding a piece of bread in his hand, "Allah's Apostle, here he is. I have weaned him and he eats food." He entrusted the child to one of the Muslims and then pronounced punishment. (Imam Muslim XVII: no. 4205)

Theologians conclude from this *hadith* that pregnancy as a result of illegitimate sex should be carried to term.

Islam and Abortion Because of Rape

The Grand Imam of Al-Azhar (1993) indicates that termination of a pregnancy because of rape is not allowed in Islam. The argument is that the angel has breathed the soul into the child and it has to be treated as a human being. The Grand Imam is one of the most important authorities in relation to what is and what is not allowed in the Islamic world. Of course, his statements are important in the medical institutions of Al-Azhar University itself. This opinion was a reply to a question regarding some Bosnian Muslim women who were raped by Serbians and became pregnant. He urged the Muslim communities to help raise those children who had resulted from rape to be good Muslims. Sudan, however, although it is a Muslim country, allows abortion when pregnancy is the result of rape.[4] The laws of Islamic states may differ from the majority of *fiqh* scholars and leave sometimes more and sometimes fewer possibilities compared with the majority of *fiqh* scholars.

Islam and Abortion Because of Fetal Deformities

With the advance of modern prenatal diagnosis and with considerable accuracy, one can safely diagnose some of the congenital anomalies. But Sheikh Gad El Hak, Grand Imam of Al-Azhar (1992), in reply to questions on that subject indicates that the religious opinion (*fatwa*) was that abortion cannot be per-

---

[4] www.un.org/esa/population/publications/abortion/doc/sudan. doc.

mitted on such grounds. Nonetheless, in some Islamic countries, Kuwait for example, the abortion of such fetuses was sanctioned if the defect was incurable (Hathout 1989).

Discussion regarding abortion in many countries worldwide has nowadays polarized into two positions, neither of which has universal consent. In one, the fetus is regarded as a physical part of a woman's body that she is free to remove at will; her right to decide whether or not to bear a child conceived in her is absolute, thus overriding all rights that are incompatible with it. At the other extreme the fetus is invested with such an absolute right to life that no consideration could prevail to secure its termination. In Muslim culture, however, neither view is accepted. For instance, Hathout, a prominent Islamic scholar and medical doctor, challenged the idea of the mother's "right to choose." He argues that a woman does not create a fetus but receives it; the fetus is entrusted to her. It is not part of its mother's body and may have different biological attributes; it cannot be considered as a tumor or a lump to be removed. He suggests that a woman's freedom with regard to her body cannot entail killing "another" human being merely because that human being is inside her (Hathout 1989).

Islamic ethics is between the two extreme positions. It is a position that seems more consistent with the tradition of medical ethics on safeguarding life in general. This position permits abortion if it endangers its mother's life or health. But this position would not allow abortion for social or economic reasons.

Conclusion

Muslims' view of the beginning of life influences the rules that regulate abortion. There is a consensus among the theologians that abortion after 120 days is not allowed except to save the mother's life. Before 120 days, the majority of Muslim scholars allow abortion but only for health reasons. Also, Islam gives women the right to terminate a pregnancy in cases of severe maternal health problems. On other indications, these rights are relative and should be weighed against other alternatives.

Bibliography

Abdul-Ati, H. (1975). *Islam in Focus.* Kuwait: American Trust Publications/Mogahwi Press.

Haseeb, Farouk. (2001). "Early Development, and Types of Abortion." In: Farouk Haseeb. *Basics Obstetrics.* Cairo: University Book Center. Pp. 38-40.

Gad El Hak, A. Younis, M., and A. Ragab. (1992). "Abortion in Cases of Congenital Anomalies." In: G.I. Serour (ed.). *Some Gynecological Problems in the Context of Islam.* Cairo: IICPSR, Al-Azhar Publications. Pp. 114-29.

Grimes, David A. *et al.* (2006). "Unsafe Abortion: The Preventable Pandemic." *The Lancet.* Sexual and Reproductive Health Series 4 (October): 1908-19. www.who.int/reproductivehealth/topics/unsafe abortion/article unsafe abortion.pdf.

Hathout, H. (1989). "Ethics and Human Values in Family Planning: Perspectives of the Middle East." In: Z. Bankowski, J. Barzelatto, and A.M. Capron. *Ethics and Human Values in Family Planning: Conference Highlights, Papers, and Discussion.* XXII's CIOMS Conference, Bangkok, Thailand, 19-24 June, 1988. Geneva: Council for International Organizations of Medical Sciences.

Imam Muslim. *Sahih Muslim.*

Madkour, M. (1974). "Muslim Outlook on Abortion and Sterilization." In: *Proceedings of Islam and Family Planning Conference in Rabat (Morocco), December 1971.* Vol II. Lebanon: IPPF (Middle East and Africa). Pp. 263-86.

Mussallam, B. (1978). *Sex and Society in Islam.* Cambridge: Cambridge University Press.

Omran, A. (1992). *Family Planning in the Legacy of Islam.* New York and London: United Nations Population Fund/Routledge.

CHAPTER XII

Human Organ Transplantation

Ahmed Ragai El-Gindi

Introduction

Human organ transplantation was unknown in ancient times, except in a primitive form in one case where one of the Prophet's Companions lost an eye and Muhammad put it back. In another case, a Companion lost his nose during a war, and the Prophet ordered that it be replaced by gold. Apart from these two cases, the history of Islam does not record any attempts at transplanting an organ from one person into another.

The main objective of transplantation is to save a person's life through medical intervention and to preserve the goal of medicine. But transplanting an organ from a person who has just died is not recommended in most Islamic countries because it is tantamount to an offense against the human body. In his contribution to this volume, Mostafa Salem summarizes the recent Egyptian Law on Organ Donation (2010) that, as he states, for the first time provides a framework, including regulations and restrictions, for organ transplantation.

In this chapter I will discuss the crucial issues that have led to objections to organ donation. I will describe how Muslim medical specialists have come to ethical conclusions and have formulated rules for dealing with cases in practice. The first issue we will discuss is the question of what should be decisive for ascertaining the donor's end of life: in short, the organ has to be "alive" while the patient has "died." The second section concerns the integrity of the body of the dead (and living) person who is prepared to provide an organ. In Islam, the integrity of the body—which God has trusted to an individual—is important. This section deals with whether an incision in the body and removal of an organ is permitted. Also, living persons can be donors. The third section discusses criteria for the (healthy) donor who is willing to give one of his organs. Fourth, I will make some remarks on organ trafficking and the financial exploitation of poor people who offer their organs. After a short conclusion, I will provide an appendix that contains a proposed form for issuing a brain death certificate as prepared by the (international) Islamic Organization for Medical Sciences (IOMS) based in Kuwait.

Ethical Issues in Retrieving Organs from the Deceased

In ancient times, a person was considered dead when his heart stopped beating and his lungs stopped breathing. But, in light of the new developments in intensive care units and critical care units, there is a great demand for organ transplantation due to the huge number of accidents. For the same reason, there are a number of casualties of persons declared brain dead or brain stem dead with healthy organs that can be used to save others who are suffering from very bad health conditions due to the failure of one of their vital organs. They can be saved by the transplantation of organs from persons with irreversible brain or stem brain death. These developments encouraged the surgeons to make use of the healthy organs from dead persons.

Organ transplantation was recently introduced, and the technology around it has developed immensely. At the same time, the drugs for immune suppression have also been highly improved so that the problem of rejection of the donated organs can be avoided. This is reflected in the great demand for donated organs in the face of the scarcity of those available.

For dying persons, the only group of people whose organs can be used are those with irreversible brain and brain stem death. In fact, the moment of death has to be declared at the moment of irreversible brain stem death so that a healthy organ can be extracted from a person who has died. It is very important to define death accurately because retrieving organs from a non-dead person has many consequences in Islamic jurisprudence (*fiqh*). Death is a very important occasion in Islam and involves two aspects: the ritual and the social. The ritual aspect concerns issues such as washing the dead body, performing the funeral prayer, etc., and the social aspect has to do with the family, relatives, and friends of the deceased, inheritance, etc. In Islam, the decision on the moment of death is a joint decision between medical experts and Muslim jurists.

There are many ethical questions involved in extracting and transplanting the organs of a dead person. In this section I will deal with the following issues:

1) What is the exact moment that a person should be declared dead?
2) What are the criteria for determining that death has occurred?
3) Who has the right to make this decision?

To answer these questions, we have to know the exact state of the new technology in the field of intensive care and critical care. According to recent developments, it is possible to keep the heart beating and other main organs alive for a certain period of time in spite of brain damage and/or stem brain damage. Although this process will not change the moment of death, it will prolong the process of death and increase the pain of the deceased's families (especially their spouses and children) and relatives. Nevertheless, the best sources for obtaining healthy organs are healthy individuals who die.

So, the moment of death needs to be defined accurately from the medical point of view for those who are suffering from brain damage and stem brain damage and are considered dead because this damage is irreversible and the vital organs will gradually die if they are not supported by the external supply of oxygen and nutrition. Therefore, all organs will die gradually, although the length of time varies from organ to organ. But the conflict between the Muslim jurists and the medical team has to do with how the jurists will issue a decision or a certificate or agree that this person is dead while his heart is still beating and his lungs are still breathing. So, guidelines were adapted to help ascertain when an individual is dead and if decisions can be made concerning, for example, the retrieval of the organs.

The Islamic View of the Medical Definition of Death

The advent of new medical technologies especially in critical care and intensive care units and the introduction of organ transplantation have made the task of defining death the most pressing issue in the field of biomedical ethics. The previous traditional view of death, which focused upon the cessation of circulatory and respiratory functions as criteria for determining the departure of the spirit, is still used for the majority of people who die normally. But it cannot be used in certain cases either in intensive care or critical care units or in accidents, especially if death can be postponed by artificially maintaining a patient's normal heart beat, blood pressure, respiration, liver, and kidney functions. The answer to the question of the timing involves an attempt to understand the moment of imminent death. Any error in judgment could lead to a legally questionable decision.

For Muslims, the definition of death cannot be based on medical facts or scientific investigations alone. Muslim jurists should be consulted. So, the IOMS was very keen to discuss the problem by inviting physicians from different specialties, lawyers, jurists, sociologists, psychiatrists, and other specialists to two different meetings in 1985 and 1996.

In 1985, the IOMS held a symposium to study "The End of Human Life" (El-Gindi 1985). A select group of top religious jurists, medical scholars, legal experts, and authorities in the humanities participated in the discussions. After these detailed discussions, the symposium endorsed the following conclusions.

(1) There is usually no difficulty in diagnosing death based on its publicly known features or an external clinical examination distinguishing the dead from the living.

(2) In some (very few) cases, usually under close observation in the intensive care units or similar specialized hospital wings, there is a pressing need for establishing the diagnosis of death, even at the phase when life-like phenomena persist, either spontaneously or by means of artificial life support machines.

(3) The old jurisprudence books were scrutinized in search of signs that prove death. These were mainly human interpretations based on available medical knowledge and the absence of a clear-cut definition of death in the Qur'an and the traditions of the Prophet. Since the diagnosis of death and its signs has always been part of the medical domain, on which the jurists based their ruling, the medical experts presented to the symposium the current medical opinion on the definition of death.

(4) After the medical scholars presented the case, the following points became clear:

- The death of that part of the brain responsible for the primary vital functions, which is called the brain stem, is a reliable indicator of the occurrence of death.
- The diagnosis of brain stem death is based on clear-cut and reliable evidence and excludes well-known clinical entities that might give a false positive diagnosis.
- A vital organ or function like the heart or respiratory system might stop temporarily but can sometimes be restored, but only if the brain stem is alive. If the brain stem has died, there is no possibility of such recovery, and the person's life has for all intents and purposes come to a end, even if other organs or systems have not yet died but will inevitably after a certain period of time.

(5) It was on these medical data that the religious jurists based their view that a person is dead if it is determined with certainty that a person is in the state of brain stem death and some of the rulings concerning death are applicable to him. This is in analogy—although not completely similar—to the juridical ruling about the person who has attained "movement of the slain."[1] The jurists preferred to defer discussing the applicability of other rulings to another occasion.

(6) In view of all this, there was a consensus that if the death of the brain stem is diagnosed with certainty, then disconnecting the person from artificial life support apparatus can be carried out.

The IOMS, keen to pursue any scientific developments on the matter and feeling obligated to address a recent campaign in the press and public media discrediting the universal standard acceptance of brain death with brain stem death as diag-

---

[1] "Movement of the slain": If a person is seriously injured by someone but does not die, and if another person hits him and he does die, Islam considers the first person who hit to be the killer, and this process is called "movement of the slain."

nostic of death, decided to hold another symposium in December 1996. In November 1996, three members of IOMS participated in an international conference in San Francisco organized by the American Association of Bio-ethics and the network to study the definition of death. They reported that there was no departure from the standing definition of death by brain death together with brain stem death. No individual for whom brain and brain stem death was correctly diagnosed ever recovered, and none of those who recovered had been given an established diagnosis of brain and brain stem death. Questions on more curious aspects were confined to philosophical views or the relative evaluation of confirmatory procedures after the diagnosis was established.

The second IOMS symposium was convened in Kuwait, 17-19 December 1996, with an interdisciplinary group of distinguished scholars.[2] The subject was comprehensively discussed over three days, including a meticulous appraisal of the clinical cases presented in support of the dissent—no case properly diagnosed as brain or brain stem death ever recovered, and in all those who recovered an obvious and flagrant error in diagnosis had been made, omitting, misreading, or violating the standard criteria.

Reviewing the global situation and the regional experiences and safeguards taken (for which the contribution of the Saudi team was particularly commendable) and in full awareness of the scientific and religious dimensions, the IOMS found no reason to discard, modify, or alter the recommendations of its previous symposium on "Human Life: Its Inception and its End" (1985) or the rulings issued by another organization, the

---

[2] Specialists in neurology, neurosurgery, anesthesiology, intensive care, neurophysiology, cardiac surgery, organ transplantation, medicine, pediatrics, obstetrics and gynecology, general surgery, medical jurisprudence; who came from Kuwait, Saudi Arabia, Egypt, Lebanon, Turkey, and the United States of America, were invited. It was also attended by the Director of the Eastern Mediterranean Regional Office (EMRO) of the World Health Organization.

Fiqh Academy (a department of the Organization of the Islamic Conference) in Mecca in 1986.[3]

Criteria and Safeguards

The following standards, criteria, and safeguards were spelt out by the 1996 symposium, [4] and the IOMS herewith presents them for the benefit of formulating legislation and bylaws regulating this subject.

Signs that Indicate Death
    An individual is considered dead in one of the following two situations:
    1) complete irreversible cessation of respiratory and cardiovascular systems;
    2) complete irreversible cessation of the functions of the brain including the brain stem.

This should be confirmed by accepted medical standards.

Guidelines for Diagnosing Brain and Brain Stem Death
    1) The presence of a reliable medical specialist well experienced in the clinical diagnosis of brain and brain stem death and the various implications of such diagnosis;
    2) Prescribed observation necessitates complete medical coverage in a specialized, suitably equipped institution;
    3) A second opinion should be accessible whenever needed.

Preconditions for Considering the Diagnosis of Brain Death
    1) The person must be in continuous deep, uninterrupted coma;
    2) The cause of the coma can be explained by extensive damage of the structure of the brain, such as severe traumatic concussion, massive intracranial hemorrhage, after intracranial surgery, a large intracranial tumor or obstructed blood supply to the brain: confirmed by adequate diagnostic measures;

---

[3] http://www.islamicvoice.com/july.98/dialogue.htm#ORG.

[4] http://www.islamset.com/bioethics/death/state.html.

3) At least six hours have passed since the onset of the coma;

4) There is no spontaneous breathing.

Requirements of Diagnosis of Complete Irreversible Cessation of Brain and Brain Stem Function

1) deep coma with complete unreceptivity and unresponsiveness;

2) the clinical signs of the absence of brain stem functions, including absence of the pupillo-corneal reflex, absence of occulocephalic reflex, absence of occulovestibular reflex, absence of the gag reflex, and absence of the cough and vomiting reflexes;

3) absence of spontaneous breathing as confirmed by the apnea test when the respirator is temporally disconnected.

It should be borne in mind that:

- some spinal reflexes may persist for some time after death; this is not incompatible with the diagnosis of brain death;
- conclusions ensuing from "decortications," "decerebration," or "epileptic seizures" are incompatible with the diagnosis of brain death.

Exclusion of all Cases that may be Reversible or Curable, such as:

1) if the patient is under sedatives, tranquilizers, narcotics, poisons, or muscle relaxants, or in hypothermia below 33°C, or in an untreated cardiovascular shock;

2) metabolic or endocrine disturbances that might lead to coma;

3) a certainty of complete cessation of brain functions over a period of

- 12 hours since the onset of irreversible coma
- 24 hours if the coma is due to cessation of circulation (such as cases of cardiac arrest).

Children:

- in children under 2 months, the observation period is extended to 72 hours, followed by the repetition of electroencephalograpy or tests for cerebral circulation

- children between 2 and 24 months require a longer observation period of 24 hours followed by repletion of encephalography
- children over one year are treated like adults.

Requirements of Team Authorized to Diagnose Brain Death
1) The team comprises two specialists with experience in diagnosing brain death. A neurologist's opinion is also sought if necessary;
2) One of the two doctors of the team should be a specialist in neurology, neurosurgery, or intensive care.
No member of the team should
- be a member of the organ transplantation team;
- be a member of the family of the deceased person;
- have any special interest in the declaration of death (such as an inheritance or bequest)
- have been accused by the family of the deceased of having committed any professional misconduct.

The appendix shows a proposed form for issuing a brain death certificate.

With all of these precise regulations in mind, the IOMS advised that further public upheaval and campaigns be prevented. Therefore, it appealed to all concerned to confine the discussion of such a sensitive issue to the relevant medical and scientific circles. It chooses this path instead of presenting it in a sensationalist way to the lay media, shattering the confidence and trust of the public, which was not given the complete and correct data.

The IOMS would also like to urge the relevant authorities in Muslim countries to issue legislation defining, regulating, and safeguarding the diagnosis of death and the practice of organ donation and transplantation based upon *shari'ah*, for a legal vacuum only results in confusion or malpractice. The creation of a venue enabling the organ transplantation centers in Arab and Muslim countries to communicate, network, and exchange views and experiences should be given the appropriate priority.

Incisions in the Body

General Rules

Having established that organs can be taken from the body, we have to discuss the question if it is permissible from an Islamic point of view to make the necessary incisions.

There are three main Islamic situations similar to this situation. Islam pays full respect to both living and dead persons. All people should be treated with dignity during their lives and after their death. The Prophet says "The breaking of a dead person's bones is just like the breaking of his bones while he is alive" (Ibn Majah, Abu Dawud, Ibn Hibban, and Al-Bayhaqi). At the same time, dead people should be buried immediately after complete washing, shrouding, and performing the funeral prayer. The body should be kept from mutilation. Although these are individual rights, they still include the right of Allah, a right that may not be waived.

All these rituals should be performed for people who die a normal death. But in case of brain or brain stem damage, all these rituals cannot be observed because there are some duties that should be done to retrieve the organs to be donated to another person waiting for an organ to replace the failed one in order to relieve his sufferings.

Muslim jurists agree that it is permissible to autopsy the body to identify the real cause of death. They also agree that autopsy or desiccation can be done for teaching purposes. In addition, they condone the practice of removing a living fetus from her dead mother by making an incision in the abdomen. They also agree that the abdomen of a dead person who swallowed a valuable object belonging to someone else can be opened.

The public interest is the main rule used in this case. On the other hand, some other Muslim jurists considered this a desecration of the body. But by the calculation of the benefits and harms that could result from this, it is clear that the benefits outweigh the harm. So, from the Islamic point of view, it is acceptable (Ghaly 2011/2: 8f.). At the same time, the organ taken from the dead person will save the life of the other person who is suffering from the failure of his organ and has no hope for a cure except by organ transplantation. Thus, giving an organ is perhaps the best form of altruism in which one can act in the way recommended in the Qur'an: "...if any saves a life it is as if he saves the lives of all mankind" (Surah Al-Ma'idah (5):32).

Incision in the Body to Retrieve the Organ

Is it permissible to take an organ without getting free and informed consent from a person before his death? If it was impossible to obtain such consent, should the immediate family (spouse and children) have the authority to issue it after his death?

It is essential to get someone's free and informed consent before his death, and it is obligatory in Islam for each person to write down his/her advanced directives in the case of his/her serious illness, and after death in the form of a will and testament not only with respect to this but also for the way that he/she should be treated after his/her death. Nevertheless, if this is not available, the immediate family (spouse and children) are authorized to issue such consent. If they are not known, the official authority is the representative of those who do not have any family to issue the consent (Resolutions 1985-2000: 54, No. 26).

Does One Have the Right to Donate an Organ?

This will lead us to the question of the rights and ownership of the human life and the human body. In Islam, God has rights over and ownership of the human life and body. God allowed human beings to be partners on His behalf, and the human being is responsible for taking care of his body by taking the appropriate measures of prevention and treatment in order to enjoy his life. If he does not take these measures, he will be judged in the Hereafter as having sinned. In Islamic jurisprudence we have two types of rights, namely, the right of God and the right of the individual.

Types of Rights Pertaining to the Human Body

Muslim scholars divide rights into two major categories: the right of Allah, and the right of the individual. The right of Allah is what pertains to public interest and not that of a particular individual (Al-Maqdisi 1997: II, 414; Al-Abdari 1994: II, 254; Ibn 'Abd al-Salam 1968: I, 102). The legislator, by determining the right of Allah, was protecting the interest of the community.

The fact that the right of Allah is indicated does not mean that Allah gains any interest from such a right. In fact, Allah the Almighty is in need of no one, whereas all His creatures need Him. This designation was used, however, to enhance the importance, significance, and comprehensiveness of the right of the community that is covered by this designation. On the other hand, the right of the individual *(haqq al-'abd)* is that which pertains to the interest of a particular individual.

Rights Pertaining to the Body of the Living Human Being

The body of the living person involves two types of rights; namely, the right of Allah and the right of the individual, according to the majority of scholars. Al-'Izz ibn Abd al-Salam states that

> the crime of a person against his own body or organs varies in its sinfulness in accordance with his personal loss, and the losses and injustices that may befall others as a result of his actions .... No one has the right to destroy that part of his body, as this is a joint right shared by the individual and his God .... (In: Ibn Nujaym 1983: II, 247; Al-Suyuti 1985: 178; Ahkaam al-Gerah, Al-Shinquiti 1994: 326)

The right of Allah with respect to the human body is confirmed in many *shari'ah* rulings. Some examples are the following.

1) The agreement of *shari'ah* on the prohibition of suicide, as well as considering it one of the deadliest sins *(al-kaba'ir)* as the Almighty says: "Nor kill (or destroy) yourselves: for verily God hath been to you Most Merciful" (Surah Al-Nisa' (4):29). The Prophet said: "He who kills himself with an iron, his iron will be in his hand poking his stomach in the fire of hell, for all eternity. He who has taken poison will continue to take it for all eternity in the fire of hell. And he who throws himself from a mountain to kill himself will fall in the depths of hell fire for all eternity" (Muslim; Al-Tirmidhi; Ibn Hibban). The reason is that he who kills himself is transgressing against the right of Allah Almighty (Ibn Nujaym 1983: 93; Al-Suyuti 1985: 173).

2) The scholars prohibit anyone from harming himself in any way. They forbid anyone to cut off part of his body

or injure himself without a reason. If the individual had full rights over his body, he would not have been forbidden from doing so (Qawaid al-Ahkam, I: 130, Al-Muwwafaqaat, II: 376; Al-I'tisaam by Al-Shatibi, II: 24; Bada'i al-Sana, VII: 177).

According to Maliki and Shafi'i scholars, it is imperative the murderer be punished even if he is forgiven by the victim's blood relatives. These scholars justify this ruling by pointing out that the forgiveness of the blood relative erases the individual's right. But it does not erase the right of Allah or the right of the community and that is why he has to be punished, since this is in the interest of all people (Al-Shinqiti 1994: II, 318, III, 247; Al Qarafi, al-Furuq: I, 140; Ibn 'Abd al-Salam 1968: I, 153).

1) Some of the rulings proving what we have previously put forward are those dealing with the prohibition of alcoholic drinks and the imperativeness of implementing the prescribed punishment (al-hadd) for committing such an offense. Even though the drinker does not really transgress against anyone, he does, in fact, transgress against his own mind. This indicates that mental health pertains to the right of Almighty Allah (Al-Taftazani (1996): II, 151; Al-Shinqiti 1997: II, 318; 'Usda 1984: II, 484-85; Al-Dirini 1984: 70).

2) The right of the community in the individual's body is further supported by the shari'ah texts that indicate the unity of the Muslim community and the brotherhood of believers. This necessitates cooperation and sharing among Muslims in profits and losses.

3) The Prophet said: "Believers to each other are like parts of a structure, each part supporting the other" (Al-Bukhari; Muslim). He also said that "Believers are one organic body, if part of it is impaired, then all other parts will suffer similarly from fever and sleeplessness" (Muslim; Al-Bayhaqi).

On the other hand, a number of *shari'ah* rulings indicate the right of the individual over his body and organs, such as the following.

1) The right of retribution *(qisas)* is imperative if an organ of the body is injured in an attack. It is also made imperative for the victim's heirs if the offended party is deliberately and unjustly killed. *Shari'ah* makes paying compensation obligatory for causing bodily harm and injury and blood money *(diyah)* or compensation to the heirs of the victim if retribution is abandoned or not mandated for some reason. Furthermore, giving the victim or his heirs the right to grant pardon from retribution or compensation signifies that a transgression against an individual right has occurred. If this was not so, pardon would not be the right of the individual, since the rights of God cannot be possibly pardoned by any human being (Ibn 'Abd al-Salam 1968: I, 130; Makki 1998: I, 141, 157; Al-Shinqiti 1994: II, 376).

2) This is further supported by the ruling of the majority of jurists that the victim's acceptance of his own killing cancels the right to retribution *(qisas)*. If a person tells another to kill him and the latter does so, then the right of vengeance is waived, according to Abu Hanifa and his colleagues al-Shafi'i and Ahmad and a few Maliki scholars (Al-Shinqiti 1997: II, 376; Ibn 'Abd al-Salam 1968: I, 130; Makki 1998: I, 141; 'Usda 1984: I, 447-48).

3) The majority of scholars hold that if a person asks another to cut off his hand, and the latter does so, then no retribution is mandated. In justifying this ruling, al-Kasani, a Hanafi scholar, says, "If someone says: cut off my hand and another obliges, then the majority of scholars rule that the latter has committed no offense, since limbs are just like money, and the possession of money can be surrendered by the permission of the owner. If the owner says: 'Destroy my wealth,' and the latter does, then no offense has been committed" (Ibn 'Abd al-Salam 1968: I, 130; Al-Shinqiti 1997: II, 315, 376, VII, 124; Al-Hatab al-Ru'ayni 1992: VI, 268; Al-Shatibi 1992: II, 24; Al-Kasani 1982: VII, 177).

4) Maliki scholars believe that the permission to injure or cut someone is valid only if the injured party continues to hold on to it after the injury or cutting has been sustained. If the victim withdraws his permission after the injury has been sustained, the required *shari'ah* punishment for the offense becomes mandatory. This is either retribution or the paying of compensation.

Therefore, the majority of jurists believe that the permission of an individual to remove one of his organs allows the perpetrator to escape worldly punishment, while simultaneously stating that one is prohibited from cutting any part of himself or permitting others to do so. One might believe that there is some form of contradiction here, but in fact there is none. This may be explained by noting that they believed that two rights pertain to the human body, namely the right of Allah and the right of the individual. The permission grants pardon only for the right of the individual, but the offense is still there since the right of Allah has been ignored, and the only way to remove it is to repent. Maliki scholars have gone so far as to ignore the right of the individual over his organs, since they determine the impact of the pardon only if it occurs after the offense, and they void any permission prior to the perpetration of the offense and do not regard it as a valid pardon. Pardon is one form of surrender, and the surrendering of a right prior to determining it is not valid for them.

Rights Pertaining to the Body of the Deceased

One might ask how far the right of Allah and the right of the individual can be transferred and waived? Many Muslim scholars have stated that the right of Allah and the right of the individual differ in how far each of them can be transferred and waived. They noted that the fundamental rule in relation to the right of the individual is that it is in the interest of its owner, and hence he has the right to waive it or transfer it, and to undertake various other acts vis-à-vis his body. But the fundamental rule in relation to the right of Allah is that it is not permitted to waive or transfer it except in accordance with *shar'iah* justification, which is governed by specific rules. We will summarize the main rules and exceptions.

In determining these two fundamental rules, Ibn Qayyim al-Jawziyyah says:

> Rights are of two kinds, the right of Allah and the right of the individual. The right of Allah does not allow any form of compromise.... As for the right of individuals, it permits compromise, waiving and compensation for it. (In: Ibn 'Abd al-Salam 1968: I, 167; Al-Hatab al-Run'ayni 1992: VI, 268; Al-Shinqiti 1997: II, 315; Al-Baji 1913: VII, 124)

Muhammed al-Shinqiti says that "the right of Allah is that in which the individual has no interest, whether it makes sense or not to the individual" (1997: II, 376). Elsewhere he says "all the rights of Allah bear no interest for the individual, whereas the right of the individual bears his interest" (1997: II, 354-55).

Imam al-Qarafi (d. 684/1285) says:

> we mean by the right of the individual that which when waived is waived. Otherwise, there is no right of the individual which does not involve the right of Allah Almighty; this must be delivered to its true recipient. This is known as the validity of waiver. Everything that an individual can waive is the right of the individual, and anything that an individual cannot waive is the right of Almighty Allah. (Al-Qarafi, *Al-Furuq*; Al-Kasani 1982: VII; Al-Ramli 1984: II, 49; Al-Hatib 1992: IV, 346-47; Al-Bahuti 1981: III, 343).

There are certain exceptions to these two fundamental rules, however, in which the right of the individual becomes impossible to waive or transfer and in which the right of Allah becomes valid for waiving or transfer. The exception is based on the Islamic concept that such a right is a gift from Allah to his worshippers and that it only holds through Islamic religious law. It is Almighty Allah who legislated these rights and mandated his worshippers to a specific course in the application and use of these rights. If an act vis-à-vis these rights contradicts the course determined by Allah, then such an act is forbidden. Ibn 'Abd al-Salam says, "there are hardly any individual rights which they may waive that do not involve the right of Allah as well; this is the right of Allah to be obeyed and affirmed" (cf. Al-Kasani 1982: VII, 236). "The most prominent feature of this is that it prevents man from unfairly using his right to the detriment of the rights of others" (Ibn 'Abd al-Salam 1968: I, 167).

Consequently, on the basis of this rule, the individual is prohibited from acting vis-à-vis his right either through transfer or waiving, if his actions lead to waiving or to damaging the rights of others, whether the injured party is an individual or the whole community. It is not permitted for a person to act in his property in a way that may injure his neighbor or his partner. A husband is not permitted to transfer his right to enjoy his spouse as soon as the marriage is consummated. All these acts are transgressions against the right of the community to maintain and preserve the honor and the kinship line in it. There are many examples of this. But if a person uses his right within the given course determined by religious law, the basic rule then is to allow him to do so without any encroachment on his rights.

Regarding the exception, in which it is legislated that one act vis-à-vis the right of Allah either by transfer or waiving, it occurs in a conflict of rights and mixing of benefit and harm, and there is no way out except through the waiver or transfer of some of these rights. This then becomes imperative or permitted in accordance with rules set in Islamic religious law and deduced by scholars. The most important is the choice for the lesser of two evils in order to prevent the worse evil, or the sacrifice of the least of two interests to bring about the greater.

There are many applied examples for this rule:

- the permission to eat from a dead animal in case of extreme starvation or hunger;
- drinking alcohol if it is the only available drink when a person is choking;
- uttering heresy under compulsion;
- permission to eat the flesh of a dead person when under compelling necessity to do so, at least according to some scholars (Ibn Qayyim al-Jawziyyah 2002: 108);
- permission to pay Muslim money to disbelievers if it is the only way to escape siege or to pay Muslim money to save Muslim prisoners of war;
- permission to amputate a diseased hand to save a life (Al-Shinqiti 1997: II, 318, 375-78);

- permission to cut open the abdomen of a dead pregnant woman to extract her living fetus if the fetus's life can be saved (al-Qararfi, *al-Furuq*: I, 141);
- permission to discredit witnesses and reveal secrets before court;
- and permission to inspect taboo areas of the human body for diagnosis or therapy, etc. (Ibn Nuyaym 1983: 93; al-Suyuti 1985: 173).

The principle of "necessity knows no law" was used to explain God's permission to allow prohibited acts in case of severe duress or life-threatening conditions like thirst or starvation. The Prophet emphasizes this relaxation of the rules by God by saying, "Allah loves His Permission to be used the way He likes His Obligations to be performed" (Al-Tabarani; Ibn Hibban). In our case, the principles of "there should be neither harm nor reciprocation of harm," "choosing the lesser of two evils to prevent the worse one," and "hardship compels relief" are decisive here ((Ibn 'Abd al-Salam 1968: I, 65; Ibn Nujaym 1983: 95; al-Suyuti 1985: 176; Qasim 1982: 114). All these principles are subordinate to the most indispensable value in Islam, i.e. the "sanctity of the human life," where Islamic jurisprudence urged the preservation of the five objectives of *shari'ah*, namely, the preservation of religion, life, honor, progeny, and commodity. The preservation of life means that everyone has to take precautionary measures to keep him- or herself healthy and follow a healthy lifestyle, i.e. eat healthy food, live in a healthy environment, abstain from drinking or eating forbidden foods, have sex within the bonds of marriage, and earn and spend money through legitimate means. Allah instructed in the Qur'an: "Never should a Believer kill a Believer; but (if it so happens) by mistake, (compensation is due): If one (so) kills a Believer, it is ordained that he should free a believing slave" (Surah Al-Nisa' (4):92);

> Nor take life which God has made sacred except for just cause. And if anyone is slain wrongfully, We have given his heir authority (to demand *qisas* or to forgive): but let him not exceed bounds in the matter of taking life; for he is helped (by the Law). (Surah Al-Isra' (17):33)

The Prophet commanded people to find treatment for themselves: the God who creates diseases, also creates treatment for it (Abu Dawud).

The other principles in the five objectives are all equally important to the sanctity of the life, which should be reflected in all aspects of life. It is clear that incision does not violate human dignity if it saves the life of another.

Healthy Donors

The second source for the organs is the living person. The ethical issues in this case are that this person should be healthy, not in need of surgery, and the fact that his life is at risk in one way or another (there is a percentage of risk during the operation). The question now is: Is this person violating God's right by donating one of his organs? Allah says:

> if anyone kills a person—unless in retribution for murder or spreading corruption in the land—it is as if he kills all mankind, while if any saves a life it is as if he saves the lives of all mankind. (Surah Al-Ma'idah (5):32)

The healthy donor should be informed about the details of the operation and all the expected risks he might face. The donor should sign freely without any pressure or coercion or undue payment on the informed consent that he approved to donate one of his organs. Nevertheless, this informed consent will be of no value and will be meaningless if this organ is a vital organ and will affect his/her health. Accordingly, the donor should be adult and have the capacity and capability to understand what is mentioned to him and capable of making a decision on such a very important occasion. The surgeon has the right to remove the organ if he is sure that the removal will not affect the patient's health to the extent that that he will not be capable of leading a normal life. This act is permissible from the Islamic point of view because, as will be mentioned below, the human being does not have the right over his body to harm himself or to cut an organ from his body, but God obliged him to take care of himself in the right way. At the same time, God sanctifies human life, and Muslim jurists emphasized the principles of "harm should be removed" and "necessity knows no law," and "hardship necessitates relief" (Ibn Najaym 1983: 93; Al-Sayuti 1985: 173).

From the above rules and principles, it seems that the decision of the donor to donate does not violate God's right over human life and the body of the human being. To the contrary, the donation is a very clear indication of the sanctity of human life that God emphasized in the Qur'an.

This is compassion and mercy among all individuals. So the donation of an organ is one of the supreme noble virtues in Islam and in accordance with the rules and principles put forward by Muslim jurists in the conditions stated above. This duty is a collective religious obligation. If there is only one person capable of helping the one in need, saving the latter is an obligatory act for this person, otherwise, all of society will have sinned.

Maintaining the individual's health is the collective responsibility of the society that has to ensure it by any means without inflicting harm on others. This comprises the donation of body fluids or organs such as providing blood transfusion to one who is bleeding or a kidney transplant to a patient with bilateral irreparable renal damage.

This is another collective duty, a duty that donors fulfill on behalf of society. Apart from the technical procedures, the onus of public education falls on the medical profession, which should also draw up the procedural, organizational, and technical regulations and policy priorities. Organ transplantation should never be the outcome of compulsion, family embarrassment, social, or other pressures of exploitation of financial need.

Donation should not entail the exposure of the donor to harm. The medical profession bears the greatest portion of responsibility for issuing laws, rules, and regulations for organ donation during life and after death by a statement in the donors' will or the consent of the family, as well as the establishment of tissue and organ banks for tissues amenable to storage. Cooperation with similar banks abroad should be established on the basis of mutual aid.

'Umar Ibn Al-Khattab, the second caliph, decreed that if a man living somewhere died of hunger, then the community should pay his blood money (diyah) as if they had killed him. The analogy of people dying because of lack of a blood transfusion or donated kidneys is very similar to this (Ibn Nujaym 1983: 96; Al-Suyuti, 1985: 178; Al-Shinqiti 1994: 326). One tradition of the Prophet is quite relevant in this respect. He said, "Believers are one organic body, if part of it is impaired, then all other parts will suffer similarly from fever and sleeplessness" (Muslim; Al-Bayhaqi). In the Qur'an Allah says what this means: "They give them preference over themselves, even if they too are poor" (Surah Al-Hashr (59):9).

If living human beings are able to donate, then the dead are even more able, and no harm will afflict the cadaver if the heart, kidney, eyes, or arteries are removed to be put to good use in a living person. This is indeed a charity and directly fulfills God's Word.

Organs

Types of organs from the living organs can be classified as follows.

a) Renewable Parts of the Body

This includes blood, bone marrow, parts of the skin, milk, etc. All of them, if donated, will not cause any permanent harm or irreversible damage to the donor. While such donation is of greater value and benefit for the recipient, especially the blood, this act is considered a collective duty and acceptable according to the views of Muslim jurists.

b) Vital Organs without which Life Cannot Continue

It is not very difficult to determine the juristic opinion in cases where they prohibited this type of donation since it will seriously affect the life of the donor. If this is committed by any individual it will be considered a sinful act.

c) Singular Organs Not Vital to the Continuation of Life

If the organ is singular, then the fundamental rule is that it is not permitted to donate it to another, even though its loss might not lead to the death of the donor. This refers to organs like the tongue or kidney.

d) Organs that Are Not Singular

We can divide this into three classes. First, the donation of the organ should be a definite means for saving the recipient's life and it does not lead to permanent damage to the donor, as in the case of donating one of the two kidneys. This type of donation is highly appreciated and permissible according to the rules of Islamic law with the following prerequisite conditions: 1) the certainty of not endangering the donor's health, and 2) the likelihood of the success of the kidney transplant. Second, if the donation saves the life of the recipient but seriously adversely affects the health of the donor, it is not acceptable according to the rules of Islamic law.

Third is when the donation of an organ that is not singular does not lead to saving the recipient from death and does not lead to the death of the donor, such as the donation of the cornea of the eye or any similar organ. This can be subdivided into the following three categories:

1) the donation of all parts of the organ is not allowed because this leads to a loss of the utility of this organ for the donor;

2) donation of one member of the organ to a recipient who already has one member of the organ such as the donation of one eye to a recipient who has one eye; the rule here is that it is not permissible;

3) the donation of one organ to a recipient who totally lacks the use of a donated organ, such as the donation of an eye of a normal person to a blind person is controversial, but most Muslim jurists did not accept it.

e) Reproductive Organs

These are the organs that contribute to reproduction, such as female ovaries, ova, and womb and male testicles, penis, and sperm. These organs, especially the ovaries and testicles, differ from other organs of the body in that they are linked to specific activities of religious legislation, which are the preservation of lineage and the prevention of mix-ups in parenthood and kinship. Thus, donation of these organs (testicles and ovaries) is prohibited. But donation of the womb from living women, although it has no effect on the mixing of lineage, is not accepted unless the ovaries have been lost and the woman thus has no use for her womb.

It is forbidden to donate the penis because it is a single organ and has a vital function in sexual intercourse between husbands and wives. At the same time, the donation of sperm and ova is also prohibited in Islam.

The Problem of Financial Exploitation

Financial exploitation is a universal problem that appears in media in the form of announcements for purchasing a kidney or another organ. This kind of organ trafficking is rejected by Muslim jurists, who consider it an insult to human dignity. The individual's organs are not for sale, and the individual has no right to sell any of his organs. At the same time, this is considered a kind of exploitation committed by both the donors who exploit the needs of the sick and the sick who exploit the poverty and financial needs of the donors.

Jurists agree that the human body is not a commodity that can be turned into a commercial advantage. *Shari'ah* forbids treating humans who are endowed with dignity and honor as merchandise in commercial transactions. Furthermore, the nature of the right of the individual over his organs is the right of exclusive use and enjoyment throughout his life and that he does not have the right to transfer that use. The human body, whether that of a Muslim or a non-Muslim, has the same inviolability and dignity that is afforded to all humankind as stated in the Qur'an.

Conclusion

Muslim jurists discussed the subject of organ donation and reached the following conclusions. 1) Organs can be classified as renewable or non-renewable. 2) Renewable organs are blood, bone marrow, skin, etc., and the donation of these organs is not prohibited. 3) Permanent organs can be classified under different categories: singular, double, vital, and non-vital organs that can disfigure the person although the individual can live without them.

Muslim jurists discussed the general ruling on the donation of each and every type of human organs. The most important rules for deciding whether it is prohibited or not are the sanctity of the human life and the ownership and the rights of God and the individual over the human life and body. At the same time, they apply the following juristic rules: public good, neither harm nor reciprocating harm is allowed, harm must be removed, and the balance between benefits and harm must be preserved. Also, the jurists mentioned certain conditions for the approval of organ transplantation to avoid any harm to the donor and protect his dignity so as to save the life of the recipient. Organ transplantation is possible, but the question was how to define the moment of death. That has been resolved; consensus has been reached about brain stem death. Living donorship is allowed only out of altruism, not for commercial purposes, and under strict rules. Gamete donorship, however, is not allowed when kinship issues play a role.

Bibliography

Al-'Abdarī, Muhammad ibn Yūsuf ibn Abī al-Qāsim ibn Yūsuf. (1994) *Al-Tāj wa al-Iklīl*. Beirut: Dār al-Kutub al-'Ilmiyyah.

Al-Bukhari. (1993). *Sahih al-Bukhari*. Cairo: Dar al-Maarif.

Abū Dāwūd. *Sunan*.

Al-Bahūtī, Mansūr ibn Yūnus ibn Idrīs. (1981). *Kashf al-Qinā' 'an matn al-Iqnā'*. Beirut: Dār al-Fikr.

Al-Bājī, Abū al-Walīd Sulayman ibn Khalaf. (1913). *Al-Muntaqā Sharh Al-Muwata'*. Cairo: Dār al-Sa'ādah.

Al-Bayhaqī. *Sunan*.

Al-Dirīnī, Fathī. (1984). *Al-Haqq wa Madā Sultān al-Dawlah fī Tatbīqih*. Beirut: Mu'assasat al-Risālah.

El-Gindi, Ahmed R. (ed.). (1985). *Human Life: Its Inception and End as Viewed by Islam*. Kuwait: IOMS Publication Series.

Ghaly, Mohammed. (2011/2). "Organ Donation and Muslims in the Netherlands: A Transnational Fatwa in Focus." https://openac-cess.leidenuniv.nl/bitstream/handle/1887/20115/Ghaly-Organ-donation-Muslims-Netherlands.pdf?sequence=2.

al-Hatāb al-Ru'aynī, Muhammad ibn Muhammad ibn 'Abd al-Rahmān. (1992). *Mawāhib al-Jalīl li-sharh Mukhtasar Khalīl*, Part IV. 2nd printing. Beirut: Dār al-Fikr.

Ibn 'Abd al-Salām, 'Izz al-Dīn ibn 'Abd al-'Aziz. (1968). *Qawā'id al-Ahkām fī Islāh al-'Ānām*. Cairo: Maktabit al-Kulliyyat al-Azhariya, Dar Al-Sharq Lil-Tiba'a.

Ibn Hibbān. *Sunnan Ibn Hibbān*.

Ibn Hazm, 'Alī ibn Ahmad ibn Sa'īd. (1990) *Al-Muhallā*. Beirut: Dār al-Fikr.

Ibn Illaysh, Muhammad ibn Ahmad. *Sharh Manh al-Jalīl 'alā Mukhtasar Khalīl*. Cairo: al-Ryyān.

Ibn Mājah. *Sunan*.

Ibn Nujaym, Zayn al-Dīn ibn Ibrāhīm. (1983). *Al-Ashbāh wa al-Nazā'ir.* Beirut: Dār al-Kutub Al-'Ilmiyyah

Ibn Qayyim al-Jawziyyah, Muhammad ibn Abī Bakr ibn Ayūb. (2002). *I'lām al-Muwaqqi'īn 'an Rabb al-'Ālamīn.* Riyadh: Dār Ibn al-Jawzī.

Al-Kasānī, Ala al-Din. (1982). *Badā' al-Sanāi' fī Tartīb al-Sharāi'.* 2nd printing. Beirut: Dār al-Kitaab al-Arabiya.

Makki, Muhamamd ibn 'Alī ibn Husayn. (1998). *Tahdhīb al-Furūq wa al-Qawa'id al-Saniyyah fī al-Asrār al-Fiqhiyyah,* printed on the margin of al-Qarāfī's *Al-Furūq fī al-Anwār al-Burūq fī Anwā' al-Furūq.*

Al-Maqdisī, Muwaffaq al-Dīn ibn Qudāmah. (1997). *Al-Mughnī.* Beirut: Dār al-Kutub al-'Ilmiyyah.

Muslim. *Sahīh.*

Al-Qarāfī's *Al-Furūq fī al-Anwār al-Burūq fī Anwā' al-Furūq.* Beirut: Dār al-Kutub Al-'Ilmiyyah.

Qāsim, Yūsuf. (1982). *Nazariyat al-Darūrah fī al-Fiqh al-Jinā'ī al-Islāmī wa al-Qānūn al-Jinā'ī al-Wad'ī.* Cairo: Dār al-Nahdah al-'Arabiyyah.

Al-Ramlī, Muhammad ibn Shihāb al-Dīn. (1984). *Nihāyat al-Muhtāj Ilā Sharh al-Minhaj.* Cairo: Dār al-I'tisām.

Al-Shāfi'ī, Muhammad ibn Idrīs. (No year). *Al-Risālah.* Beirut: Dār al-Kutub al-'Ilmiyyah.

Al-Shātibī, Abū Ishaq Ibrāhīm ibn Mūsā ibn Muhammad al-Gharanātī. (1992). *Al-I'tisām.* Jeddah: Dār ibn 'Affān.

Al-Shīnqītī, Muhammad ibn Muhammad al-Mukhtār. (1994). *Ahkām al-Jirāhah al-Tibiyyah wa al-'Āthār al-Mutarattibah 'alayhā.* Jeddah: Maktabat al-Sahabah.

(1997). *Al-Muwāfaqāt.* Jeddah: Dār ibn 'Affān.

Al-Suyūtī, Jalāl al-Dīn. (1985). *Al-Ashbāh wa al-Naza'ir.* Beirut: Mu'assasat al-Risālah.

Al-Tabarānī. *Al-Mu'jam al-Kabīr.*

Al-Taftazānī, Sa'd al-Dīn Mas'ūd Ibn 'Umar. (1996). *Sharh al-Talwīh 'alā al-Tawdīh.* Beirut: Dār al-Kutub Al-'Ilmiyyah.

Al-Tirmidhī. *Sunan.*

Resolutions and Recommendations of the Islamic Fiqh Academy 1985-2000. (1988). Jeddah: Islamic Fiqh Academy.

'Ūsda, Abd al-Qādir. (1984). *Al-Tashrī' al-Jinā'ī al-Islāmī.* Cairo: Dār al-Fikr al-'Arabī.

Appendix

Proposed Form for Issuing a Brain Death Certificate

(a space for the signature of every member of the medical team in front of each item is preferable)

	First Examination At initial diagnosis of brain death	Second Examination Six hours after initial diagnosis
A - Preconditions:		
- Extensive non-curable brain damage (mention cause)	-----------------------	-----------------------
- Six hours passed since onset of coma	-----------------------	-----------------------
- Absence of spontaneous breathing	-----------------------	-----------------------
B - Exclusion of confusing causes:		
- Is temperature below 33°C?	-----------------------	-----------------------
- History of sedatives, tranquilizers, poisons, muscle relaxants	-----------------------	-----------------------
- Laboratory assay of above drugs?	-----------------------	-----------------------
- Is this a case of untreated cardiovascular shock?	-----------------------	-----------------------
- Have metabolic and endocrine factors been excluded?	-----------------------	-----------------------
C - Clinical examination:		
- Is there unresponsiveness to external stimuli?	-----------------------	-----------------------
- Are the following brain stem reflexes absent?	-----------------------	-----------------------
- Pupillary reactivity to light	-----------------------	-----------------------
- Response to touching cornea	-----------------------	-----------------------
- Cephalo-occular reflex	-----------------------	-----------------------
- Vestibule-occular reflex	-----------------------	-----------------------
- Vomiting reflex	-----------------------	-----------------------
- Cough reflex	-----------------------	-----------------------

D - Confirmatory tests:
(if necessary):

- Standard electroencephalography   no electrical activity
     Or
- Imaging for cerebral circulation   no cerebral circulation

E - After all the above has been fulfilled:

- Has the apnea test been done? ---------------------------- ----------------------------
- What was its result? ---------------------------- ----------------------------

CHAPTER XIII

Receiving a Donor Organ
and Muslims in Europe

Theological and Intercultural Dimensions

K. Schipper, M. Ghaly, and T.A. Abma

Introduction

Dutch research carried out on organ donation and Muslim communities showed different results relevant to this study. First of all, they acknowledged that people's (religious) belief systems inform their views on organ donation (Zwart and Hoffer 1998; Lex 2000). Further, both supporters and opponents of organ donation can be found among various religious and philosophical traditions, and each individual will base his or her view on specific assumptions and arguments that are valid within his or her own tradition (Zwart and Hoffer 1998; Gillman 1999). Recent reports, however, still show that there is uncertainty about the question of how Islamic scholars and Muslims evaluate organ donation in the context of European health care. One example is the Dutch report *Support for Organ Donation* by the National Institute for Health Promotion and Disease Prevention (NIGZ), which considers "uncertainty about the position of religion" to be a stumbling block among immigrants, including those with a Muslim background (Van Thiel and Kramer 2009). Previous studies have primarily and often exclusively focused on the ethical issues surrounding the *donation* of organs and not on *receiving* organs.

The main thesis of this chapter is that receiving organs can raise complex ethical issues among Muslims. This chapter pays attention to these ethical issues to inform those involved in the process of organ transplantation. We will shed light on these issues by looking at the story of Yusuf (not his real name), a Muslim Turkish kidney patient, and will reflect on a number of theological and intercultural dimensions, namely the two

schools within Islam that have different views on organ donation and the differences in doctor-patient relations. We will conclude with recommendations meant to remove obstacles in the
doctor-patient relationship and communication and to inform
doctors and patients about the perspective on donor organs endorsed by the majority of Muslim scholars, which allows for
receiving a donor organ if this is necessary and effective.

Method

The case study presented is drawn from a larger study on research priorities of renal patients (Abma *et al.* 2007; Schipper
and Abma 2011). From a series of interviews we chose Yusuf's
story because of its learning potential (Stake 1994) in illuminat-
ing theological and cultural issues related to receiving a donor
kidney. Yusuf was recruited through the patient organization;
he received a letter announcing the study and was called a
week later. The interview took place at his home and lasted
about two hours. Two interviewers, an academic researcher and
patient research partner, completed a semi-structured interview
(Schipper *et al.* 2010; Nierse *et al.* 2012). Topics included his illness and personal history. The interview was recorded with approval and fully transcribed. It was analyzed following an in-
ductive approach, reading the transcript line by line and looking for recurring themes. The coding process was completed by
two researchers, who compared and discussed the codes. The
analysis was returned to Yusuf so he could check its validity
(member check), and he approved it.

For the literature study, relevant texts within Islam were
analyzed systematically regarding organ donation. Theological
debates among Muslim scholars about organ transplantation
compose part of the contemporary Islamic biomedical ethics
(Sachedina 2007). Muslim scholars find few direct references to
organ donation in the two main sources of Islam: the Muslim
Holy Scriptures, the Qur'an, and the sayings, deeds, and tacit
approval of the Prophet Muhammad, the *Sunnah*. Therefore,
these scholars often use secondary sources and interpretation
techniques such as the concept of *maslaha* (public interest) and
fiqh al-muwazanat (weighing the possible benefits against possible harm) of medical treatments. Since the 1980s, a number of
international Islamic organizations, including the Islamic Or-

ganization for Medical Sciences (IOMS) in Kuwait, played an important role in these discussions (Ghaly 2010).

Case Study

Yusuf immigrated to the Netherlands with his parents when he was a child. At the age of twenty, he had to start dialysis on an acute basis. Three times a week he had to go to the hospital, where a machine took over his kidney function for four hours. After four years Yusuf received a donor kidney from a deceased donor, but after several years the transplanted kidney was removed. This caused a lot of pain: "Back to where I started. Again dialysis. It is a deep inner pain that you cannot explain. A part of your body is dead." After eight years of dialysis Yusuf received a kidney from a deceased donor for the second time. Because the first had failed, the second transplantation evoked thoughts of Allah in Yusuf: "If I were not religious, I would say that nature determines whether my kidney will survive or not, but, because I have faith, I say that it is in God's hands."

The varying responses of his fellow believers to the first kidney transplant worried Yusuf. He began to wonder if it was permissible in Islam to be the recipient of a donor kidney. Some of his friends expressed doubts that Islam would allow the acceptance of an organ donation. Some even joked about it: "You could get a kidney from a non-religious person! Is it permissible to pray with such a kidney?" Yusuf's first spontaneous reaction was: "If a person is sick and you can help him, why would God not allow that?" In response to the comment regarding the kidney of a non-believer, he said: "The kidney is only flesh and it doesn't matter if the flesh is religious or not."

Yusuf took the doubts and jokes of his fellow believers very seriously and consulted a Turkish imam to inform him about the organ donation and his questions. The response from the imam was not very different from what he already thought:

There is nothing in Islam against seeking a cure for your illness, any illness. But we must not first seek our salvation with the more profound and complex treatments as these may entail certain risks, while less invasive treatments are available that may be equally effective.

As to the religious character of the donor kidney the imam re-marked: "Within Islam what counts is the soul, and the soul cannot be transplanted."

When asked what he expects from his medical doctor, Yu-suf referred to his doctor in Turkey with whom he still has contact and whose way of working he appreciates:

> My Turkish doctor always said: "Don't be nervous, every-thing will be okay, we are going to do this treatment." Be-cause he did this I got the feeling that everything would be all right. While knowing that my kidney was being rejected, I needed the hope, and he gave it to me. I expect things like this from my doctor.

Yusuf wants relief and expects a consoling attitude from his doctor. He wants his doctor to decide for him and feels that Dutch doctors are not as directive as Turkish doctors tend to be. He explained that many Turkish people want their doctor to make a decision regarding a certain treatment. Also, Yusuf em-phasized the need for personal recognition: "He called me Yu-suf. That doctor was a good man. I mean he was more like a brother or father for me." Yusuf is heavily dependent on his doctor. For instance, after the transplantation he waited pas-sively: "I did not know what to do after the transplant. Do you have to drink a lot? What about the medicines and diet? I didn't think about it; that's what the doctor's for." Yusuf sees his atti-tude towards doctors as the norm among fellow patients: "They leave everything to the doctor because doctors know every-thing and can solve everything."

Theological Dimensions

Two Schools in Islam

Theological discussions among contemporary Muslim scholars on organ transplantation started as early as the 1960s. Since then, numerous *fatwas* (religious opinions on Islamic law issued by an Islamic scholar) have been formulated, dividing these scholars into proponents and opponents.

The opponents held that organ transplantation is not allowed in Islam and based their contention on two main arguments. First, they quote the Qur'anic verse 17:70[1] and the Prophetic tradition: "Breaking the bones of the dead is [as forbidden] as breaking the bones of a living person." They emphasize the concept of *hurma* (respectability, sanctity) of the human body and state that organ transplantation conflicts with *hurma*. The body must remain intact for the resurrection on the Day of Judgment. The second argument is that the body does not belong to humankind but is only given in trust (*amana*) by its Owner, Allah. Therefore it is not up to humans to decide about their own bodies (Al-Qaradawi 2010).

The proponents argue that organ transplantation implies no infringement of *hurma*. Transplantation is redefined as a serious attempt to recover the body and save the life of a patient by means of another human body. Proponents acknowledge that God is the true owner of the body but argue that God entrusted humans with the responsibility of caring for the body. They refer further to the Qur'anic verse 5:32,[2] which portrays saving the life of another person as a great ethical value. They also rely on commonly acknowledged ground rules in Islamic law, such as "necessity makes prohibited deeds permissible" and "a lesser harm should be tolerated in order to prevent a greater one." Organ transplantation is thus tolerated in an emergency situation to save a man's life. The lesser harm (causing an injury to a dead body) should be tolerated to avoid the greater harm (the death of a living person). Finally, this group refers to the principle of *maslaha*: the public interest and welfare of society (Al-Qaradawi 2010; Albar 1994).

---

[1] "We have honored the sons of Adam; provided them with transport on land and sea; given them for sustenance things good and pure; and conferred on them special favors, above a great part of our creation."

[2] "… and if any one saved a life, it would be as if he saved the life of the whole people."

On the basis of studies available in Western languages, some researchers expressed doubt that the majority of Muslim scholars are in favor of organ transplantation (Zwart and Hoffer 1998). But in his study of organ transplantation in Islam, the Muslim physician and bioethicist Albar concluded that the proponents outnumber the opponents. In his recent study, the Muslim religious scholar Yusuf al-Qaradawi quoted 13 *fatwas*, all advocating organ transplantation from an Islamic perspective (Al-Qaradawi 2010). Also, most leading Muslim scholars and collective councils advocate organ donation (Albar 1994). Furthermore, some of the opponents change their positions over time, joining the proponents' camp. For instance, in 1988 the council of Muslim scholars in Singapore produced a revised *fatwa* that permits organ donation. The topic of organ transplantation was also discussed in a conference held in the Netherlands in March 2006 whose final declaration states that there is no objection to organ transplantation, provided that:

- it is necessary for the patient;
- there is no financial gain;
- the decision to become a donor is made freely;
- the deceased's wishes are respected;
- the removal and transplant procedures takes place with the greatest medical and social care (www.nigz.nl).

Supporters of organ donation are also gaining ground as the process of organ transplantation has become increasingly reliable and the beneficial effects of transplantation are increasingly apparent (Beck and Wiegers 2008).

The Role of the Doctor

Yusuf and his imam were thus in line with the majority of Muslim scholars in holding that there was no bar to organ transplantation in Islam. But there are two conditions for accepting a donor kidney, namely necessity and effectiveness. Transplantation is allowed when no less invasive procedure is available and when there is a high probability (*zann râjih*) that the organ of the donor will be effective in curing the disease. Muslim scholars agree that the only one who can judge if these two conditions apply is the treating physician (Al-Qaradawi 2010; Sharaf al-Din 1981).

Here is a clear preference by Muslim scholars for an active role of the medical doctor in the assessment of the situation. It is the doctor who assesses if receiving an organ is necessary and/ or effective. This also holds true for the doctor-patient relationship. The former Grand Imam (Sheikh) of al-Azhar, Jad al-Haqq, stated in his answer (*fatwa*) to a question from an American Muslim that a Muslim patient should listen to and obey his doctor (Jad al-Haqq 2005). Here we see a clear preference for a paternalistic relation between doctor and patient. Yusuf's story also shows that Muslim patients might tend to give the physician's discretion great value. We will explore below how this philosophy relates to Western bioethics.

Western Bioethics

Principles that play a role within Islamic debates about organ donation can also be recognized within Western bioethics, a discipline derived from Christianity in which the sacredness of life is a central notion (Widdows 2007). What is called *hurma* comes close to what is known as bodily integrity. Bodily integrity implies that no one can be touched or medically treated without consent (Slatman 2008). Both bodily integrity and *hurma* stress the importance of the integrity and value of the body. In contrast to the notion of bodily integrity, however, *hurma* also entails that the body should remain intact even if the person in question has given his or her consent. Other notions we recognize within Western bioethics are the principles of doing good and preventing harm, both of which resonate with the Islamic idea of saving life and *maslaha* (Beauchamp 2007). Also, in both traditions reference is made to the effectiveness of treatment and proportionality.

The principle of respect for autonomy constitutes an exception. This is a major principle in Western bioethics and in debates on organ donation (Price 2007). Whereas Islam accentuates the authority of the doctor, Western bioethics stresses respect for the autonomy of the patient (Tronto 2007). But this difference should not be exaggerated. Within Islam, the notion of consent is considered to be of importance, but the idea of autonomy is reframed as a "bounded autonomy." "Bounded" refers here to the idea that one's autonomy is limited by the rules of Islam. Sometimes this is referred to as the difference between "freedom by God" (Islam) versus "freedom from God" (West). The self within Islam may decide for him- or herself, but always in the context of devotion to God. See the table below for an overview of the principles within Islam and Western bioethics concerning organ donation.

Table 1: Comparing Principles Related to Organ Donation

	Islamic bioethics	Christian, Western bioethics
Opponents	*hurma*	bodily integrity
Proponents	*maslaha*	beneficence
	non-magnificence	non-magnificence
	effectiveness	effectiveness
	proportionality	proportionality
	bounded autonomy	respect for autonomy
	freedom by God	freedom from God

We have outlined the theological dimensions of organ donation above. Yusuf's story illuminates, however, the fact that socio-cultural dimensions also play a role in the decision-making process about organ transplantation. Yusuf refers, for instance, to the responses from his community and how he relates to his doctor. We will therefore now focus more closely on the doctor-patient relationship.

Intercultural Dimensions

The Doctor-Patient Relationship

There are several models in ethics that describe the relationship between doctor and patient. Emanuel and Emanuel (1992) describe four models: the paternalistic, the informative, the interpretive, and the deliberative models. These models vary with regard to respect for autonomy. The paternalistic model starts from the idea that the doctor is an expert and should decide for the patient. There is hardly any respect for the patient's autonomy since the doctor's attitude does not originate in close collusion with the patient. This is reversed in the informative model. Here the doctor provides information using his expertise, but the patient decides on the basis of his or her autonomy. The two other models are more dialogical in nature. The relationship be-

tween doctors and Muslim patients may lead to a collision because doctors tend to work within the informative model while
patients expect a more paternalistic approach. On the basis of
respect for the autonomy of the patient, doctors are more likely
not to insist on treatment, even if that treatment is deemed the
best option from a medical perspective.

Bridging Intercultural Differences?

A solution to this intercultural dilemma is not to simply state
that the medical doctor must adapt to the needs of Muslim patients by a direct recourse to the paternalistic model. Nor is it an
option to force the patient to the informative model.

Matching expectations and developing a unique doctor-patient relationship on the basis of consultation is a way to discuss
differences and to bridge these gaps (Walker 1998). Only then,
in joint consultation, can an appropriate treatment policy be formulated. The alignment of expectations and determination of
who is responsible for what are considered important. In this
process we should not overestimate cultural and religious differences. Knibbe and Verkerk (2007) show that even in the case
of a Dutch liver transplant patient and health care professionals
need to carefully negotiate responsibilities. Equally important is
an exchange on what is considered good hope as this is a driving force for patients and families to remain motivated in the
process towards organ transplantation (Knibbe and Verkerk
2007). Hope can, after all, be seen as connected with the information given by professionals and to the way patients handle
this information. Patients desire, partly based on the received
information, a certain outcome and belief that this outcome is,
to a higher or lower degree, probable but not certain. This may
lead to certain moral dilemmas: Should professionals inform
patients in a realistic way and take away all hope or should
they give hope and therefore not inform patients about the actual outcomes? Hope can, after all, also be seen as important
since it motivates patients. In any event, it is important to distinguish real hope and giving real hope from false hope based
on manipulative giving of information. Hope can also be influenced by contacts with fellow sufferers and the way patients
deal with information. Professionals should discover how to
handle and how to guide the hopes of patients and how to sup-

port them in hoping well. How hope is created and trust is inspired should be part of the negotiation between patients, families, and doctors, despite their religious or cultural background (Knibbe and Verkerk 2007).

While Muslims in general might expect the doctor to act as an authority, doctors should never simply presume they know what their immigrant patients need. Those who are younger and more integrated into society may have other expectations, some more in line with the informative model. Doctors are already aware that such intergenerational differences may affect their relationships with patients. Gender is also a dimension that needs to be taken into account. It may help to consider each immigrant as a unique person, with needs and expectations that arise out of a particular confluence of religious, cultural, gendered and intergenerational dimensions. These dimensions are not just added on but intersect with one another. Given the uniqueness of each immigrant, doctors should negotiate their relationship each time anew.

The interpretation of Islamic discourse on organ transplantation in its proper context is also an important element in overcoming or minimizing religious and cultural differences. Authoritative Islamic legal rulings on donation are largely drawn from the Islamic world, where doctors might be more inclined to follow paternalistic model. Time, circumstances, and the context of Muslims living in the West, where other medical norms prevail, need to be taken into account when interpreting Islamic rulings.

Conclusion

Although there are two trends in Islam on organ transplantation, the majority of Muslim scholars allow it. It seems that this view does not easily find its way to ordinary Muslims and medical doctors. Therefore, better education is needed. Doctors should take any cultural or religious barriers to organ transplantation into account. Different and sometimes conflicting expectations may exist between Muslim patients and doctors regarding their communication and decision making on organ donation. The alignment of the mutual expectations and negotiation on responsibilities and hope are essential to overcoming or minimizing misunderstandings.

Bibliography

Abma, T. *et al.* (2007). *Leren over lijf en leven. Een agenda voor sociaal-we-tenschappelijk onderzoek door nierpatiënten.* Eindrapportage ten behoeve van nierstichting en Nierpatiënten Vereniging Nederland.

Albar, M. (1994). *Al-Mawqif al-Fiqhî wa al-Akhâlqî min Qadiyyat Zar' al-A'dâ'.* Damascus/Beirut: Dar al-Qalam/al-Dar al-Shamiyya.

Beauchamp, T.L. (2007). "The Four Principles' Approach to Health Care Ethics." In: R.E. Ascroft *et al.* (eds.). *Principles of Health Care Ethics.* Chichester: Wiley. Pp. 3-10.

Beck, H., and G. Wiegers. (2008). *Moslims in een westerse samenleving. Islam en ethiek.* Zoetermeer: Meinema.

Emanuel, E.J., and L.L. Emanuel. (1992). "Four Models of the Physician-Patient Relationship." *Journal of the American Medical Association* 267: 2221-26.

Ghaly, M. (2010). "Human Cloning through the Eyes of Muslim Scholars: The New Phenomenon of the Islamic International Religio-scientific Institutions." *Zygon* 45: 7-35.

Gillman, J. (1999). "Religious Perspectives on Organ Donation." *Critical Care Nursing Quarterly* 22: 19-29.

Jad al-Haqq. (2005). *Buhûth wa Fatâwâ Islâmiyya fî Qadâyâ Mu'asira.* Vol. 3. Cairo: Dar al-Hadith.

Knibbe, M., and M. Verkerk M. (2007). "Economies of Hope in a Period of Transition: Parents in the Time Leading Up to Their Child's Liver Transplantation." In: H. Lindemann, M. Verkerk, and M.U. Walker (eds.). *Naturalized Bioethics.* Cambridge: Cambridge University Press. Pp. 182-98.

Linsen, Lex. (2000). *Levensbeschouwing doorslaggevend bij orgaandonatie. Ethiek en Beleid.* The Hague: NWO.

Nierse, C. *et al.* (2012). "Collaboration and Co-Ownership in Research: Dynamics and Dialogues between Patient Research Partners and Professional Researchers in a Research Team. *Health Expectations.* 15: 242-54.

Price, D.P.T. "Organs and Tissues for Transplantation and Research." In: R.E. Ascroft *et al.* (eds.). *Principles of Health Care Ethics.* Chichester: Wiley. Pp. 475-82.

Al-Qaradawi, Y. (2010). *Zirâ'at al-A'dâ' fî Daw' al-Sharî'a al-Islâmiyya.* 1st ed. Cairo: Dar al-Shuruq.

Sachedina, A. (2007). The Search for Islamic Bioethics." In: R.E. Ascroft *et al.* (eds.). *Principles of Health Care Ethics.* Chichester: Wiley. Pp. 117-26.

Schipper K. *et al.* (2010). "What Does it Mean to be a Patient Research Partner? An Ethnodrama." *Qualitative Inquiry* 16: 501-10.

Schipper K., and T.A. Abma. (2011). "Coping, Family, and Mastery: Top Priorities for Social Science Research by Patients with Chronic Kidney Disease." *Nephrology, Dialysis and Transplantation* 26: 3189-95.

Sharaf al-Din, Ahmad. (1981). *Al-Ijrâ'ât al-Tibbiyya al-Hadîtha wa Hukmuhâ fî Daw' Qawâ'id al-Fiqh al-Islâmî.*

Slatman, J. (2008). *Vreemd lichaam. Over medisch ingrijpen en persoonlijke identiteit.* Amsterdam: Ambo.

Stake, R.E. (1994). "Case Studies." In: N.K. Denzin and YS Lincoln (eds.). *The Handbook for Qualitative Research.* Thousand Oaks: Sage. Pp. 236-47.

Thiel, L. van, and P. Kramer. (2009). *Draagvlak orgaandonatie. Kennis, houding en gedrag van Nederlanders.* The Hague: NIGZ-Donorvoorlichting.

Tronto, J. (2007). "Consent as a Grant of Authority: A Care Ethics Reading of Informed Consent." In: H. Lindemann, M. Verkerk, and M.U. Walker (eds.). *Naturalized Bioethics.* Cambridge: Cambridge University Press. Pp. 182-98.

Walker, M.U. (1998). *Moral Understandings: A Feminist Study in Ethics.* New York/London: Routledge.

Widdows, H. (2007). "Christian Approaches to Bioethics." In: R.E. Ascroft *et al.* (eds.). *Principles of Health Care Ethics.* Chichester: Wiley. Pp. 99-108.

Zwart, H., and C. Hoffer. (1998). *Orgaandonatie en lichamelijke integriteit. Een analyse van christelijke, liberale en islamitische interpretaties.* Best: Damon.

CHAPTER XIV

Palliative Sedation

An Exploration
from a Christian Ethical Point of View

Theo A. Boer

Introduction

In this chapter we will explore some ethical questions concerning palliative sedation from a Dutch and Christian angle. "Dutch and Christian" is not as easy as it may sound. Until the 1960s, it was safe to describe the Netherlands as a Christian country. Historically, we could point to the roles played by churches and believers in establishing and running health care institutions. But in recent decades the relationship of the Dutch to their religious origins has become more ambiguous. Despite protests from conservative Christian churches, organizations, and politicians, abortion, birth control, assisted reproduction (including the use of donated gametes), and euthanasia[1] were accepted and made legally possible. Patient (or client) autonomy became a major competitor to the allegedly paternalistic approach of Christianity. The former connections between Christianity and medicine have not dissolved, but a self-evident identity between the two can no longer be assumed either. The further the emancipation of medical ethics from Christian ethics progresses, the more urgent it becomes to ask if a Christian view (*the* Christian view does not exist) differs from a view prop-

---

[1] Since the 1980s, the term "euthanasia" in the Netherlands has always implied, by definition, a life-terminating intervention by a physician as well as the request from the patient. Both "active euthanasia" and "voluntary euthanasia" are pleonasms. "Non-voluntary euthanasia" is now referred to as "life termination without request"; "passive euthanasia" is referred to as "withdrawing treatment."

agated by, for example, the Dutch government or the Royal Dutch Medical Association (hereafter RDMA (Dutch: KNMG)).

Unlike abortion or gay marriage, however, palliative sedation does not create similar sharp disagreements beforehand between Christians and others. Most doctors, irrespective of their religion or worldview, are convinced that the number of euthanasia cases should be as limited as possible. Palliative sedation has been welcomed by many as an alternative to euthanasia provided that the conditions of serious suffering, refractory symptoms, a patient's consent, and the absence of the intention to shorten the patient's life apply. There seems to be a relatively broad, and in my eyes beneficial, societal consensus on the moral acceptability of palliative sedation. But even so, important questions remain. In what follows I will identify the most pressing ones.

Palliative Sedation Only Hours or Days
before an Expected Natural Death?

Palliative sedation means the administration of drugs to keep the patient in deep sedation or coma until death without artificial nutrition or hydration (Rietjens *et al* 2004: 179). The RDMA distinguishes between intermittent sedation and continuous sedation until death. The latter is also known as terminal sedation. In the Netherlands, it is estimated that in 2010 12.5% of all deaths were preceded by palliative sedation, a considerable increase in comparison to an estimated 8.2% of all deaths in 2005 (Van der Heide *et al* 2012: 107). The majority of patients receiving palliative sedation suffer from cancer in a terminal phase. The growing incidence of palliative sedation can be seen as a consequence of the development of medical technology that can be operated both institutionally and at home without continuous attendance of a physician or nurse. A more intriguing explanation, applying specifically to the Netherlands, may be found in a preference on the side of many doctors, patients, and others to avoid euthanasia.

Technically, palliative sedation is a form of medical treatment. As Lieverse, Hildering, and Klaasse-Carpentier (2009) convincingly argue, however, it is an uncommon form of normal medical treatment. After all, a patient *and* his[2] autonomy are put to sleep for the rest of his life, and the dying process may be shortened. Possible criteria we will consider here are: (1) the suffering must be intolerable; (2) the symptoms should be refractory, i.e. they cannot be sufficiently relieved by using less radical palliation—painkillers, tranquillizers, anti-emetics, etc.; (3) the patient must consent to being sedated; (4) a natural death is expected within days or weeks; (5) the palliative sedation should not shorten his life.

According to the RDMA guidelines, no nutrition and hydration are administered in cases of palliative sedation.[3] One reason for this policy is that hydration may deteriorate a patient's condition by, for example, contributing to his ascites or by increasing the quantity of fluid in the lungs. When death is expected within hours or days, withholding hydration will hardly hasten a patient's death, nor will it do much good. And, since *any* dying patient at some point stops eating and drinking, why force hydration on patients in a state of sedation when they are dying?

The issue becomes more complicated when a patient has longer than a week to live: without hydration, *any* sedated person, terminally ill or not, will die within days or weeks. In order to preclude the possibility that palliative sedation causes a patient's death, the RDMA has ruled that palliative sedation may only be given when a natural death is expected within 1-2 weeks. But how accurate can the assessment of a patient's life expectancy be? An experienced doctor may be reasonably certain in saying that a patient will die within hours or a day or two: the patient's breathing changes, his skin becomes pale. He may also be reasonably certain in predicting that natural death can roughly be expected to occur within weeks or months from

---

[2] The words "he" or "his" are used inclusively in this chapter.

[3] Officially, the guideline speaks of "withholding nutrition and hydration." In this chapter I will refer to hydration, not only for the sake of brevity but also because one of the most problematic aspects of palliative sedation—its life-shortening effect—seems to be caused mainly by the dehydration of a patient.

now. But it is hard to claim convincingly that natural death will occur within, let us say, five or eight days. In the end, the patient may die much sooner of much slower.

So what about the RDMA's requirement that a natural death be expected within one or two weeks? That a patient in a terminal stage of a disease will die is certain. But no prediction is infallible. Some patients outlive the most "optimistic" predictions of their doctors; others die much sooner. Even if the RDMA's guidelines are followed, it cannot be ruled out that a decision to start palliative sedation will in effect shorten a patient's life because the patient would have lived much longer without being sedated.

This brings us to the following question: If the principal objective is palliation, why restrict this kind of treatment to patients with a life expectancy of less than 1-2 weeks? What about patients with a longer life expectancy who suffer from the same refractory symptoms—anxiety, pain, nausea, fatigue, dyspnea? According to the RDMA, they do not qualify for palliative sedation. From my own observations,[4] it becomes clear that a doctor's refusal to administer palliative sedation sometimes leaves patients no other option than a euthanasia request, despite a *prima facie* aversion for euthanasia.

Is There a Moral Obligation to "Feed the Hungry"?

Since the Christian thinker Thomas Aquinas (1225-1274), the principle of double effect (PDE) has been pivotal for making difficult decisions regarding life and death. According to Aquinas, many actions have two kinds of effects: (1) a foreseen and *intended* effect, such as pain relief as the effect of administering painkillers, and (2) a foreseen but *unintended* effect, such as an earlier death as a consequence of painkillers. The PDE holds

---

[4] Unpublished; during my participation in a Regional Review Committee for Euthanasia, I reviewed about 3,100 euthanasia cases reported by physicians in the years 2005-2013. Observations from these materials provide important indications but do not stand the test of statistics. Quotations from the reports have been changed to protect the privacy of those involved.

that some things may be permissible if they are the unintended effect of an action performed with the intent to bring about something else. Most Christian thinkers consider the intentional killing of an innocent human being (even at his request) to be wrong. Yet if a death is the foreseen but unintended result of another action and this death is not in itself a means, the PDE holds that such a death may sometimes be justified, provided that everything has been done to prevent this effect (Wogaman 1994: 92; Biggar 2003: 59ff.). Applied to the context of palliative medicine, the PDE means that we may be excused if we have caused the death of a suffering person provided that this death is the unintended result of the necessary and proportional administration of painkillers and/or sedatives and provided that this death could not have been avoided. Euthanasia cannot be justified on the basis of the principle because death is the intended effect here.

With the principle of double effect in mind, we may ask some questions about the RDMA's guideline, which seems to imply the following logic on the criterion of life expectancy:

(1) palliative sedation implies withholding hydration;
(2) without hydration, people will die within 1-2 weeks;
(3) palliative sedation should not be the cause of a patient's death;
(4) therefore, patients with longer than 1-2 weeks to live do not qualify for palliative sedation.

The first question that comes to mind is: Why would palliative sedation necessarily imply withholding hydration? We indicated some of the reasons above: hydration can deteriorate a patient's condition, and *any* dying patient will at some point stop eating and drinking. But what if these reasons do not apply, such as when a patient has longer than 1-2 weeks left?

This equation of "artificial hydration" and "prolonging life" in the case of palliative sedation will not be convincing to all. We can reverse the logic and argue that the real issue is not the alleged *life-prolonging effect of artificial hydration* but the *life-shortening effect of palliative sedation*. In line with the PDE, we can argue that the life-shortening effect of palliative sedation is acceptable only if measures have been taken to prevent an earlier death from occurring. Administering hydration would meet this requirement.

Is there a moral obligation to administering some hydration then? A distinction frequently made in medical and nursing practice is the distinction between (medical) treatment and care (Teeuw 2003). The duty to provide care is, all other things being equal, harder than the obligation to give treatment. A doctor's decision to refrain from surgery on a dying patient, for example, is less problematic than a decision to refrain from feeding that same patient. Correspondingly, a patient's claim to care is more difficult than his claim to treatment. In the Christian tradition, the obligation to "feed the hungry" has always had high status. The RDMA's decision to restrict palliative sedation to patients with only 1-2 weeks to live may be understood in the light of this "preference for life": no life-shortening effect of palliative sedation! But instead of limiting the option of palliative sedation to patients shorter than 1-2 weeks to live, why not discuss the option that only patients with a life expectancy of hours or days will not be administered hydration, and why not consider the option that all other forms of palliative sedation should include the possibility of administering hydration? Why not give access to palliative sedation to *all* patients with refractory symptoms, irrespective of their life expectancy? Such a less rigid approach would be congruent with practices found in other countries. In Italy, for example, 65% of the patients receiving palliative sedation *do* receive artificial hydration, compared to 36% in Denmark and the Netherlands (Simon *et al.* 2007). Why not discuss the risks, benefits, and goals of fluids before initiating terminal sedation instead of rejecting such a discussion beforehand?

But the RDMA may be more "right" than suggested here. A Dutch survey indicated that about two thirds of the physicians who administer palliative sedation not only intend to alleviate the suffering but also to hasten death. Moreover, a patient has the right to refuse treatment and care. If a patient suffers from a terminal disease and wishes to be placed in an artificial coma, this probably indicates that that patient does not want to be kept alive by artificial means. Many of those who qualify for palliative sedation will use their right to refuse food and drink —a right based on considerations of patient autonomy and bodily integrity. There can be no obligation on the part of the patient to accept artificial hydration.

So if palliative sedation is made accessible to *all* patients with refractory symptoms, irrespective of their life expectancy, some doctors, along with their patients, may be tempted to use palliative sedation instead of euthanasia. In light of this, the 1-2 weeks of life expectancy in the RDMA guideline can be better understood. Still, we can consider another option: if a patient has longer than a week or so to live, why not issue a *second* guideline in which sedation is offered intermittently—and *only* in combination with the administration of hydration? Cooney suggests so-called "respite" sedation of a predetermined duration, followed by a lightening of unconsciousness to assess response (Cooney 2000). Patients have a right to refuse artificial hydration, but a doctor may, in turn, refuse to administer continuous sedation to such a patient. If a patient nevertheless refuses hydration during sedation in a non-terminal state, there are good reasons to consider this analogous to a euthanasia request. The patient not only wants relief for the suffering; he also wants a termination of his life. We will return to this below.

Other Religious Questions

Palliative Sedation as Unnatural?

In the Christian tradition, Roman Catholics especially have insisted that human life be lived as much as possible in accordance with the "natural order of things" or within the "creation order." Thomas Aquinas stands out as the most influential representative of religious natural law thinking. Protestant Christians have traditionally been more skeptical about the normativity of "nature" or "creation" for human actions. Within a religion that considers sickness and death a consequence of human sinfulness, it is indeed hard to argue for a "natural way to die." Still, influential voices within the Christian tradition argue that both life and death should be as "natural" as possible. Palliative sedation takes an interesting position here, since it is found somewhere between the "unnatural" death of euthanasia and the "natural" death of dying in consciousness and distress. Christians who strongly oppose euthanasia tend to be strongly in favor of palliative sedation.

Palliative Sedation as the End of Human Autonomy?

In health care in Western countries, patient autonomy has become one of the most important moral principles, if not the most important (Beauchamp and Childress 2001). Important contributors to this stress on autonomy were the Reformation (Lutheran) theologian Martin Luther (1483-1546) and the Enlightenment philosopher Immanuel Kant (1724-1804) who interpreted human self-determination in terms of personal responsibility. Given the fact that modernism and postmodernism reinterpret autonomy in terms of individual liberties, Christian churches have developed an increasingly paradoxical attitude: following Kant, they welcome human autonomy; but, also following Kant, this autonomy does not consider the human will to be the *source* of our morality. Autonomy is not "doing as we please" but rather "directing our wills to affirming a moral law which transcends our subjectivity." Franz Böckle describes this ambiguity in terms of "theonomous autonomy" (Böckle 1972: 233). Likewise, the Dutch theologian Harry Kuitert states that "autonomy" is intended to free an agent from undue pressure from his fellow human beings and not to liberate him from obligations issued by God (Kuitert 1993: 73).

If autonomy (or the more "traditional" concept of responsibility) is seen as a human characteristic and a human duty, an obvious problem of the practice of palliative sedation is that it can be interpreted as "putting an end to human autonomy." Kant's main argument against suicide is that through it a person abandons his autonomy. (John Stuart Mill compared suicide to a person's decision to sell himself into slavery.) A reconstructive interpretation of the Christian tradition and Kant in the context of sedation may imply the view that palliative sedation should be rejected *prima facie* for exactly the same reason: through it the individual abandons his capacity to act autonomously or responsibly. This objection pertains all the more to cases of sedation in which no hydration is administered and in which the sedation will go on until death. In the case of intermittent sedation, a person abandons his autonomy only temporarily.

Palliative Sedation as an Answer to Experiences of Meaninglessness?

The most common reason for palliative sedation is to relieve symptoms of physical suffering: dyspnea, pain, incontinence, nausea, and fatigue. Part of the suffering is of a psychological, psychosocial, or existential nature: meaningless waiting, the absence of social contacts, the loss of freedom, being dependent on others for one's daily needs. Christianity, like most religions, searches for meaning in situations of suffering (cf. Boer and Groenewoud 2011: 29ff.). It may even be said that religions as such are attempts to discover or create meaning in seemingly meaningless circumstances. This meaning can contribute to alleviating suffering: religion in itself may function as a form of "palliative care." Suffering is not seen as intrinsically good; it may even be seen as intrinsically bad. Nevertheless, it may be used instrumentally for the realization of intrinsic goods. First, the meaning of suffering is sometimes found in its contribution to establishing loving, caring, faithful, and trusting personal relations. Second, the dying person himself may be able to discover or create meaning in the final stretch of his life. The *ars moriendi*, the art of dying well, is often considered a means to obtaining moral virtuousness: by praying, by detaching oneself from the life one has lived, by repenting for one's failures, and by reconciling oneself with one's adversaries, a human being may become more virtuous, more patient, more courageous, more hopeful (cf. Verhey 2011). From a Christian point of view—an interesting aspect in an Islamic-Christian dialogue—an example may be found in the conviction that God, incarnated in a human being, suffered an undeserved death without becoming bitter, cynical, or resentful.

Suffering consists in part in the awareness that most of the things that make life worth living—happiness, health, prosperity, growth, creativeness, communication—are losing ground. Traditionally, religions have developed practices of consolation in which this loss of human goods was relativized. They acknowledged the fact that humans may lose their health, independence, and well-being, but this does not, in the view of these religions, in any way threaten their value or humanity. In contrast to the somewhat hedonistic *adagium*, "life should be enjoyed," that sometimes pops up in contemporary Western culture, the Christian *adagium* may better be stated as "life should be lived"—including in the harder and hardest of times.[5] Frequent reference is also made to the Christian hope of a final "restoration of all things." The prospect of life after death motivates people not to give up hope. Despite some differences between Islam and Christianity on suffering, they share the conviction that God will, in the end, grant the faithful a life that may be all the more rich and rewarding, depending on the degree of patience and faith that one has learned during one's earthly life. All these views do not render palliative sedation wrong or redundant as a category of acts. In some cases, they may even help to *motivate* the choice for palliative sedation.

Is Palliative Sedation Always the Proportional Answer to Suffering?

We return now to a more medical perspective. Not all palliative sedations are the same. The American Hospice and Palliative Nurses Association defines palliative sedation as "the monitored use of medications intended to induce *varying degrees of unconsciousness*, but not death, for relief of refractory and unendurable symptoms in imminently dying patients" (HPNA 2003, italics mine). Generally speaking, the sedation should not be deeper than necessary to keep the patient unconscious: "First stage anesthesia," not deep sedation, is the goal. Higher dosages may increase the chance that a patient's death is hastened.

Before referring to the common answer that a patient in an artificial coma cannot experience suffering, we need to address the question if the sedation is always sufficiently deep. Depending on the depth of the coma and on the effectiveness of the sedatives given, sedated persons may display expressions of discomfort, such as rattling and irregular breathing (Cheyne-Stokes respiration), and groaning. The Hospice and Palliative Care Federation of Massachusetts suggests that heavy snoring and abrupt onset of apnea may be caused by too high a dosage of sedatives (HPCF/MA 2004). In other cases, the dosage of sed-

---

[5] It is said that Dutch writer Harry Mulisch, who died in October 2010 from cancer, rejected the option of euthanasia because he wanted to feel what it is like not only to live but also to die.

atives may have to be increased. In one of the euthanasia reports a physician writes:

> Patient was sedated but continued to express pain: groaning, grimacing, gesturing, mumbling, "help me." The relatives insisted that I would perform the euthanasia the patient had requested, and that is what I did.[6]

Another doctor writes:

> Palliative sedation would be an option but patient has traumatic memories of her husband dying in a state of palliative sedation: staring at the ceiling he was waiting for his death for days.

And a third doctor states:

> Patient is afraid that if I give her palliative sedation, she will still be suffering from her pain, but without the possibility of expressing herself. For this reason, she requests euthanasia.

From these and other reports in the euthanasia review procedure, it becomes clear that some terminal patients reject palliative sedation out of fear that it will not lead to the intended effect. A properly conducted sedation implies a coma that is deep enough to preclude experiences of suffering in a patient. On the other hand, the dosage should not exceed the patient's need for palliation. When sedation is properly conducted, it may be proper for a physician to explain to the bystanders that irregular breathing or rattling may be unpleasant for bystanders to witness, but the patient himself is no longer suffering.

The Netherlands was the first country in which euthanasia and physician-assisted suicide (PAS) were made legally possible (Boer 2007: 529-30). For some years, palliative sedation was heralded by some as *the* alternative to euthanasia: a natural death that spares all the involved parties the moral and legal hassles connected to euthanasia. If administered in accordance with accepted medical standards, the chances that palliative se-

---

[6] This and the following citations are from the reports mentioned above. See note 4 above.

dation will shorten the patient's life are small: it is *not* "slow euthanasia." The next question, especially in a Dutch context, is: If palliative sedation takes away all the patient's suffering, why would euthanasia be even necessary?

A euthanasia case that was reported in 2006 to a review committee may serve to illustrate the moral complexity of this question. The case involves a physician who was to perform euthanasia on a terminally ill cancer patient. All the criteria set by Dutch law were met. The evening before the agreed date, the patient called the doctor in a state of distress. He insisted that euthanasia be performed right away. Since the physician did not yet have access to the lethal drug until the next morning, she administered a medication that induced a coma. The next morning she returned and, without waking the patient, performed the euthanasia as agreed. The review committee decided to report the case to the prosecutor. It based its verdict on a report written for the RDMA that suggests that a patient in a coma cannot experience unbearable suffering (Legemaate 2005: 40). In the view of the committee, the physician should either have awakened the patient to ask him or should not have proceeded.

The verdict discloses a pivotal and ever recurring issue in almost any euthanasia discussion: if a patient can be made comfortable with the help of advanced palliative techniques, including terminal sedation, what justification is there left to take the most radical measure and terminate both the suffering and the life of the patient? In a technical sense, the committee's verdict applies to most euthanasia cases in the Netherlands. Following RDMA guidelines, most physicians induce a coma (usually by using sodium thiopental) before the actual life termination takes place (usually through pancuronium bromide, a neuromuscular muscle relaxant). In the minutes between the administration of the two drugs, the patient is in a coma and seems to be free from suffering. Why would it be wrong to administer the pancuronium to a patient who has been in a coma for about twelve hours and right to do the same when the patient has been in a coma for three minutes?

This question, of course, cannot be discussed here. At the center of the discussion lies the question whether the primary goal of palliative care (including euthanasia and palliative sedation) should be to alleviate a patient's suffering, to alleviate a patient's suffering *in a way acceptable to him*, or to fulfill a patient's autonomous wish. Many patients who are convinced that palliative sedation will end their suffering still opt for the much more radical option of euthanasia. Not only do they reject the prospect of suffering, but they also reject the prospect of existing unconsciously. In the terminology of the British philosopher Richard Hare, such a wish can be called a "now for then" preference (Hare 1981: 101). It remains to be seen if such wishes are irrelevant from a Christian point of view. But that the wish not to exist anymore carries a heavier burden of proof than the wish not to suffer can hardly be denied.

Concluding Remarks

In this chapter I have explored some questions with regard to palliative sedation from a Christian and Dutch perspective. I share the RDMA's contention that palliative sedation is a good option as long as death is not the underlying intention. Moreover, I share the view that palliative sedation should only be administered in case of refractory symptoms. It also seems safe to assume that, for Christian and secular (medical, professional) positions alike, palliative sedation is preferable to the more "unnatural" option of euthanasia or physician-assisted suicide.

There are also some concerns on my part. First, Dutch medical practice may be criticized for the fact that palliative sedation is not accompanied by the administration of hydration. As a result, patients who are not in a terminal stage of their illness are excluded from receiving sedation and some patients may even be forced to make a euthanasia request because they do not fill the criterion of terminality. The alternative would be to offer intermittent sedation to patients who are not in a terminal stage and to continue administering hydration during the sedation or between periods of sedation.

A second concern is based on a Christian and Kantian understanding of human autonomy: just as suicide is rejected because it puts an end to our capacity to be autonomous and responsible agents, palliative sedation may be considered problematic. Offering intermittent sedation would help to ease this moral tension: human agency would not be altogether abandoned. A third concern is that palliative sedation may sometimes be an inadequate *medical* answer to questions regarding *meaninglessness*. Neither concern is conclusive: notwithstanding both arguments, palliative sedation may in many situations still be the best alternative.

A fourth concern has a more medical character: sometimes the sedation is not deep enough, and the patient still experiences considerable suffering. In other cases, sedation may be deeper than necessary to ease the refractory symptoms. This leads to a final concern: it can clearly be rational and moral to wish to not suffer. But when the symptoms can be relieved without using sedation, can it still be rational to have a wish to be not conscient?

Bibliography

Beauchamp, T.L., and J.F. Childress. (2001). *Principles of Biomedical Ethics*. 5th ed. Oxford: Oxford University Press.

Böckle, F. (1972). "Theonome Autonomie: Zur Aufgabenstellung einer fundamentalen Moraltheologie." In: J. Gründel, F. Rauh, and V. Eid (eds.). *Humanum: Moraltheologie im Dienst des Menschen*. Festschrift für R. Egenter. Düsseldorf: Patmos Verlag. Pp. 17-46.

Boer, T.A. (2007). "Recurring Themes in the Debate about Euthanasia and Assisted Suicide." *Journal of Religious Ethics* 35: 529-55.

Boer, T.A., and A.S. Groenewoud. (2011). *Vroegchristelijke denkers en hedendaagse morele zorgdilemma's*. The Hague: ZonMw.

Cooney, G.A. (2013). "Palliative Sedation: The Ethical Controversy." http://cme.medscape.com/viewarticle/499472 (Accessed 24 February 2013).

Hare, R.M. (1981). *Moral Thinking: Its Levels, Method, and Point*. Cambridge: Cambridge University Press.

Heide, A. van der et al. (2012). *Tweede evaluatie van de Wet toetsing levensbeëindiging op verzoek en hulp bij zelfdoding*. The Hague: ZonMw.

HPCF/MA (Hospice and Palliative Care Federation of MA). (2004). "Palliative Sedation Protocol, 2004." http://www.hospicefed.org/hospice_pages/reports/pal_sed_protocol.pdf (Accessed 21 November 2010).

HPNA (Hospice and Palliative Nurses Association). (2003). "Position Statement Palliative Sedation at End of Life, Pittsburgh 2003." http://www.hpna.org/pdf/PositionStatement_PalliativeSedation.pdf (Accessed 24 February 2013).

Keizer, B. (2005). "Vluchtweg naar de dood? De werkelijkheid van terminale sedatie." *Denkbeeld* 17/2: 48-50.

Kimsma, G.K. (2010). "Death by Request in The Netherlands: Facts, the Legal Context, and Effects on Physicians, Patients, and Families." *Medicine, Health Care and Philosophy* 13: 355-61.

——— (2000). "Het lijden beoordeeld: Een voorstel voor een conceptueel kader." *Medisch Contact* 55: 1757-59.

KNMG (Royal Dutch Medical Association). (2010). *Euthanasie bij verlaagd bewustzijn. KNMG-richtlijn.* Amsterdam: KNMG.

Kuitert, H.M. (1993). *Mag er een einde komen aan het bittere einde?* Baarn: Ten Have.

Legemate, J. (2005). *De zorgverlening rond het levenseinde: Een literatuurstudie naar begripsomschrijvingen en zorgvuldigheidseisen.* Utrecht: KNMG.

Lieverse, P., P. Hildering, and M. Klaasse-Carpentier. (2009). "Palliatieve sedatie. Een glijdende schaal." *Medisch Contact* 64: 1881-83.

Rietjens, J.A.C. *et al.* (2004)."Physician Reports of Terminal Sedation without Hydration or Nutrition for Patients Nearing Death in the Netherlands." *Annals of Internal Medicine* 141 (3 August): 178-85.

Simon, A. *et al.* (2007). "Attitudes towards Terminal Sedation: An Empirical Survey among Experts in the Field of Medical Ethics." *BMC Palliative Care* 6:4. http://www.biomedcentral.com/1472-684X/6/4.

Teeuw, A.A. (2003). *Niet starten om staken te voorkomen? Een morele beoordeling van niet-starten en staken van sondevoedingstherapie bij CVA-patiënten in een verpleeghuis.* Ridderkerk/Veenendaal: Landelijk Bureau of the Patiënten Vereniging (NPV).

Verhey, A. (2011). *The Christian Art of Dying: Learning From Jesus.* Grand Rapids: Eerdmans.

Wij,k E. van *et al.* (2009)."KNMG-richtlijn Palliatieve sedatie: Meer houvast voor arts." *Medisch Contact* 65: 194-97.

Wogaman, J.P. (1994). *Christian Ethics: A Historical Introduction.* London: SCM Press.

CHAPTER XV

Islamic Care Ethics
between Law and Conscience

Arslan Karagül

Introduction

In this chapter I will show how Muslims make difficult medical decisions. They need to take into account medical practice and state law, ethnic customs, and the rules of their religion while being counseled by medical specialists and by Islamic spiritual caregivers. I will first give an example from actual political discussions in Turkey on abortion and Ceasarean sections in 2012. This example will show the tension between law, religious ethics, and the decision-making process by those involved here and there. Discussions in Morocco, Egypt, and Turkey influence the thinking of most Muslims in Western Europe who have roots in those countries. Then I will discuss cases concerning organ donation, stopping pointless treatments, and palliative care. The Muslims in these cases are not only from Turkey. I will also present an abortion case from my own experience. I will do so as a former Muslim spiritual caregiver without issuing a *fatwa* on it. The decision is ultimately left to the patient's conscience, as a Turkish proverb states: "Ask the mufti [issuer of *fatwas*], but leave the ultimate decision to your heart or conscience." As a lecturer in Islamic spiritual caregiving, my perspective is that the attention in care should not only be directed to the physical aspect. The spiritual aspect is crucial as well. That is why I emphasize the role and presence of a Muslim spiritual caregiver in care institutions. Let us begin with the discussion on abortion.

Abortion: Murder or Necessity?

Turkish Law, Islamic Jurisprudence *(Fiqh)*, and Practice

The relation between secular law and (Islamic) faith is complicated. "That is murder, murder," the Turkish leader *(imam)*[1] Prime Minister Recep Tayyip Erdogan repeated on his political pulpit, speaking about abortion. This threw Turkey into an uproar in May and June 2012. The current president of the Turkish Union (Diyanet) for Religious Affairs, Mehmet Görmez, immediately confirmed this view: "According to Islam, abortion is murder and is therefore forbidden *(haram)* except if it is strictly necessary to save the life of the mother." [2] Both the "feminists," as Erdogan called them, and the political opposition strongly opposed these statements by Erdogan and Görmez.[3] The "feminists" organized demonstration after demonstration with the slogans that were heard in the 1960s in the Netherlands as well, such as "Our womb, our life, our decision" and "Keep your hands off me." Some young women even tried to "chain" themselves to the door of the ministries. After these protests, the proposed change in the abortion law was dropped.[4] The abortion law in Turkey, which took effect in 1983, allows abortion until the 10th week of pregnancy. The Caesarean procedure was limited to medical necessity or fear in connection with the normal

---

[1] Prime Minister Erdogan of the Republic of Turkey is often greeted in Turkey with the words, "We are proud of our prime minister who graduated from the *Imam Hatip school* (Imam Hatipli başbakanımızla gurur duyuyoruz). The phrase *Imam Hatipli* also means to be an "imam" (leader).

[2] http://ensonhaber.com/diyanet-isleri-baskanindan-kurtaj-aciklamasi-2012-06-04.html (accessed 4 June 2012).

[3] http://haberturk.com/polemik/haber/748260-diyanet-kurtaj-cikisi (accessed 5 June 2012).

[4] Ceasarean sections were indeed limited to medical necessity or fear of a normal birthing, according to the Minister of Health, Recep Akdağ. This was to prevent major costs for the state and to insure less harm to the body. See: http://video.cnnturk.com/2012/haber/7/11/illegal-kurtaja-buyuk-darbe (accessed 11 July 2012).

birth, according to the Minister of Health, Recep Akdağ.[5] The Caesarean procedure is a thorn in Erdogan's eye because it has become an expensive business in Turkey. Abortion is also a thorn in the eye of the prime minister—if not absolutely necessary—because he wants the Turkish population to grow more quickly and Turkey to play a larger role on the world stage. He sees this medical procedure as a check on the growth of the young Turkish population, which is crucial to Turkey's future. Abortion and Caesareans are an attempt to check this growing "power." Erdogan is well known for thinking that each Turkish family should have at least three children.[6] As far as the relation between "church and state" (religious authorities and the authority of the state) is concerned, Turkey is an interesting country because, on the one hand, it is a secular state that excludes religion from state laws whereas, on the other hand, there is a large Islamic majority and an Islamic oriented party that has held a parliamentary majority for a number of years.

Ultimately, it seems that this is a matter of political power, but in fact it is a matter of faith.[7] On the one hand, Muslims have to deal with secular laws and, on the other, with their faith tradition that recommends or forbids certain things. In the secular state, however, the concrete situation and their own consciences have become more important. It is remarkable that it is thought that the decision of a mother to abort her child would be a frivolous one. What mother would consider abortion or a Caesarean unless it was necessary?

In addition to the *fiqh* arguments on why abortion on certain grounds is permitted for a certain period or not, Islam also follows the rule "necessity knows no law" (*al-darûrat tubiyh al mahdurât*). This *fiqh* rule goes back to a verse in the Qur'an where, after forbidding certain types of meat, an exception is

---

⁵ http://video.cnnturk.com/2012/haber/7/4/dogum-korkusu-da-tibbi-zorunluluk (accessed 04 July 2012).

⁶ http://nederlandersinturkije.nl/nieuws/wijziging-turkse-abortus wet-zorgt-voor-veel-ophef/ (accessed 30 May 2012).

⁷ Islam's position regarding abortion is presented in this volume by Hegab (chapter XI).

made for people who are forced for one reason or another to eat such forbidden food: "But whoever is forced, not out of willingness or transgression, no sin rests on him. God is forgiving and merciful" (Surah al-Bakara (2):173). People apply the rules themselves in practice—given their situation. The decision is left to their own conscience in the discussions they have on what they should do, as the Turkish proverb quoted above already says.

A legal prohibition by the state will cause people to turn to illegal means—sometimes with serious consequences. Aside from the life of the mother being in danger, there are two practical reasons to consider abortion: rape or a medical indication that the child has severe handicaps, defects, or innate illnesses. Both cases confront the mother with a heavy question of conscience. The broad discussions among law schools on the precise number of days within which abortion is or is not allowed are ultimately secondary matters.[8] In agreement with the word of the Qur'an that only humans have been given only a little knowledge of the *mind* or spirit (Surah al-Israa' (17):85), people should not speculate about the exact state of the human spirit (*rûh*) but consider what someone's needs are and what that person can and cannot do. This is because, according to Islam, ev-

---

[8] The Islamic law schools have different views on the moment when the breath of life (*rûh*) is blown into the fetus. Most (*jumhûr*) assume that this happens after four months; some think that it occurs around the 40th day of pregnancy. They hold that abortion, if it is necessary, should be done before the breath of life is blown into the fetus. These differences of opinion are based on a few vague traditions (*hadiths*). See: http://www.diyanet.gov.tr/turkish/DIYANET/ilmi der-gi/ilmi/ main. asp?makno=6 (accessed 13 February 2013). In addition, there are Muslim scholars who hold that removal of a living being (human) is prohibited from the moment of conception unless the mother's life is in danger. (http://www.HayrettinKaraman.net/sc/ 00104.htm (accessed 13 February 2013).

Although Turkish law is not based on religious sources (which is even prohibited in Turkey), the law here (abortion is permitted up to 10 weeks) agrees more or less with the view of most Muslim scholars (permitted between 6-16 weeks if there is a good reason).

eryone is ultimately responsible for his or her own acts. The Qur'an states that God does not burden anyone beyond his ability (Surah al-Bakara (2):286). Just like all care ethics, in my view, Islamic care ethics also lies between state legislation, religious rules, and one's conscience. I will now present two cases from my own experience.

Case I

During my ten years as a Muslim spiritual caregiver, I have been confronted a number of times with questions concerning abortion and I have spoken with the women in question, either in the presence of their husbands or alone. It was apparent that no one simply has an abortion. Everyone has her own argument and story and reasons for having or not having an abortion. I was approached once by a gynecologist in the VU Medical Centre in Amsterdam. She had difficulty with the fact that one Muslim woman was some months pregnant with her third child who would most probably be born with severe birth defects. Her earlier children (then eight and six years old) had a serious chronic illness: a kind of dissolving of the bones in the fingers and feet through which the hands and feet wasted away and as a result they could not be expected to live long. I talked to the father a few times at the hospital, but I was also able to visit the children and the mother at home. The state of the children was shocking. Their fingers and bones were becoming very thin. The parents had sought advice abroad via the telephone. Without having viewed the situation themselves, the scholars they contacted advised against the permissibility of an abortion. The mother was already four months pregnant. My "advice" was different. Instead of stating my view, I attempted to deal with the woman's feelings and abilities, to support her against the fear of committing a serious sin. She said, "I already find it difficult with caring for these two handicapped children. How can I take care of the third sick child? I don't want it anymore." Her husband was against abortion. After a long talk with both parents I left the house with my mind at ease. I do not think the third child was ever born. I impressed upon the mother to ultimately make the choice herself and present her reasons to the Merciful God. I found her argument convincing. Who was I to make a religious declaration (issue a *fatwa*) by stating what was not permitted, knowing that God never gives someone a burden greater than he or she can bear (Surah al-Bakara (2):86) or was allowed, knowing that everyone is accountable before God for his or her own actions, according to Islam. For an outsider, it is easy to make a quick judgment because he or she will not have to deal with the burden (caring for a handicapped child). As a spiritual caregiver, I was thus not concerned with discussing the pros and cons of a *fatwa* (religious opinion) but wanted to explore with her what alternative would be best for her spiritual well-being. My job is to listen to what the patient/client feels, intends, and what that will mean for her or his future life. Spiritual caregivers in hospitals have a hard time with the fact that they see a patient only a few times and are not be able to be part of the processing. This also holds for those who give advice or issue a *fatwa* from a distance.[9] The spiritual caregiver needs to show the advantages and disadvantages of various alternatives (opinions) in an interactive conversation with the patient so that the latter can make choice him- or herself.

Case II

I will use this case to make clear what position I chose in a similar crisis. My wife and I had three children and wanted to wait a while. Despite the IUD, however, my wife became pregnant unexpectedly: the IUD had disappeared into the uterus. The doctor could not find it either and warned my wife that the IUD, if it was inside, could rust and severely harm the child. My wife panicked. She called me from Germany where she still lived. I felt that I could not take the risk either and left the decision up to her. "If the doctor said that the child could be born with a severe defect, then you can abort it," I said. She also

---

[9] The difference between a *fatwa* and advice is that the latter allows the patient him- or herself to choose between the various alternatives, looking at the advantages and disadvantages of them. A *fatwa* simply allows or prohibits it. That is, it states what is and what is not a sin, with all the attendant consequences: each sin is a threat with a punishment (if it is not compensated for or God forgives it), according to Islam, both in this life and in the hereafter.

found out that a fetus under nine weeks could be removed while the mother was anaesthetized. Neither of us have negative psychological effects or a sense of having sinned. I was aware of my decision and she trusted that. Why should I deliberately cause a problem for us and later regret it? I can address God with my own argument, knowing that He is the Merciful and Just One. For the Almighty does not burden anyone beyond their ability (surah al-Bakara (2):286), as stated above. After a few years' rest, we were rewarded with a fourth healthy child.

Organ Donation

In comparison with abortion, which we just discussed, organ donation is a more comprehensive and complicated theme. It is more comprehensive in the sense that more people are, relatively speaking, involved in organ donation than in an abortion. Moreover, an abortion is often performed in private. Organ donation is more public and relational. With abortion, one thinks of a baby or fetus that has not yet been born. With an organ donation, one is confronted with the hard reality of pain and loss and all kinds of expectations arise. There is a donor and a recipient, who are connected with each other to a more or less degree if the donor is still alive. The recipient is dependent on the donor; the donor on the advice of the doctors. Both are more or less involved with each other. While abortion has to do with allowing or not allowing a fetus to live, organ donation has to do with extending or not extending a life. People cannot decide to be born or not, but once they have been born, most want to live long and happy lives. But not everybody is granted happiness in this life. In Islamic culture, happiness is often postponed until the afterlife or, better, a balance is sought between happiness in this world and happiness in the afterlife. Because of that, attention for what can be done to achieve a happy life in this world is sometimes weak. The (Islamic or other) caregiver encounters many people every day who want to live longer and do not want to say good-bye to their loved ones. On the basis of these experiences one learns, already with young people, to be positive in principle with respect to organ donation, which can extend the life of the patient. But, in fact, the situation is more complex, for the entire success of the organ transfer is never certain, not for the recipient nor for the donor. I will give an example of this uncertainty:

The 25-year-old Steven Goossens tells about his kidney transplant:

> I was given a kidney in the Antwerp teaching hospital eight years ago. I had one diseased kidney, atrophied, and that spread very slowly to the other kidney. They didn't have a clear idea of how that happened. I started with dialysis when I was 15 and I was immediately put on the list for a transplant. Two years later I received a kidney. Everything's alright with the kidney now, but in the last eight years I have had all possible complications. The kidney was accepted at first; that took almost a month. Fluid accumulated in my lungs. Four years ago a piece of my hip began to die because of all the medication I was taking. They had to put in a prosthesis, and calcium began to collect on the prosthesis. That was very painful: the muscles around the prosthesis chafed against the calcium. They took it out after a year.
>
> But it came back and I was operated on again. Afterwards, I heard that it was a very difficult operation. As a result, I now live with constant pain. No, given the situation now, I would never want to have another kidney transplant. Everything was going much better before the operation. My dialysis period went well. I went to school and I was also studying to be a commercial artist but had to stop. Now I sit at home the whole day on disability. If I leave the house, it's usually in a wheelchair. Before the transplant, they only talked about possible rejection of the kidney, but never about all the other complications.[10]

This is an example of a medical complication. Doctors can only rely on their experiences with patients and, in the event of transplants that are done quite often, on statistics on success and complications. But for the individual patient, this is diffi-

---

[10] *NRC Handelsblad* (19 March 1998): 35; for other examples see: http://retro.nrc.nl/W2/Lab/Profiel/Orgaandonatie/interviews.html (accessed 25 June 2012).

cult to judge. Even if the law leaves the decision ultimately up to the patient or next of kin, they are usually not able to come to a decision without medical advice and spiritual counseling. For Muslims, in addition to the medical complexity, there are also religious sensitivities and uncertainties that cannot always be resolved by arguments. A sad example of this is my mother-in-law, who needed heart valve transplants. The doctors wanted to use porcine heart valves. Although no one had told her that this was forbidden by the Islamic commandments, she rejected the use of heart valves from an unclean animal. Because no donor valves could be found, she chose artificial valves that later caused complications. She died within a year at 57. If she had had a deep discussion with a Muslim spiritual counselor from the hospital, she would probably have consented to the doctors' first choice.

With respect to organ donation, many Muslims wonder if they are allowed to donate their organs to a non-Muslim or if they can accept an organ from a non-Muslim. Should they not be satisfied with the body they were given? Am I responsible if someone with my organ lives a bad life? Such religious reservations also explain why only 27% of Muslims are ready to donate organs as compared to 61% of the non-religious population in the Netherlands, even though most Muslim scholars allow organ donation in principle.[11]

---

[11] According to Statistics Netherlands, 61% of those without religious conviction are prepared to donate their organs at their death. That is a higher percentage than religious people. Only 27% of Muslims are prepared to do so. The differences between the other religious groups are less on this point and the percentages lie around 50. See: http://cbs.nl/nl-NL/menu/themas/gezondheid-welzijn/publicaties/artikelen/archief/2012/2012-3585-wm.htm (accessed 23 June 2012). In a statement on "Islam and Organ Donation in the Netherlands" (28 January 2006) by the CMO (Contact Organ for Muslims and the Government) and the Shi'ite Islamic Council, the following conditions for organ donation were mentioned: It must be necessary for the patient; there must be no involvement of financial profit; the decision to become a donor should be made in freedom; the wishes of the deceased are to

The constant discussions in European countries like the Netherlands and Belgium on the pros and cons of the laws surrounding organ transplants of those who have died reinforce the uncertainty of people. The fact that the one country has a "no, unless" policy and the other a "yes, unless" shows that transplants from those who have died is a serious operation that also affects the integrity of the dead body. In countries like Belgium and Austria, a person's organs can be used after his death unless the person has explicitly expressed his objection while alive. In the Netherlands this is permitted only if the person has given permission for this by signing a donor declaration.[12] In Turkey the policy is "no, unless," but removing organs is permitted in case of brain death as the result of a traffic accident or natural disaster.[13] The shortage of organs and rumors of organ trafficking in this country creates an attitude of suspicion and can reinforce prejudices that organ trafficking could arise.. Nevertheless, it remains that quick action can save the lives of those who need an organ even though the operation on people who are brain dead can be traumatic for the family. Organ donation by a living person is of course always dependent on his consent—if not on his initiative.

The doubts mentioned are very alive among Muslims. Even though *fiqh* scholars and Muslim doctors accept brain

---

be respected at all times; the operations should be done with the strictest medical precision and social scrupulousness. http://ws10.evision. nl/donorvoorlichting/index.cfm?act+structuur.tonen&pagina=232 (accessed 23 June 2012); cf. http://ntvg.nl/publicatie/islam-staat-orgaan donatie-toe/volledig/print (accessed 23 June 2012).

12 Wet op de orgaandonatie (Organ Donation Act): http://wetten. overheid.nl/BWBR0008066/geldigheidsdatum 21-02-2013; Turkey: Law no.: 2238 (29-05-1979); the added article Ek fikra 21-01-1982-2594/1).

13 Turkey: Law no.: 2238, 29-05-1979; the added article Ek fikra: 21-01-1982-2594/1. Turkey requires a declaration of brain death before the organs of a deceased person can be removed: bkz. Hekimler ve Tabibler Odası Yöneticiler için Mevzuat, Yürütme, madde 35, E K: 2 (Ek: 05-03-2010 27512).

death as death so that the organs of the deceased can be used,[14] Muslims have many doubts as to whether it is good. No simple consensus has emerged yet in 50 years. Already in 1960 a committee of the Turkish Union gave positive advice about heart transplants, whereas it was known that the still functioning heart of the deceased person had to be removed quickly after brain death occurred. According to the High Religious Council of the Diyanet in Turkey, for example, brain death is not always viewed as death. Ibrahim Çalışkan, then vice-chairman of this High Religious Council, responded negatively in writing on 25 November 1996 to a question if brain death can be seen as death.[15] The former chairman of the Turkish Union, Mehmet Nuri Yilmaz, declared in 2006 that in his view there were no objections to organ donation.[16] Sheik Mohammed Sayyed Tantawi, head of the leading Al-Azhar University in Cairo, made his organs available after his death.[17] But there are also dissenting voices.[18]

The uncertainties with their pros and cons can lead to a certain reservation with respect to organ donation. The general decisions of most expert medical committees and the most authoritative spiritual authority do not translate directly into decisions by individual people in their unique circumstances, with their own body or their own faith and experience of the world. The concrete decision on the treatment of a specific

---

[14] See the chapter by El-Gindi in this volume (chapter XII).

[15] From a personal letter to me on 25 October 1996; sayı (no.). B.02.1.DİB.0.10.214/1138.

[16] Sayı (no.): B.02.1.DİB.0.10.-214/1138. Decision 492, 25 October 1960;   http://kurul.diyanet.gov.tr/sorusor/duyurular.aspx?haber=47#div47 (26 May 2011; accessed 25 June 2012); http://arkasokak.net/dini-konular/27099-umutlari-sonduren-fetva/ (3 June 2006; accessed 25 June 2012).

[17] *Trouw* (2 May 1997); *NRC* (2 May 1997).

[18]   http://arkasokak.net/dini-konular/27099-umutlari-sonduren-fetva/ (accessed 28 June 2012); http://expliciet.nl/content/view/74/52/ (accessed 18 July 2012).

patient is largely dependent on the report of the doctors on the patient's condition and his alleged prognosis after treatment. In addition, the patient must fit the decision into his or her own value system and that of his closest family—on whom the patient depends in the recovery period. The rules in law, the ethical codes of the hospital, and the statements by *fiqh* scholars on what is permitted or forbidden constitute the environment in which the patient and the people around him or her arrive at a decision. For believers, the spiritual caregiver from their own tradition is a comforting and mediating conversation partner here more than he is an advisor. The donation of an organ by a living person to a sick one is a major step that, despite the risks for the donor and the recipient, extends life for many people and increases the quality of life. Removing organs from a deceased person can, primarily with one who has died suddenly, go against the feelings of those closest to him. The detached medical, *fiqh*, and juridical-political decisions about organ donation and brain death are of course necessary and important, but the concrete application of general insights and rules requires spiritual guidance and care: the medical treatment has to concur with the religious value system and self-esteem of the patient—which is a specific area of expertise that requires that the value systems of patient and spiritual caregiver be close enough to communicate on this deeper level of identity.

Euthanasia or Suicide

The third topic is euthanasia.[19] The Greek word "euthanasia" means a good, clean, gentle death. In medical ethics, this does not have to do with a slow, natural process in which someone's life ends or a natural sudden death but death through requesting toxins that at a certain time ushers in a gentle death that ends the life of a terminally ill person who is suffering great pain.

In the discussions on euthanasia until recently a distinction was made between active and passive euthanasia. The given

---

[19] Euthanasia is also dealt with in the chapters by Boer and Salem in this volume (chapters 14 and 16).

description above is then a matter of active euthanasia, i.e. euthanasia in the actual sense of the word: a treatment that ends life quickly and intentionally. Passive euthanasia rests on the decision to end treatments that do not appear to be able to heal the patient and treatments for pain that could have the side-effect that the patient dies earlier. These treatments are criticized for leading indirectly to death; others say that death is the result of the illness and not from stopping treatment. To prevent the suggestive conceptual confusion, the term palliative sedation is preferred. I will discuss that form of treatment as a fourth case. There the question if and under what circumstances treatment can be stopped will be discussed as well.

Here the concern is thus euthanasia in the actual meaning of the word: putting someone to death at his request. From the perspective of Islamic jurisprudence (*fiqh*), euthanasia in that sense is absolutely forbidden. It is considered to be suicide (and murder by the one who does it). The Qur'an clearly warns against suicide: "... do not commit suicide" (Surah an-Nisaa' (4):29). For a Muslim patient or one of his family members, it is therefore difficult, if not impossible, to agree to treatments of patients (whether terminal or not) that would lead to death. No Muslim, scholar or not, would agree with euthanasia in any form and under any circumstances. Suicide was considered such a serious sin that it was also asked if imams were allowed to recite the traditional prayer (*janaza*) at a suicide's burial. Two of the great Hanafite scholars from the second century AH differed in their views: Imam Mohammad al-Shaybânî (d. 804 C.E.) and Imam Abu Yusuf (d. 798 C.E.). According to the latter, it was not permitted, but Mohammad al-Shaybânî and his teacher Abu Hanifa himself thought otherwise. In their view, it was permitted from a religious point of view. They based their view on the fact that a suicide did not choose death in complete freedom but was probably acting compulsively in a hopeless situation.[20]

That meant that, as a Muslim, a suicide still merited a final prayer by Muslims, regardless of whether he was a sinner or

---

[20]   http://muslumangenc.com/kiptaplar/oku/ek/tk/kuranahkami/094.htm (accessed 29 June 2012).

not. Simply on the basis of this discussion one can already conclude that a religious opinion (*fatwa*) in a normal situation can
change when it concerns an abnormal, hopeless situation. I referred above to the rule "necessity knows no law," and situations where necessity is involved should be assessed appropri-
ately (*al-daruûrat yuqaddar bi mikdariha*). This requires time and
again juridical or ethical assessments that are in line with the
seriousness of the situations of necessity. That is why there is
no religious law regarding euthanasia in Islamic countries except for the above-mentioned Qur'anic prohibition against suicide (4:29, cf. 12:87) and rules derived from them.

It is different in Western countries. Let us look briefly at
Dutch law regarding euthanasia. After years of discussion, the
euthanasia law went into effect on 1 April 2002: the "Termination of Life on Request and Assisted Suicide (Review Procedures) Act."[21] The law permits euthanasia in situations of unbearable suffering with no hope of healing under strict conditions. That is already apparent from the description of euthanasia as "assistance in suicide by a doctor under the supervision
of an authorized committee, at the voluntary and well-considered explicit request of the patient who is in a situation of
hopeless and unbearable suffering." [22] The doctor has to submit

---

[21] http://wetten.overheid.nl/BWBR0012410 (accessed 6 July 2012).
In 2009 2500 cases were submitted to this committee; cf. http://nu.nl/
wetenschap/2154520/toename-aantal-euthanasiegevallen.html.

[22] The act (http://wetten.overheid.nl/BWBR0012410) sets strict
conditions (Article 2.1), i.e., that the doctor a) believes that the patient
has presented a voluntary and well-considered request; b) believes that
the patient is experiencing hopeless and unbearable suffering; c) has
informed the patient about his situation and his prospects; d) together
with the patient has come to the conclusion that there was no reasonable alternative for the patient's situation; e) has consulted at least
one other doctor who has no involvement in the case, who has seen
the patient and indicated in writing his assessment about the requirements for caution intended in paragraphs a to d, and; f) has carried
out the termination of life or assistance in suicide in a medically precise way.

the intention to carry out euthanasia to another doctor, and report the act of euthanasia afterwards to a government committee, supplying the reasons for carrying it out. The Netherlands Society for Voluntary Euthanasia (Nederlandse Vereniging voor een Vrijwillig Levenseinde [NVVE]) opened a clinic for the termination of life (LevenseindeKliniek) on 1 March 2012 where 240 registrations for euthanasia were received within the first three months.[23] The director of the NVVE, Petra de Jong, reports that 10,000 requests for voluntary euthanasia are submitted annually, of which about one third are granted. One third of those who submit requests die before the procedure can be completely processed, and 3,500 are left to themselves. She estimates that around 1,000 people per year will appeal to the clinic for help.[24]

From the perspective of Islamic care ethics, this suicide arrangement is not in line with human dignity. Good social, material, and spiritual care can prevent such a high number of requests for euthanasia. On the other hand, one should not judge others who are in need. The judgment is God's. In Islamic countries there are no clinics for terminating life, and euthanasia is not regulated by law. There one would sooner propose other alternatives that do meet the criterion of human dignity, such as opening hospices in which people can be carefully looked after in the last few weeks before their death. Here as well the role of spiritual care is of crucial importance. I will give a few examples of this below.

Stopping Treatment, Palliative Care, and Counseling in Dying

This last example of Islamic care ethics, between law and conscience, concerns the need for spiritual care also in palliative care. Palliative sedation is one of the treatments in this care,

---

[23] http://nvve.nl/nvve2/speerpunt.asp?pagkey=150375 (accessed 28 June 2012). In 2006 the total number of deaths in the Netherlands was about 135,000; http://cbs.nl/nl-NL/menu/themas/bevolking/publicaties/artikelen/archief/2007-2280-wm.htm.

[24] http://nvve.nl/nvve2/speerpunt.asp?pagkey=146068 (accessed 28 June 2012)

which consists in relief of pain by administering sedatives during the patient's final days.[25] The underlying illness is no longer treated, with the result that the patient dies of the illness or disease and dies a natural death. This is called stopping (curative medical) treatment. I recently had a long conversation with a specialist in a hospital who wanted to stop the treatment of a Muslim patient. The community this patient was from considered this to be a form of euthanasia and insisted that curative treatment continue. According to the doctor, continued treatment was pointless because the patient's condition offered no hope. What was not discussed—understandably—was that the doctor was legally required, according to Dutch law,[26] to stop pointless treatments and to apply pain relief.[27] The family has also called upon an imam who did not speak Dutch and also viewed stopping treatment as euthanasia and thus as forbidden (*haram*). It cost me and the doctor in question an hour to explain to the family (on the telephone) that it was not euthanasia. Rather, the treatment that was not helping would be stopped and the dying woman would no longer receive medicine or fluids any more. The woman's husband could not accept the latter. He found it incomprehensible that his wife would no longer receive any fluids. The doctor explained to him that this would not bring any relief but only extend her life and pain unnecessarily. A lengthy discussion between the husband and the doctor led to a small but meaningful compromise: he would give his wife a glass of water (*zamzam*) himself towards the end. When I spoke with him later on the telephone, he said she was no longer able to drink the water, so he

---

[25] Cf. the chapter by Boer in this volume.

[26] "Voor verrichtingen ter uitvoering van een behandelingsovereenkomst is de toestemming van de patient vereist" (For actions intended to implement an agreement for treatment, the permission of the patient is required) (VGBO, article 450); http://www.rbng.nl/user files/file/wetten/WGBO (accessed 22 February 2012).

[27] See the commentary by the professor of health law, Aart Hendriks, in Hendriks 2012: 748-49.

carefully dabbed her lips with it—which is viewed in Islamic culture as a very tender gesture. She died a half hour later.

Without the support supplied by his faith, the husband—and other family members—found it impossible to stop medical curative treatment. Aside from the fact that this is a difficult decision, he believed that it went against his faith and therefore did not want to bear the responsibility of not being able to endure the test and helping to speed her death. In these and similar situations people need to "view" their lives from that faith that is part of their identity and make their decisions with a good conscience—honestly before their families and honestly before God. Here the support of the spiritual caregiver is important, the support of one who shares this faith, knows the language and intentions of the doctor and is acquainted with the considerations people have to make in such situations and whose judgment can be trusted.

This counseling of people in crisis situations is at the heart of Islamic spiritual caregiving. People who are terminally ill suffer two kinds of pain: physical and spiritual, and while there are many means at present for treating physical pain, there are no pills or injections for spiritual pain. As far as counseling is concerned, there is only understanding and respect by the nursing and medical staff. The process of saying good-bye, evaluating, and dying means that the patient asks profound questions about life. Here the course of one's life, one's experience, faith, values and norms, as well as one's life with its high points and its sorrows and failures are central. It is here, in our view, that true spiritual care begins. We will discuss that via a final case.

Medisch Contact recently described a case in which the oldest son opposed stopping the treatment of his 63-year-old mother who was no longer responding to that treatment. He was also opposed, for reasons of faith, though not supported by his brother and sisters, to giving her morphine as part of the palliative treatment (Kluge, Brewster, and Kuipers 2012).[28]

---

[28] As a result of this article, Bert Keizer, doctor and a columnist for *Trouw*, a Dutch newspaper, wrote a column that goes far beyond the article in *Medisch Contact* with the suggestion that, as indicated al-

This was a 63-year-old Muslim woman, a widow and mother of two sons and three daughters. She had been admitted to intensive care with severe respiratory problems and a hole in her intestines as a result of cancer of the large intestine. After eight months the situation deteriorated significantly, and the doctors came to the conclusion that there would be no improvement. They wanted to limit treatment and not reanimate her if she suffered a heart attack or a new infection but allow her to die. After hearing the explanation and consultation, the rest of the family agreed to stop treatment and to give her morphine to prevent her from dying by suffocation while fully conscious. This is called palliative sedation. Suffocation while fully conscious is considered as one of the most fearful ways of dying. It is allowed by strict procedural rules that are followed stringently. The morphine would allow her to lose consciousness—but not cause her death. The oldest son vehemently refused this intention for religious reasons. Attempts at mediation by the imam chosen by the family failed. The oldest son "stated that his mother, if given morphine, would then 'come dazed before Allah,' which is unacceptable from a religious point of view." The specialist felt obligated to not administer morphine, as a result of which the woman died after five hours in severe respiratory distress.

What happened here does not testify to a great deal of wisdom and expertise. In addition to mental, emotional, and social factors, there is also a spiritual factor in care that the policy by the hospital staff did not take account of, although it is essential in the experience of Muslims—and other believers. The religious and ethical side of the treatment is viewed as private and left to the family. The search for an imam was also left up to the family—as if any local imam is able to bring together the complexities of medical treatments, the values of the Islamic tradition, the sensitivities of the family, and the acute situation of the dying patient. Hospitals should care for the patient as a human being, i.e. it should be able to see to it that the patient is

---

ready in his title, Islam offers little room for palliative care: Keizer 2012: 10. I responded to his column in *Trouw/Podium* (16 April 2012) but will not go further into the issue here.

treated adequately not only in a medical and technical way but also as the physical and spiritual being each human being is (cf. note 25). The problem here is not one approaching an imam to get a black-and-white "yes" or "no." Every care institution with a large number of Muslim patients, should in fact also have a regular Muslim spiritual caregiver on staff who can counsel Muslim families as part of the care provided by the institution.

As a supervisor of students being trained as Islamic spiritual caregivers, I have to state that few hospitals have hired trained Muslim caregivers who are truly acquainted with Islamic norms and values, know the hospital rules, and can assess complex situations in consultations with the doctors. These Islamic experts would then, if necessary, also be able to mediate, if necessary, between the professional norms of the medical staff and the Islamic families with their (often traditional) values and norms, sorrows, and fear. Such discussions concern understanding the patients and their families in their faith as they experience it, even if it seems to conflict with the medical treatment that is in the patient's interest. With such counseling, Muslim patients can comply with an easy conscience in the doctors medical-ethical decisions. Where no meaningful medical treatment is possible, religious rules also have nothing to offer. It is then a matter of acceptance. That is the work of spiritual caregivers and not of doctors. Islam does offer room for palliative care.

Summary and Conclusion

In this chapter care ethics was discussed from an Islamic perspective, and four elements were studied: first, law and conscience, i.e. secular law and a faith perspective, and, second, the body and the spirit in care. The accent here lies on the importance of spiritual caregiving in care. This is clarified by means of a few cases in abortion, organ donation, euthanasia, and palliative care.

The law on these topics varies from country to country. In the Netherlands abortion and Caesarean sections are no longer a subject of discussion. In contrast, however, in Turkey, for example, vehement discussions have recently taken place and these practices were permitted under strict conditions. (Secular) law in Turkey is more or less in agreement with an Islamic faith perspective. Euthanasia is an undiscussed or absolutely forbidden topic in Islamic countries, although permitted in the Netherlands after an intricate process. There are strict conditions under which it may be performed: "assistance in suicide by a doctor under the supervision of an authorized committee, at the voluntary and well-considered explicit request of the patient who is in a situation of hopeless and unbearable suffering."

That is why there are organizations that want to help in the process of ending people's lives at their request, like the NVVE, which was founded on 1 March 2012 and received 240 requests for euthanasia within the first three months. From an Islamic perspective this would be viewed as inhuman. In Islam people would choose rather for an alternative more worthy of humans, an alternative in which not only the body but the spirit is also crucial. That is why people are often trapped between law and conscience.

That obtains also for organ donation and palliative care. The Netherlands has a "no, unless" policy regarding organ donation, i.e. it is permitted to take organs from a body only if the donor has given permission. Countries like Belgium and Austria, in contrast, have a "yes, unless" policy. Organs can be used after a person's death unless that person has declared his or her express objections to that practice. Turkey follows the *"no, unless" policy, but the removal of organs is permitted after brain death as a result of an accident or natural disaster.* That sometimes leads to rumors of organ trafficking, etc. All in all, the role of expert Muslim spiritual caregivers in the care process is crucial. It is time that care institutions also pay attention to that.

In each of the cases discussed above—and in all of my experience as a Muslim spiritual caregiver and as supervisor of the training of my master's students—it has been and is my conviction that attention must be paid not only to care for the body but also to care for the spirit so that people do not feel trapped between state law, worldview and religious opinions, and their conscience. The presence of a Muslim caregiver in care institutions is a "must."

Bibliography

Hendriks, Aart. (2012). "Waardig sterven, godsdienstvrijheid en het recht van de oudste zoon." *Medisch Contact* 2012/13 (30 March):

748-49; http://medischcontact.artsennet.nl/nieuws-26/archief-6/tijd-schriftartikel/112688/waardig-sterven-gods dienstvrijheid-en-het-recht-van-de-oudste-zoon.htm.

Keizer, Bert. (2012). "Islam biedt weinig ruimte voor palliatieve zorg." *Trouw* (7 April): 10.

Kluge, Georg, Ellen Brewster, and Saskia Kuipers. (2012). "Waardig sterven, godsdienstvrijheid en het recht van de oudste zoon." *Medisch Contact* 2012/13 (30 March): 748-49; http://medischcontact.artsennet.nl/nieuws-26/archief-6/tijdschriftartikel/112688/waardig-sterven-godsdienstvrijheid-en-het-recht-van-de-oudste-zoon.htm.

Rutenfrans, Chris. (1998). "Wie is goed genoeg om een orgaan te geven." *Trouw* (2 April).

CHAPTER XVI

The Islamic Legal System
vis-à-vis
Euthanasia and Organ Transplantation

Mostafa Salem

Introduction

The aim of this chapter is to present the position of *shari'ah* and *fiqh* vis-à-vis recent emerging issues regarding euthanasia and organ transplantation. One question raised by this volume is if and to what extent Islamic law and the practice of Muslim states are in line with the Western attitude towards such arising issues.

It must be admitted at the outset that Muslim states have responded in a variety of ways to the forces of modernity. These responses cross the lines of tradition, sect, and school. They affect the ways in which *shari'ah* is interpreted by individuals in their personal lives and the extent to which *sharia'h* is implemented in the laws of the state. These diverse movements can be referred to collectively as "contemporary" *shari'ah*.

In this chapter I will describe and analyze what factors play a role in rules on euthanasia and organ donation. The various practices and circumstances of organ donation have been described in the chapters by El-Gindi and Schipper, Ghaly, and Abma in this volume. Here I will briefly describe the sources and methods of Islamic ethics and jurisprudence (*fiqh*). I will show the divergences in the application of *shari'ah* in the laws of various states with a majority of Islamic inhabitants. Then I will deal with the pros and cons of euthanasia and organ transplantation as presented by *fiqh* scholars. After these considerations I will describe the rules of Egyptian State law on organ transplantation and draw conclusions.

What is Meant by Shari'ah?

Before we discuss Islam's attitude towards the emerging issues of transplantation I need to typify what is generally meant by

Islamic "law," *shari'ah*. A fuller exposition of *shari'ah* can be found in the chapter by Marzouk Aulad Abdellah in this volume, to which I refer for a broader explanation of the legal terms that I use.

In its original sense *shari'ah* meant the road to the watering place, the path leading to the water, or the way to the source of life. The technical application of the term as a reference to the law of Islam has been traced directly to the texts in the Qur'an in which God indicates that adherents of Islam—*the believers*—must follow the clear and right way, the path of *shari'ah*. One verse of the Qu'ran expresses this as follows: "... then we put thee on the (right) Way of religion; so follow thou that (way), and follow not the desires of those who do not know ..." (Surah Al-Jathyah (55):18)

Shari'ah deals with many topics addressed by secular law, including crime, politics and economics, and personal matters like sexuality, hygiene, diet, prayer, and fasting. All Muslims believe *shari'ah* is God's law, but there are many differences concerning what it entails exactly. Modernists, traditionalists, and fundamentalists all hold different views of *shari'ah*. During its long history, various law schools developed their own interpretations. In addition to these developments in the circles of acknowledged Islamic scholars, the leadership of different countries applied varying interpretations of *shari'ah* in their laws.

Shari'ah law is founded on and derived from two primary sources, the divine revelations set forth in the Qur'an and the sayings of and the example set by the Prophet Muhammad and his companions (*Sunnah*). Valid reasons to think that a certain judgment is truly Islamic include the consensus of the religious scholars (*ijma*) and clear analogy (*qiyas*) with texts in the Qur'an and *Sunnah*, though Shi'a jurists replace *qiyas* by *aql* ("reason").

The majority of Muslims regard themselves as belonging to either the Sunni or Shi'a sub-traditions. Within these sects are different schools of religious study and scholarship. The schools within each sect have common characteristics, although they differ in the details. The major schools of Sunni *fiqh*, such as the Hanafi, Shafi'i, Maliki, and Hanbali schools accept *ijma, qiyas*, and some other principles like public interest as means to adapt the authoritative traditions in new situations, such as modern medical ethics.

Local and national developments and applications of *shari'ah* law depend on other factors as well. In different Islamic countries present *fiqh* practices also have roots in comparative law and local customs—and it is debatable if rules based on customary laws are always fully in accordance with the Qur'an and *Sunnah*. Some scholars think that Islamic law consists of long, diverse, and complicated intellectual traditions; it is not a well-defined set of specific rules and regulations that straightforwardly can be applied to life situations. Others consider *shari'ah* to be a shared opinion of the Islamic community based on literature that is extensive but not necessarily coherent or authorized by any single body. The commonality between those scholars is a warning that *shari'ah* does not refer to a unified and well-defined body of rules that can direct Islamic life but to sets of principles and rules that have grown in different contexts throughout the course of history. One scholar who stresses this complexity and supports this view is J.M. Otto who studied Islamic law in various Islamic countries and concludes that

> Anthropological research shows that people in local communities often do not distinguish clearly whether and to what extent their norms and practices are based on local tradition, tribal custom, or religion. Those who adhere to a confrontational view of sharia tend to ascribe many undesirable practices to sharia and religion overlooking custom and culture, even if high ranking religious authorities have stated the opposite. (Otto 2008: 30)

Indeed, local circumstances and customary law keep being influential in the laws and practices of justice in many Islamic states. This implies that not all practices in Islamic countries can be understood as applications of *shari'ah*. Therefore, if people in Islamic countries have practices that others might judge to be "undesirable" and maybe even as intolerable, it is important to investigate carefully, first, if these practices conform to national laws and, if they do, how such national laws follow *shari'ah*. This implies that not all "undesirable practices" can be attributed to *shari'ah*. Otto distinguishes three forms of how *shari'ah* law influences state law (Otto 2008: 8f.). He distinguishes between secular states, states with mixed systems, and states with classical *shari'ah*. First, Turkey, amid its Muslim majority and pressure from a religious political party, has declared itself to be secular. Religious interference in state affairs, law, and politics is prohibited. Second, in Pakistan, Afghanistan, Egypt, Nigeria, Sudan, Morocco, and Malaysia laws have blended sources. Their legal systems are strongly influenced by *shari'ah*, but the constitution and state laws are binding. These countries conduct elections, and it is their politicians and jurists, rather than their religious scholars, who make the laws. Most of these states have modernized their laws and have legal systems with significant differences compared to classical *shari'ah*. The third group comprises the Islamic states that derive their laws relatively straightforwardly from classical *shari'ah*, such as Saudi Arabia and some of the Gulf States. They do not have constitutions or legislatures. Their rulers have limited authority to change the laws, which are based on *shari'ah* as their religious scholars interpret it. Iran shares some of these characteristics but also has a parliament that legislates in a manner consistent with *shari'ah*.

In what follows, I will discuss two cases of medical ethics, euthanasia and organ donation. In the discussion on euthanasia I will stress the difference with the laws of some European countries. The discussion of organ donation from the perspective of *fiqh* will be followed by a summary of the recent Egyptian Law on organ donation.

Islamic Law vis-à-vis Euthanasia ("Mercy Killing")

Let me first explain the terminology. Euthanasia is a direct act of the physician to end the life of a patient, under whatever circumstances. Euthanasia may be classified into three types. The term *voluntary euthanasia* refers to the situation where the explicit consent of the patient is obtained. In situations of unbearable suffering voluntary euthanasia is—under strict conditions—legal in some smaller countries in Europe and some states of the USA. When the patient brings about his or her own death with the assistance of a physician, the term *assisted suicide* is often used. *Non-voluntary euthanasia* refers to situations in which the consent of the patient is unavailable.

Euthanasia has sometimes been divided into passive or active variants. In that case, the term passive euthanasia refers to withholding common treatments, such as antibiotics, necessary for the continuance of life, while the term active euthanasia refers to the use of lethal substances to let the patient die. This is the most controversial issue. But some believe that all the above terms and classifications are only seemingly precise and useful.

With regard to the position of Islam, we need to consider first the question if people have a right to bring about their own death—in one form or another. As a matter of fact, the question of euthanasia is not discussed often in Islam and if it is, it is dismissed as religiously unlawful. The terms euthanasia or mercy killing are not found in Islamic studies. According to Islamic teaching, we did not create ourselves nor do we own our bodies; rather, we are entrusted with them for care, nurture, and safekeeping. God is the owner and giver of life, and His rights in giving and in taking are not to be violated or questioned. Attempting to kill oneself in whatever way is a serious sin. The Qur'an says: "Do not kill (or destroy) yourselves, for verily Allah has been to you most Merciful" (Surah Al-Nisa' (4):29).

The Prophet Mohammed warned against suicide:

> Whoever kills himself with an iron instrument will be carrying it forever in hell. Whoever takes poison and kills himself will forever keep sipping that poison in hell. Whoever jumps off a mountain and kills himself will forever keep falling down in the depths of hell. (Al-Ahwadi: 165)

He also taught:

> There was a man in older times that had an infliction that taxed his patience, so he took a knife, cut his wrist and bled to death. Upon this God said: My subject hastened his end, I deny him paradise. (Imam Muslim: 2254)

As for *mercy killing,* as euthanasia is called in Islamic medical ethics discourse, we must make clear that the idea that a life might not be worth living any more does not exist in Islam. The justification for taking a life to alleviate suffering is not acceptable in Islam. Islamic law listed and specified the indications for taking life, i.e. the exceptions to the general rule of the sanctity of human life, and they do not include mercy killing or make allowance for it. Human life is a value to be respected unconditionally, irrespective of other circumstances. Evidence that mercy killing is forbidden can be seen from the following *hadith* as authentically narrated by Ibn Kathir:

> Among those who lived before you was a man who had a wound. He cut his hand with a knife in a way that the bleeding did not cease until he died. Allah, the Almighty and Majestified then said, "My salve has killed his own self. I made Paradise prohibited for him." (Ibn Kathir 2007: I, 316; cf. Al-Bukhari: VIII, 603; Yusouf and Fauzi 2012: 65)

During a military campaigns one of the Muslims was killed and the companions of the prophet kept praising his gallantry and efficiency in fighting. To their surprise, however, the Prophet commented, "His lot is hell." Upon inquiry, the companions found out that the man had been seriously injured so he put the handle of his sword on the ground and plunged his chest onto its tip, committing suicide (Al-Bukhari: XXIII, 446; Yusouf and Fauzi 2012: 65-66).

The Islamic Code of Medical Ethics endorsed by the First International Conference on Islamic Medicine states:

> Mercy killing, like suicide, finds no support except in the atheistic way of thinking that believes that our life on this earth is followed by void. The claim of killing for painful hopeless illness is also refuted, for there is no human pain that cannot be largely conquered by medication or by suitable neurosurgery. (Islamic Organization of Medical Ethics 1981: 8)

In addition, it is mandatory in Islam to seek medical treatment for illness, according to two sayings of the prophet: "Seek treatment, subjects of God, because for every illness God has made a cure" (Al-Bukhari: IV, 450), and "Your body has a claim on you" (Al-Bukhari: IV, 456). The needs of the body may not be neglected.

The issue of suffering pain raises the question of what profit and gain a Moslem can achieve from bearing such severe pain? Patience and endurance are highly regarded and highly rewarded values in Islam. "Those who patiently preserve will truly receive a reward without measure" (Surah Al-Zomar (39):10). "And bear in patience whatever (ill) maybe fall you: this, behold, is something to set one's heart upon" (Surah

Luqman (31):17). The Prophet Mohammad taught: "When the believer is afflicted with pain, even that of a prick of a thorn or more, God forgives his sins, and his wrongdoings are discarded as a tree sheds off its leaves" (Imam Muslim: 2573; Al-Bukhari: 5642).

In fact, when the means to prevent or alleviate pain fall short, this spiritual dimension can be very effectively called upon to support the patient who believes that accepting and enduring unavoidable pain will be to his/her credit in the hereafter, the real and enduring life. If the above is true, then for a person who does not believe in a hereafter this might sound like nonsense, but to one who does, euthanasia is certainly beyond what is good (Tahan 2004: 40).

Yet a dilemma arises in situations when the treatment holds no promise. Of course, stopping treatment that will have no success is different from euthanasia. According to a majority of scholars, the treatment ceases to be mandatory. This applies both to surgical and/or pharmaceutical measures, and, according to many scholars, to artificial animation equipment. Ordinary life needs those things that every living person needs and has a right to—and those are not categorized as "treatment."

Finally, on euthanasia, there is agreement that the financial cost of treating incurably ill persons is a growing concern, so much so that some groups have gone beyond the concept of the "right to die" to that of the "duty to die." Some people claim that when the human "machine" has outlived its productive span, its maintenance is an unacceptable burden on the productive stratum of society and it should be disposed of abruptly rather than allowing it to deteriorate gradually. As a matter of fact, this logic is completely alien to Islamic society where values take priority over prices. The care for the weak, old, and helpless is a value in itself for which people are willing to sacrifice time, effort, and money.

Islamic Criteria and Conditions for Transplantation

In Islam, respect for the living person has a bearing on respect for the dead person and his or her body. That respect includes the prohibition against taking organs from a dead person because violation of the dead is unacceptable. On the other hand, Muslims have also been instructed that when doubt persists as to the right thing to do according to the meaning of classical sources and uncertainty continues, the use of *ijma* and *qiyas* allows Muslims physicians to make intelligent decisions and recommendations on how to treat the patients that are critically ill. While supporters of the traditional *fiqh* schools opposed organ transplantation, contemporary scholars such as Al-Qaradawi made it permissible (cf. Sharafo 1987: 24-26). [1]

Therefore, the central question is if organ transplantation is permissible and under what conditions. Those who think that it is permissible under circumstances have to decide when the organs can be taken from the dead person, and, therefore, how the surgeons can declare a person dead. This subject was treated extensively in El-Gindi's chapter in this volume. In this chapter I will concentrate on the considerations in the Islamic discussion for or against organ transplantation in general, with respect to the use of organs from both deceased and living persons. In this section I will describe the main arguments against using organs and then the arguments for.

Islamic Arguments against Organ Transplantation

The majority of scholars who belong to the traditional *fiqh* schools hold that organ transplantation cannot be deemed permissible because the harm it does and its ill effects weigh more heavily than its potential benefits. I will mention the five main arguments.

The *first* and foremost argument is that God has honored the human body. The Qu'ran says: "And verily we have honored the children of Adam" (Surah Al-Isra (17):70). As such, it is a well-established principle of *shari'ah* that all the organs of a human body, either Muslim or non-Muslim, are sacred and must not be tampered with. To benefit from any part of a human is unlawful (*haram*). God made humans the best of His creatures and created everything else for their benefit. The Qur'an says: "It is He, who has created for you all things that are on earth" (Surah Al-Baqarah (2):29). Thus, it is permissible

---

[1] Sheik Yusuf Al-Qaradawi is a well-known and influential Muslim leader; see, e.g., http://best.topic-ideas.com/t1075-donating-organs (2010).

for a human to benefit from each of Allah's creations, including animals (under certain conditions), plants, and inanimate things. It would be unreasonable to place humans in the same category as animals by allowing them to use parts and benefit from human bodies, if it requires cutting, chopping, and amputating parts of the body. This is certainly unreasonable and unlawful to do to a human body. The Messenger of Allah said: "Breaking the bone of a dead person is similar (in sin) to breaking the bone of a living person" (*Sunan Abu Dawud*, *Sunan Ibn Majah*, and *Musnad Ahmad*).[2] Another saying of the prophet, narrated by Asma bint Abi Bakr, relates Allah's cursing of a woman who wears false hair (from humans) or arranges it for others (*Sahih Muslim*: 2122). Imam Nawawi, a famous Muslim Scholar, commented on this *hadith*:

> If human hair is used, then it is unlawful by consensus, whether it's the hair of a man or woman, because of the general narrations that prohibit this. And also, it is unlawful to take benefit from the hair and all other organs of a human body due to its sanctity. The hair of a human along with all his body parts must be buried. (Nawawi: 1600)

Similarly, Islamic scholars (*fuqaha*) have stated that in the case of extreme necessity and if there is no alternative, even unlawful things, such as pork and alcohol, become permissible. But even in such a situation consuming or deriving benefit from a human body still remains unlawful. Several famous *hadith* sources point in this direction. In *al-Fatawa al-Hindiyya* it states:

> If a person feared death due to hunger and another person said to him: "Cut off my hand and consume it" or he said: "Cut off a part of me and eat it," it will be unlawful for him to do so. Similarly, it is impermissible for a desperate person to cut part of his own self and eat it. (*al-Fatawa al-Hindiyya*: V, 310)

According to Ibn Abidin, the flesh of a human remains unlawful even in forceful situations (*Radd al-Muhtar*: V, 215). Ibn

---

[2] These are well-known Islamic sources; see the explanation given in footnote 8 below.

Nujaym states: "It is impermissible for the one who is dying of hunger to consume the food of another person who is also dying of hunger; neither is permitted to consume any part of the other person's body" (Ibn Nujaym: 124). Classical Islamic scholars have also stated that if one is compelled to kill another human, it is not permitted to use parts of his body, even if someone's own life is in danger (cf. Al-Kasani: VII, 177; Ibn Qudama: IX, 331). A human body is sacred even after death. Similarly, the great Hanafi jurist and Hadith Imam, Al-Tahawi, writes in the explanation of the latter *hadith*: "The Hadith shows that the bone of a dead person has the same sanctity and honor as the bone of living person" (*Mushkil al-Athar*). The Prophet said: "Harming a believer after his death is similar to harming him in his life" (Al-Qazwini: 372). It is clear that the Qur'an teaches the holiness of the human body and the oldest traditions, the *Sunnah*, that parts of the bodies of deceased persons should not be used by the living. We can call this the *argument from the holiness of the body* that should be respected: parts of the body are *not* to be used.

The *second*, closely related, argument focuses on the mutilation and deformation of the body. The cutting of organs from the body of the deceased harms a divinely created body (*muthla*), which has clearly been prohibited in *shari'ah*. Qatada narrates that the Prophet used to encourage charitable giving and the prevention of *muthla* (Al-Bukhari: II, 206). He also recommended abstinence from *muthla* (Imam Muslim: II, 82). This is also supported by a verse from the Qur'an: "I will mislead them and I will order them to slit the ears of cattle and to deface the (fair) nature created by Allah" (Surah Al-'Imran (4): 119). In connection with the above, it may be noted that blood transfusion in cases of need is permissible because it does not necessitate the cutting of human parts or any surgical procedures on the body.[3] We can call this *the argument from the integrity of the body:* the body is not to be *harmed*.

Third, the prohibition against harming the body is also valid in the case of a living donor: it is unlawful for an individual to inflict harm upon himself or others. The Prophet said: "It is

---

[3] See: http://ar.islamway.net/fatwa/27754.

unlawful to inflict harm upon yourself and others [*la dharara wa la dhirar*]" (Al-Bayhaqi: 10984). A basic Islamic rule states: "Harm cannot be removed by a similar harm." This means that, to remove harm from another individual, it is "impermissible for one to harm himself" (Ibn Nujaym, 123). Therefore, a living person is not allowed to donate a part of his body to another person because it is harmful for himself. We can call this *the argument from the integrity of one's own body*.

Fourth, the human body and parts are not our possession; they are God's. According to this view, the human body is entrusted to us by God. Therefore, it is not permitted for one to sell, give, or donate any of his organs. Islam has forbidden suicide for the same reason. There are many texts of the Qur'an and *Sunnah* that point this out. Therefore, it is unlawful for one to give his organs to another—by life or after death[4] (Surah Al-Nissa (4): 29). We can call this *the argument of God's ownership*.

Fifth, in cases in which it is difficult to weigh the pros and the cons it is preferable to abstain. A basic rule of Islamic jurisprudence says that, "When the evidence of a prohibition conflicts with the evidence of permissibility, preference is given to the prohibition" (Ibn Nujaym). Thus, it is unlawful to transplant organs, either from a living person or a dead body, and regardless of whether there is need or not (Sharafo 1987: 89).

Islamic Arguments for Organ Transplantation

According to rules of contemporary Islamic *fiqh* scholars, the transplantation and donation of human organs would be permissible subject to certain conditions (which will be indicated below). This view is based on the following three grounds.

First is *the argument of force majeure*. It is a well-established principle (*qawa'id*) of Islamic jurisprudence, based on the teachings of the Qur'an and the *Sunnah*, that the use of unlawful means is permitted in cases of extreme need and necessity. If necessary, certain prohibitions are waived, as when the life of a person is threatened the prohibition of eating carrion or drinking wine is suspended. The Qur'an states:

---

[4] Organ donation from a living person or a dead body is prohibited.

He (Allah) has only forbidden you dead meat, and blood, and the flesh of swine, and that on which any other name has been invoked besides that of Allah. But if one is forced by necessity, without willful disobedience nor transgressing due limits, then he is guiltless. For Allah is Most Forgiving and Most Merciful. (Surah Al-Baqarah (2):173)

The Qur'an also permits the utterance of disbelief (*kufr*) in order to save one's life: "Anyone who, after accepting faith in Allah, utters unbelief, except under compulsion whilst his heart remaining firm in faith ..." (Surah Al-Nahl (5):106).

The principle and rule of *fiqh*, based on these Qur'anic guidelines states: "Necessity makes the prohibited lawful" (Ibn Nujaym: 85). According to Imam Shafi'i, it is permissible for a person dying of hunger to consume the meat of another human being (Ibn Qudama: IX, 335). Therefore, in cases of need and necessity, impure, unlawful, and *haram* measures become permissible. Thus, when a person's life is in danger and he is in dire need for transplantation, then the transplantation of organs is permitted (Sharafo 1987: 26). Actually, this is almost common practice in the case of blood donation. Almost all scholars permit the transfusion and donation of blood in cases of need and necessity. If this is true, then why should there be any difference with respect to the issue of organ transplantation?

Second is *the argument of the lesser evil*. In some cases *shari'ah* does not give priority to the sanctity of the body but to higher values, such as saving another human life. It is stated in Tuhfat al-Fuqaha:

If a pregnant woman died and the child in her stomach is still a human, then they turn her body to take him alive. This can be based on the juristic Islamic basic rule: "If one is confronted with two evils, one should choose the lesser of the two." (Ibn Nujaym, *Al-Ashbah*)

The contra argument of the integrity of the body can be rejected because the body of the deceased or living donor will not be harmed too much. Therefore, it is questionable if the modern procedure for transplantation violates the sanctity that Islam attributed to the human body whether dead or alive. Islam enjoins that we honor a human body but did not prescribe any fixed methods for such honoring. What people consider to be a disgracing of the human body will change from one time to another and from one place to another. In organ transplantation the surgery is performed in the most respectful way and it is not considered to be disrespectful. The surgical procedure of transplantation ensures that the body will not be harmed more than is necessary. The operation is similar to surgical treatment of ill persons. This is the reason why many highly respected people of the community regard the donation of organs to be a mark of merit, and they are not looked down upon. The lesser harm of the operation and loss of an organ serves the greater good of helping another person to live (Sharafo 1987: 24-26).

Third, the contra argument of God's ownership of the body does not exclude people risking severe damage to their body or even losing their lives, as when they rescue another person from drowning or from a burning house. Similarly, it is permissible to donate an organ to save the life of a fellow human being (Sharafo 1987: 120).

In view of the above arguments—according to this group of scholars—it is permissible to transplant and donate organs in order to save another person's life. Of course, these treatments are subject to certain terms and conditions (Sharafo 1987: 119).

The Egyptian Organ Transplantation Law, No. 5 (2010) [5]

In February 2010, the Egyptian Parliament passed by an over-whelming majority a law regulating organ transplants. On 5 March 2010, the Egyptian President issued Law no. 5 called "the organization of human organs transplantation." The new law is considered a milestone in Egypt's health policy, which for the first time in its history provides a legal framework, including regulations and restrictions, for organ transplantation. The law permits organ donation from a living donor or a newly dead person to a patient under very strict conditions.

As a matter of fact, the announcement of this law had been postponed for 12 years; the main obstacles to its issuance were religious objections. When, during this process of discussions, the religious scholars agreed on the compatibility of organ

---

[5] http://arabic.irinnews.org/reportarabic.aspx?sid=2714.

transplantation with Islam, the problem had shifted towards purely medical objections. Up to that point, organ transplantations in Egypt had been regulated solely by the professional code of ethics of the Egyptian Medical Syndicate, which is a nonbinding document. Therefore, the stipulations of the law were very important.

An important circumstance in the background of these discussions was that Egypt had become a focal point for organ trafficking in the decade before the law came into force. Officials believe that the law will help combat this new phenomenon of organ trafficking. The law consists of four main chapters comprising 28 Articles dealing with the rise of and controversial issues of organ transplantation. The main features of the new law can be presented and analyzed along four main lines: rules for donation, economic and social aspects, medical aspects, and sanctions.

Donation Rules: Three Situations

The law stipulates that organs cannot be sold or bought anymore. Donation has become the only permitted legal way for transplantation. Moreover, donation is not open from any person to any patient; articles 3 and 4 confine donation to three situations. First, it is permitted between relatives. Second, by way of exception, donation to non-relatives is permitted on the condition that a medical committee gives permission. Third, donation is accepted between married Egyptians and foreigners after three years of marriage. The aim of the three-year period is to be sure that this marriage does not become an avenue for selling organs.

Economic and Social Aspects

I will give a bit more information about the social and economic context in which this law came into force. Generally speaking, the new law has satisfied some important values that prevail among the majority of Egyptians. These values stem from religious and cultural sources. Because we do not own our bodies, the selling of any organ is prohibited by God (*haram*) but the donation of an organ to a very sick and needy person may be permitted. Therefore, the rules of the new law that prohibits organs sale concords with this value.

A prevalent social value in Egypt is that relatives and people from one family are closely related: they have reciprocal social responsibilities towards one another and are obliged to help members who suffer under any kind of difficulties. If the health of a donor deteriorates, the donor can count on support by his family. His family and relatives will help in overcoming health difficulties. Given this Islamic value of care for one another within the family, they will not forsake him after his good act of donating to a relative.

Official health sources revealed that Egypt has in recent years become a big market for organ trafficking where the poor, due to coercive poverty and unemployment, are offering their organs for sale. On the other hand, there is a huge demand from foreigners who visit Egypt for the purpose of buying organs. Meanwhile, there are qualified doctors and medical centers ready and able to perform the operations. The new law has an economic dimension because it deprives all individuals involved in organ trafficking from the cash flow coming through undesirable activities. Of course, this is in line with the United Nations decision that forbids organ trafficking. It is also in line with the majority of Islamic scholars who permit donation and prohibit selling. The poor must cooperate with the government to find solutions for their financial problems other than selling their organs. There is no doubt that selling of their organs is not a real solution of the problem of poverty.

The new law has made organ donation possible, but some do not expect the law to have much immediate effect. In Egyptian culture there is a deeply rooted attitude against the voluntary donation of organs. Therefore, a great deal of consciousness raising has to be done to change that common attitude and encourage people to donate organs. If some well-known political leaders, artists, or religious people would donate, it would have a major influence.

Medical Aspects

The law stipulates also the conditions under which organ donation is permitted:

a) Transplantation is allowed only in public hospitals that are under the supervision of the Medical Syndicate. A special committee has been appointed to issue licenses and supervise these hospitals.

b) The law does not allow for the transplant of sexual tissues and organs bearing the characteristics genes inherited by family. This agrees with the view of Islamic scholars who prohibit the transplant of organs that might bear and transfer the very personal characteristics of the person or his family.[6]

c) Organs of deceased persons can be taken from their body after death. The law does not mention "brain death" and does not provide further criteria for concluding that the patient has died and organs can be taken but refers the decision of death to special committees of medical doctors to decide upon, case by case.

While medical authorities widely agree on the sign and criteria for brain death, the law does not specify these criteria—which could leave the possibility of undesirable decisions in certain cases.

Criminal and Administrative Sanctions

As we have seen, the commodification of body parts is thus not allowed, and organ transplantation is allowed under strict conditions. Those who do not adhere to the rules run the risk of large fines if they are caught. In relation to organ trafficking, the new law sets out criminal penalties for all parties involved: the donor, the recipient, and the doctors (chapter 4). These penalties increase from large fines to 25 years in jail and the revocation of medical licenses. The severity of the punishments show that organ trafficking is taken seriously—although in countries with bitter poverty some people will keep trying.

Concluding Remarks

In this concluding section I will give some comments of my own. Euthanasia is not an issue in Islam. While the traditional Islamic *fiqh* schools do not permit organ transplantation on the grounds mentioned above, a majority of contemporary scholars

---

[6] http://www.al-mahad.com/manzoor.htm.

give priority to saving life and therefore permit organ transplantation according to the conditions indicated in the decisions of several conferences held by Muslim jurisprudence scholars, such as those on brain death described by El-Gindi in this volume.

There are cases in which the distinction between the dead and the living is not clear; in such circumstances Islam allows brain death to be identified with real death. Yet this must be subject to the scientific definition of the exact moment of death and in accordance with the precision and accuracy of modern scientific tools. Egyptian law adopted this attitude.

Like the majority of legal systems all over the world, Islam does not permit the selling of human organs but opposes all types of organ trafficking. An example is the Egyptian law that inflicted severe criminal sanctions on persons who participate in organ trafficking.[7]

Bibliography

Al-Ahwadi.*Tuhfat. Mohamed Ibn Al-abdi rahaman al-mobarekfori.* Part II. Beirut: Dar Al-Kutub Al-ilmiyah.
Al-Bukhari. (1993). *Sahih al-Bukhari.* Cairo: Dar al-Maarif.
Al-Bayhaqi. *Sunnan Al-kobra.*[8]
Abu Dawud. *Sunan.*
The Egyptian Organ Transplantation Law, No. 5 (2010); http://arabic. irinnews.org/reportarabic.aspx?sid=2714.
Al-Hakim. *Mustadrak.*
Ibn Abi Shayba. *Musnad.*
Ibn Hanbal, Ahmad. *Al-Musnad.*
Ibn Kathir (1428/2007). *Tafsir (Abridged).* Transl. Muhammad Anis Gad Khalil. El-Mansoura: Dar Al-Manarah.

---

[7] The Islamic countries Pakistan and Iran are exceptions in the Muslim world; they have developed policies for regulated organ donation, see Adibul Hasan S. Rizvi *et al.* 2009: 124-28.

[8] Volumes that are referred to in this way are well-known classical Islamic sourcebooks in which authors have brought together older traditions. Some classical works are also referred to in this way and are available in various editions—just as Augustine's *Confessiones* XII refers to the twelfth book of Augustine's *Confessions*.

Ibn Majah. *Sunan.*
Ibn Nujaym. *al-Ashbah wa al-Naza'ir.*
Ibn Qudama. *al-Mugni.*
Imam Muslim. *Sahih Muslim.*
Al-Kasani. *Bada'i al-Sana'i.*
Al-Qazwini, Mohamed Ibn Masom. *Kashf Al-gata, Kash, and Wojouh al-Mostafa.* Qum: Moasasat ahl al-Bayt Li-ihya al-torath.
Islamic Organization of Medical Sciences. (1981). *Islamic Code of Medical Ethics.* www.rewi.uni-jena.de/rewimedia/Downloads/LS_Ruffert/Ethical+Codes/Islamic+Code+of+ Medical+Ethics.pdf.
Mohamed ornik zib bhader (1018-1118 AH). *Al-Fatawa al-Hindiyya.*
Nawawi. *Commentary on Sahih Muslim.* Damascus: Daar Al Nawader.
Otto, Jan Michiel (2008). *Sharia and National Law in Muslim Countries: Tensions and Opportunities for Dutch and EU Foreign Policy. Law, Governance, and Development.* E-book: Amsterdam University Press.
Rathor, Yusouf, Mohammed Rathor, and Mohammed Fauzi. (2012). "Euthanasia and Physician-Assisted Suicide: A Review from the Islamic Point of View." In: *The International Medical Journal* 11 (web journal).
Rizvi, Adibul Hasan *et al.* (2009). "Regulated compensated donation in Pakistan and Iran." *Current Opinion in Organ Transplantation* 14: 124-28; journals.lww.com/co-transplantation/Abstract/2009/ 040 00/Regulated compensated donation in Pakistan and.5.aspx. (Accessed 1 June 2012).
Sharafo, Ahmed. (1987). *Al-dien Al-ahkaam Al-shariya Lil Al-amal al-tiy-biah.* 2nd ed. http://www.al-mostafa.info/data/arabic/depot2/ gap.php?file=002022.pdf.
Tahan, Mohamed Jamal. (2004). "Euthanasia and Fear and Pain Problems." (in Arabic). www.hayatnafs.com/8ar2to lak/euthanasia. htm.
Al-Tahawi. *Mushkil al-Athar.*
Al-Tamartshi Al-Gizi Al-hanafi. *Radd al-Muhtar. Al-Al-Dor Al-mokhtar Sharh Tanwir Al-Absar.*

CHAPTER XVII

The Right to Moral Independence and Its Meaning for Medical Issues

Arend Soeteman

Introduction

In 2001 Germany was shocked. The papers reported the story of a 42-year-old computer technician, Armin Meiwes, who had placed an ad for persons who were willing to be killed and eaten by him. He offered only the experience in return. The software engineer Bernd-Jurgen Brandes (43) answered the ad and was killed by his own consent. Meiwes then cut him into pieces, wrapped the pieces in plastic bags, and placed them in his freezer. When he was arrested, he had already eaten more than 20 kilos.

There were a number of legal problems in this case. The German criminal code does not contain any article prohibiting cannibalism. The defense attorney argued that this was not a case of murder, since the victim himself wanted to be killed. There was no other offense than killing on request (which is punished less severely than murder or intentional manslaughter).

But the case also gives rise to other problems. Should the law prohibit behavior like Meiwes'? Let us agree that cannibalism is morally wrong. But here the victim willingly accepted being killed and eaten. An old legal maxim states: *volenti non fit iniuria* (to a willing person, injury is not done). It might be wrong, but it is not unjust to kill and eat someone who willingly consents to it. If it is not the law's business to enforce morality, then why should the law bother about this case of cannibalism?[1] Why should the law prohibit killing on request at all?

Liberals do not view the law as an instrument for producing a morally perfect society. We have several reasons for that.

---

[1] The case is found in Sandel 2009: ch. 3.

First, the morally perfect society is something beyond human reach. We could, however, try to use the law to make society as morally good as possible. But, second, law is *part* of society. It is as much the expression of the society as it is, made by imperfect people living in an imperfect society, as it is an instrument to improve society. And, third and most important, in general we have different ideas about the characteristics of a morally good society. Every attempt to make a morally perfect society will necessarily lead to big fights.

In this chapter I will try to present a liberal position in as acceptable a way as (in my view) possible.[2] In the end I will depict some consequences of this liberal position for the legal freedom of people to decide for themselves in medical issues.

Restricted Law: The Harm Principle

Laws should be restricted. The fact that a rule is morally good is, in itself, not sufficient justification for making it a legal rule. The *locus classicus* is the *harm principle* of John Stuart Mill:

> the only purpose for which power can be rightfully exercised over any member of a civilised community, against his will, is to prevent harm to others. His own good, either physically or moral, is not a sufficient warrant. He cannot rightfully be compelled to do or forbear because it will be better for him to do so, because it will make him happier, because, in the opinion of others, to do so would be wise or even right. (Mill 1975: 15)

The clear intention of Mill's harm principle was to restrict collective coercion or, rather, coercion by law: coercion is only justified in preventing harm to others. But how restrictive this principle really is depends, of course, on our interpretation of harm. We might interpret harm in such a way that any irritation caused by behavior considered to be immoral is a kind of harm. If I

---

[2] Liberalism is a contested political philosophy that, however, is dominant in Western constitutions and in international treaties on human rights. In this chapter I will not discuss criticisms by communitarian and other thinkers.

know that my neighbors are engaging in homosexual acts, that knowledge alone could insult my feelings in such a way that I feel unhappy. Or, to use another example, a racist who sees a white girl and a black man walking hand in hand in the street, clearly in love, might be irritated in such a way that he is distracted from going about his own business. If we interpret harm rather broadly so that it includes these kinds of irritation, then Mill's limitation principle does not restrict coercion at all.

I will follow Feinberg by interpreting harm as a wrongful setback of interests (Feinberg 1984: 36). But even if we argue with Mill that the harm principle does not apply to children and to others who are mentally incapable of managing their own affairs, in this interpretation the harm principle seems to be too restrictive: there is a number of acts we all agree should be legally prohibited but do not cause harm to others.

First, there are acts that do not cause harm (in this sense) but are nevertheless so offensive that they cannot be tolerated. The cannibalism case may present an example. In the movie *Kaos* by Paolo and Vittorio Taviani (1984) some gangsters are playing bowls with the heads of their victims. Less shocking examples are public nudity or different varieties of public obscenity. The effective power of custom and public opinion to prevent more serious instances of offensive acts might make law superfluous in a number of instances, but it is doubtful whether we could do without law in this field.

Nevertheless, from a liberal point of view the legal prohibition of offensive acts is risky. We should not protect the racist who is offended by interracial sex. More generally, people might be offended by other persons who worship the wrong God, have wrong sex, play the wrong sport, or readwrong books. The fact that people are offended sometimes says more about their being quick to take offense than about the behavior that evokes their annoyance. To prevent the prohibition of offensive acts from clearing the way for legal moralism (i.e. the dominant morality being enforced by the law) we need a theory that develops some criteria (in non-moral terms) for judging when an offense is serious and may be legally forbidden. The seriousness of an offense is determined, for example, by its intensity, its duration, the extension of susceptibility to this kind of offense, the avoidability without serious inconvenience of the experience of the offense and the *volenti* maxim (when one voluntarily enters the cinema to watch a movie known to be scandalous, one cannot complain that one has been offended) (see Feinberg 1985: 35).

There is a second reason why Mill's harm principle is too restrictive. Mill presupposes that individuals can take care of their own affairs. But they sometimes make mistakes. They want to eat a piece cake but do not know it is poisoned. They smoke cigarettes even if they know that it is bad for their health. Individuals may, knowingly or unknowingly, harm themselves. But Mill accepted only harm to others as justification for collective coercion, not harm to one's self.

When individuals are compelled to do or omit some action because of their own interests we call this paternalism. It is usual to distinguish between soft and hard (or weak and strong) paternalism. Hard paternalism protects competent adults against their will from the harmful consequences of their own voluntarily chosen behavior. Soft paternalism protects individuals from the harmful consequences of their behavior if this behavior is involuntary or if they did not realize these harmful consequences or if temporary intervention is needed to establish that the individual willingly and knowingly accepts the harmful consequences (Feinberg 1986: 12).

Soft paternalism is not really a problem for Mill's harm principle. That principle only prohibits coercion and intervention *against the will* of the individuals concerned. A liberal who believes that because every person is master of his own life it is for the individual person himself to decide on the termination of his life may nevertheless require further conditions to guarantee that the decision to end one's life is voluntary. This is soft paternalism.

Legal obligations for seat belts while riding in a car are more difficult. It is clear that seat belts are in the interest of the individuals concerned. But these individuals may have objections to wearing seat belts, even if these objections might be irrational. They believe, for example, that they will not be involved in an accident (they never were before). Mill's harm principle, however, stated that one may not be coerced against one's will without any further qualification about the quality of this will. We could, perhaps, justify the obligation for seat belts by referring to the economic damage (harm) for society if the consequences of traffic accidents are more serious. But it is difficult to deny that paternalistic considerations are important in this case. It seems that legal obligations to wear seat belts violate the harm principle.

Other examples are tobacco, alcohol, and drugs. Drugs are generally forbidden (although soft drugs are tolerated in the Netherlands), alcohol is legally free (driving under the influence is prohibited, but that is justified by the risk of harm to others), and cigarettes are prohibited in public spaces. The latter prohibition is justified by the harm smoke causes to non-smokers. The prohibition of drugs stimulates criminality (as the prohibition of alcohol did in the USA in the beginning of the 20th century), but is difficult to justify on non-paternalistic grounds. The harm drugs users now cause to others seems to be a consequence of the illegality of drugs. Perhaps we should abolish the legal prohibition of drugs and smoking in areas where it does not cause harm to others. But on the face of it, the prohibitions seem to violate Mill's harm principle.

On the other hand, the law certainly does not prohibit all behavior that is risky for the individual. Car racing and mountaineering are permitted. It seems that activities that are important for the individual are legally free, even if they are very risky.

A Liberal Position

Mill's harm principle might be too restricted, but the idea that individual persons are generally free to decide on their own behavior is still dominant. Restrictions are indicated first if they seriously risk causing harm to others, second, in case of serious offenses, and third in some instances where they seriously risk causing harm to themselves and these restrictions do not interfere in an important way with the way they want to live their lives. But apart from this, individual persons are free to live according to their own values. They may be religious or not. They may believe that they have to follow the commands of God or Allah. Or they may feel themselves obliged for other reasons to follow whatever rules and principles. But other persons, and most importantly their political communities, have no right to coerce them to live according to the rules and principles of these other persons.

Even the church has no right to coerce individuals. Of course, the church may have its own principles and rules. It may, for example, strongly object to euthanasia and may prohibit its members from committing euthanasia. It may prevent individuals who are violating its rules from taking part in religious ceremonies. But the separation of church and state implies that the church has no authority to make use of the power of the state to compel individual persons to obey its rules and principles.

The dominant view in the Western world is not only that people disagree about religion, about the meaning of life, about the values that are important for their own life. The dominant view is also that people should be as free as possible to live according to their own ideas and beliefs.

Why is this? What is the justification of this liberal position? It is quite common to refer to individual human dignity. The *Universal Declaration of Human Rights* (1948) begins with recognizing this inherent dignity of all members of the human community. Religious leaders from different religions subscribe to this idea of human dignity, but the generality of the acceptance of the value of human dignity is no guarantee of its meaning as a substantial value. As a matter of fact, the concept of individual human dignity has characteristics of a container concept. The liberalization of euthanasia is defended in the name of human dignity, as a consequence of the idea that dignity implies that individuals make their own decisions. But this liberalization is also rejected in the name of human dignity: killing another person, even at his request, implies the idea that his life is not worth living anymore, which violates his dignity. The freedom of homosexuals to practice their homosexuality and to be legally recognized as couples is argued in the name of human dignity. But this legal recognition in the name of human dignity is also considered to be a fatal error.[3]

---

[3] Van Beers (2009: 677) quotes the French author P. Legendre, who even declares this legal homosexual partnership to be the conclusion of hedonistic logic that originated in Nazism.

The Skeleton of "Human Dignity"

I will try to interpret the concept of human dignity. My proposed interpretation should meet two requirements: it should make human dignity an attractive value, and it should be able to draw some normative consequences. Let me first mention four characteristics that, to my mind, are difficult to deny for any author who subscribes to the value of human dignity and that together form (part of) the skeleton of the concept of human dignity.

First, dignity is vested in human individuals, not in tribes, political communities, religious groups, etc. Of course, these organizations or collectivities of individuals are often very important for the individuals concerned. They can be instruments for human dignity (although, unfortunately, sometimes also instruments against human dignity). There is a fundamental freedom of association. But these associations, tribes, religious groups, political communities are not themselves bearers of human dignity.

Second, every human being is a bearer of this dignity. And, if every human individual has this dignity just through being human, it follows that all the particularities of individual life do not have any influence on the dignity of the individual. This means that natural characteristics such as race, sex, age, etc. do not have any influence. But the particular acts of individuals have no influence either: Hitler had the same dignity as Martin Luther King Jr., Saddam Hussein the same as Nelson Mandela. To be more exact: individuals can behave in a way that does not meet the standards of dignity, as in the case of Hitler and Saddam Hussein. Other individuals can be in situations that certainly do not meet the standards required by their dignity, which is the fate of many poor, oppressed, raped, and murdered people today.

I am not saying that the behavior of individuals or groups that conflicts with dignity merits respect: it does not. If dignity is a universal qualification, it is a qualification of human individuals, not of their behavior. We still have to see what it means to say that even Hitler had human dignity. But I am saying that if dignity is vested in us because we are human individuals, then it follows that it is vested in all human individuals. We cannot lose it. A son of a king remains a son of a king all his life, whether he likes it or not and whether he behaves as sons of kings ought to behave or not.

Third, human dignity is a normative qualification. It has to do with what we owe to others. In the terminology of rights, this means that all individuals have a right to be treated by others in conformity with their dignity. And if they have this right simply through being human individuals, then all human individuals have an equal right to be treated this way.

Fourth, political communities in particular should be organized such that all its citizens are treated in accordance with their dignity. This does not mean that all citizens should be dealt with equally; it means that they should all be treated with equal dignity. This means that the right to dignity is a political right that should be elaborated in the legal orders of global society and various states. Perhaps the right to dignity implies much more, but when we speak about law, these political aspects in particular are relevant.

I believe all this is rather clear and difficult to deny. Here we have, as I said, the skeleton of human dignity, or at least an important part of it. Racists, who nevertheless deny the right to equal dignity to blacks because they hold that whites have more dignity than blacks, are denying the presuppositions of human dignity: one cannot be a sincere racist (whatever this may mean) and at the same time hold to human dignity. Racists are wrong, I believe, because they cannot explain why race should be relevant for one's right to dignity. But now *the more difficult question arises: What are the rights contained in this equal right to human dignity, or what is the meaning of the right to human dignity?*

Two Interpretations of Human Dignity

Roughly, we can (inspired by Ronald Dworkin [1985b: 191ff.][4]) distinguish between two interpretations that I, respectively, call conservative and liberal.

The *conservative interpretation* starts with some substantial ideas about individual human good. It claims that government

---

[4] Dworkin discusses the possible interpretations of "treating citizens as equals" or "with equal dignity."

cannot be neutral on questions of the good individual life because it cannot treat its citizens as equal human beings without a theory of what human beings ought to do or ought to be or how they could flourish as human beings. It argues that the content of equal treatment and equal dignity cannot be independent of some theory about the good for humankind or the good of life because treating a person as a person with equal dignity means treating him the way the really good or truly wise person would wish to be treated.

Let us suppose, for example, that the large majority in some political society believe that a man or woman cannot really lead a good life if he or she does not worship God every day and follows what is seen as His commandments scrupulously. If that political society follows the conservative interpretation of human dignity, this implies that one holds not only that the lives of other people, the minority who do not believe in their gods, have less value but also that the equal human dignity of these unbelievers has the consequence that they should be stimulated, if not compelled, to change their view and their behavior. One can accept, perhaps, that the inner beliefs are beyond the control of the community. But speech is not, and behavior is not either. If one cannot enforce true belief, one can enforce behavior in conformity with true belief and prohibit speech that violates this true belief. This has the consequence that other people are not seduced into following false believers and that perhaps even, in the long run, the false belief loses its support.

This is a perhaps extreme, although not unrealistic, example of a conservative interpretation of equal human dignity. Other examples might be much less extreme. The majority may believe that women truly fulfill their destiny only if they have several children and spend most of their adult lives raising them. A government that follows the conservative interpretation could then take all kind of measures discouraging married women from having paid jobs. A majority also might believe that all individuals, male and female, lead a truly good life only if they are economically independent. Then the conservative interpretation of human dignity leads to measures that stimulate married couple to both perform paid jobs.

The *liberal interpretation* of equal human dignity believes, on the other hand, that government should be as neutral as possible on the question of the good life. Since the citizens of society differ in their conceptions, the government does not treat them with equal dignity if it prefers one conception to another. Even if political officials believe or the majority believes one religion to be the only good and true religion, necessary for a truly good life, it nevertheless tolerates other beliefs, religious or not. That is, it does not try to compel individuals to behave in compliance with the majority's conception of the good life. According to the liberal interpretation individuals have *a right to moral independence*: they are free to have their own ideas about what makes their life worth living as much as possible in conformity to their ideas. They

> have the right not to suffer disadvantage in the distribution of social goods and opportunities, including disadvantage in the liberties permitted to them by the criminal law, just on the ground that their officials or fellow citizens think that their opinions about the right way for them to lead their own lives are ignoble or wrong. (Dworkin 1985a: 353)

There is at least one important argument for the liberal conception. That argument is that no life can be truly good if it is not lived sincerely. Authenticity is a necessary condition of the good life. Locke already argued that worship of God has no value for God if it is compelled, that a religious belief can have any value only if it is in our hearts. This idea has now become secularized: a life has no value, cannot be really good, if it is not lived from the inside.

One can also argue from the other side. It may be the case that religious toleration is forced upon us by our own history of religious wars. But if, as most of us do, we consider religious toleration a value, then it is a value based on a liberal conception, not a conservative one. It is clear that the dominant feature of human rights as we know them in the world today is liberal (in the sense explained) and not conservative. This is not a deep philosophical argument, but it means that those among us who accept the main features of modern human rights have to accept this liberal point of view. The main philosophical argument, however, is what I stated: an insincere life cannot be a good life.

So the idea of dignity, which implies equal dignity, has the important consequence that every individual has the right to as much moral independence as possible and therefore should be able to live a life from the inside, to be king of his own life. To live a life as it has been decided by others is to be treated as an immature child. Freedom is important, but it is derived. Freedom is important because it is instrumental for our possibilities to live our own life. That means living a life we ourselves believe to be a good life.

I want to stress that this human dignity is a moral value, but it does not imply any moral judgment about the way different human individuals make use of their right to live their own lives. The moral and legally protected value of freedom of speech also encompasses the legal right of immoral speech, and the moral and legally protected right of freedom of religion also encompasses the legal right to follow false or even immoral religions.

How Much Freedom Should the Law Grant in Medical Issues?

The liberal interpretation of human dignity is also relevant for medical issues. In the medical sphere, as in others, individuals should have control over their own lives as much as possible. The doctor knows best, but if the patient does not want to follow the doctor's opinion he, the patient, has the final word.

Dutch law therefore prohibits a doctor from treating a patient against his will. If a patient does not want the treatment the doctor prescribes the decision is, in the end, the patient's. Of course, the doctor is obliged to give the patient all the relevant medical information to enable an informed decision. This may be relevant when a life nears its end. Sometimes doctors propose medical treatments that may lengthen the life but diminish its quality. It then is the right of the patient to refuse a treatment if he does not want it.

But, on the other hand, does a patient have the right to receive the medical treatment he wishes? In general, adult patients have the right to decide for themselves, in consultation with their doctors, about their medical treatment.[5] But such a right, of course, cannot be absolute. It finds its limit first in the right or even duty of the doctor to decide according to the best medical knowledge. No doctor can be compelled to give a treatment to a patient that (in his expert opinion) makes no sense from a medical point of view. Second, the medical treatment should avoid harm to others. This might be relevant for women who want some treatment so they can become pregnant. Suppose the woman drinks, smokes, uses drugs and/or is too obese. In such a case there is a medical risk that the baby she gives birth to will have medical problems. It is not evident that she has a right to the medical treatment she wants. But what about pregnant women who are mentally disabled? Third, there are financial and practical limitations. The capacities of hospitals are limited, and they have to set priorities.

There may be other limitations. But the equal dignity and the right to moral independence imply that one type of argument against some medical treatment is not allowed. Doctors may not refuse medical treatment to an informed patient for the sole reason that they believe the patient is making a morally wrong choice about his own body and/or his own life.

Let us suppose that a lesbian couple wants a baby, which is the biological child of one of them. They want IVF with the sperm of a male donor. Some doctors might object because they believe that it is wrong for a child to have two mothers and (in daily life) no father. They may, of course, believe that it is bad for the development of the child. But if this is their opinion we need empirical evidence to prove if having two mothers is indeed bad for a child's development. If such empirical evidence is absent, there is then a strong suspicion that their opinion is founded in a prejudice against homosexual couples in general and homosexual couples with children in particular. If IVF is denied to our lesbian couple because doctors believe it is wrong, this is a violation of their right to moral independence.

---

[5] In Dutch law children from the age of 16 are considered to be of age. Children from 12 to 16 have a right to decide regarding medical treatment, but they need the consent of their parents.

Gender change is another example. There are males who want to become female and females who want to become male. They feel imprisoned in a wrong body. I am sure it is difficult for most of us to understand why they would want this surgery, but they want it nevertheless. Moreover, it is possible from a medical point of view. Gender change as a medical treatment is practiced in the hospital connected with the university at which the conference where this volume originated was held (VU University Amsterdam). Again, if doctors refuse this treatment just because they believe gender change to be morally wrong, this would be a violation of the right to moral independence of these patients.

If a patient has a prima facie right to be treated as he wants to be treated, this does not imply that he can impose his will on the doctor. The doctor has his dignity as well; he is not to be reduced to an instrument of the patient. If a doctor has conscientious objections against IVF or against gender change he should not be compelled. But he should first explain to the patient what he does not want to do. Second, hospitals cannot have conscientious objections: other doctors could substitute for the doctors with conscientious objections.

Euthanasia could present another example. According to Dutch law, euthanasia is permitted at the request of the patient who is suffering unbearably and for whom there is no hope for improvement. But this does not imply that the doctor is obliged to follow the request of the patient. But he may not refuse capriciously. Usually the doctor and the patient have known each other already for some time. They should discuss the matter before the situation arises. The doctor should make clear what he is prepared to do and what not. Knowing this, the patient has of course the right to look for another doctor who is more lenient in following his wishes.

Bibliography

Beers, B.C. van. (2009). *Persoon en lichaam in het recht*. Meppel: Boom Juridische Uitgevers.

Dworkin, Ronald. (1985a). "Do We Have a Right to Pornography." In: Ronald Dworkin. *A Matter of Principle*. Cambridge MA/London: Harvard University Press.

(1985b). "Liberalism." In: Ronald Dworkin. *A Matter of Principle.* Cambridge MA/London: Harvard University Press.

Feinberg, Joel. (1986). *The Moral Limits of the Criminal Law.* Vol. 3: *Harm to Self.* Oxford: Oxford University Press.

(1985). *The Moral Limits of the Criminal Law.* Vol. 2: *Offense to Others.* Oxford: Oxford University Press.

(1984). *The Moral Limits of the Criminal Law.* Vol. 1: *Harm to Others.* Oxford: Oxford University Press.

Mill, John Stuart. (1975). *On Liberty.* In: J.S. Mill. *Three Essays.* Oxford etc.: Oxford University Press. Originally published 1859.

Sandel, Michael J. (2009). *Justice: What's the Right Thing to Do?* New York: Farrar, Straus, and Giroux.

CHAPTER XVIII

Observations and Comparisons

Petra Verdonk and Hendrik M. Vroom

Introduction

In this final chapter we will note some differences and overlappings between the contributions from the Western/post-
Christian and those from the Arab-Islamic side. We will clarify
and explain clear differences by referring to the two larger
paradigms of moral reasoning that we described in the introductory chapter to this volume. We will also try to clarify other
issues in the background, such as the role of poverty and social
security and look for commonalities between the two paradigms.

Wealth and Poverty: Different Priorities

It is clear that poor countries do not have as much money and
resources available for advanced medical apparatuses or extensive genetic population research. One of the Egyptian contributors to this volume is the director of a clinic for obstetrics
where four hundred children are born every day. The attention
and care given to the individual is very different from what is
possible in the West. This implies that more expensive treatments are not available to the mass of the population and are
just within reach of those who can afford them.

Whereas medical research in the West and the treatments it
makes possible are in some way "ends in themselves," in
poorer countries decisions to spend public money for research
are hard ones. Nevertheless, the limits of what care might cost
have also become an urgent topic of discussion in "the West."
What are "reasonable costs" for helping people above 65 live
for one more year? No country in the world can circumvent
these crucial questions of what is meaningful research, what are
accountable amounts for expensive and rare treatments, and
what it may cost compared with the expenses for other life-
threatening conditions like higher sea levels, violent storms and

increased flooding, the diminishing of oxygen levels and fresh air in mass cities? Nevertheless, in poor countries advanced research in genetics and some other areas is not a priority, as some Muslim scholars say.

Paradigms, Differences, and Internal Diversity

In the introduction we described two paradigms: a post-Christian Western one of the "secular state" with freedom of religion (and secular worldviews) and, therefore, as much freedom in making personal decisions as possible, and an Arabic-Islamic paradigm in which each moral decision is taken on the basis of Islamic sources. In this latter paradigm law has been strongly determined by *fiqh*. In our short analysis we pointed out that, beneath the surface of the central values for the West—dignity and autonomy—various groups of people do give their own meaning to these terms. The idea of the dignity of all persons has its source in the Jewish Bible—for Muslims: God's revelation to Moses—but has also become a humanist value accepted by most non-religious people. Both parts of the term "post-Christian" are equally important. The consequence of having so many independent states in Europe is that state laws vary widely—from a prohibition of abortion in Ireland to its being permitted until the 24th week in the Netherlands.[1]

The Islamic paradigm also leaves "hermeneutical space" for diversity—to some extent. The short list in Hegab's contribution showing how the various *fiqh* schools differ in prohibiting or allowing abortion is telling. Because Islam recognizes several *fiqh* schools and declares each Muslim personally accountable for following a *fatwa* from a mufti from any one of these schools, there is a high degree of freedom of personal decision in Islam—even though the social and cultural context and state laws (and not "Islam" as such) limit this freedom. Socio-cultural usages are often more determinative than religious ones.

---

[1]   http://www.rijksoverheid.nl/onderwerpen/abortus/voorwaarden-abortus.

The reader will note that Islamic states have laws that are more restrictive than the measures adopted at the meeting of the IOMS with its medical and *fiqh* scholars allowed (cf. El-Gindi's chapter above). On the other hand, the pressure of medical and *fiqh* scholars has resulted in an Egyptian law on abortion that is acceptable to politicians, medical staff, and *fiqh* scholars (see Salem's contribution). Salem stresses the internal diversity of Islam that has arisen because of the role of customary law: the customary law that obtains in Afghanistan differs from that in northern Nigeria. But if we ask what is common between all those different law systems and *fiqh* schools in Islam, we see the *proof texts* of the Qur'an (again, such biblical *loca probantia* have been usual in the Christian tradition), but, as Aulad Abdellah pointed out in his chapter, those scriptural texts have to be interpreted on the basis of the intentions of the "ultimate" Lawgiver who has revealed them in the *Sunnah*. If we ask about the intention of certain *fiqh* rules, we arrive at notions like the integrity of the body (in relation to organ donation) and the dignity of the individual. Westerners should learn to look *beneath the surface* of the Islamic paradigm for commonalities. Muslims should also look *beneath the surface* and see the roots of the inherent dignity of the individual in the revelation to Musa/Moses—that has been formulated as a generic value in the Declaration of Human Rights.

A further observation is that in both paradigms the authors have to use the basic common insights of their culture to account for their views and convince others. Accountability requires that people justify their points of view in relation to those central terms—even if these terms lie beneath the surface of the law and even more so because they are the general cultural background that is not always explained. People may stretch the meaning of the terms. Western law will stress the "autonomy" of the person, but, actually, no patient may make any decision beyond the space allowed by the medical profession; a patient will seldom completely ignore the advice of nurses, family members, or spiritual counselors—as we will see below. The doctors themselves are "guided" by their educational and professional socialization more than their explicit knowledge of rules and laws.

The Social System: "Who looks after me?"

One remarkable outcome of this project is a difference that comes up in relation to the positions of the Arab-Islamic and Western authors on different issues. We will cite them first and then make some comments. In vitro fertilization is allowed but only with eggs and sperm from the true parents; the donation of eggs and sperm is forbidden (El-Gindi). According to Egyptian law, organ donation is permitted by relatives; the law stipulates that a committee can allow donation by other persons by way of exception (Salem). Adoption is forbidden (see Mansour, Nasser, and Serour). Laws in most Western countries do not have these restrictions. This difference reflects cultures in which the extended family determines the social structure and individualism of Western laws. "Who looks after me?"—my (extended) family or "society at large"? An example of social security as organized in extended families are consanguineous marriages. Two chapters in this volume discuss consanguinity, one from a medical background and one from an anthropological background. In relation to genetic variants, research shows that cousin marriages do not show any relevant differences from other marriages on average. Only a small percenttage of consanguineous marriages have a 25% risk or higher that a child will be born with an autosomal recessive disorder. In rather closed communities such genetic diseases occur more frequently. The field research of cultural anthropologists in northern Morocco reports how educated young women who cannot find employment and have to look after themselves live in their old family town. The reason for this is that social security is the responsibility of the extended family, which in a sense co-owns the property of all family members. An individual does not live his or her own life but has a lifelong relation to the family and moral obligations to them (and only secondarily to others). Therefore, all property should be kept in the family and no people with other blood should share in these family reserves—that would harm the common responsibility of the extended family. This system necessitates families to accumulate enough money for the future. Rich people can save some capital to pay a private clinic in or outside their country.

Western culture has the opposite problem: because the law grants as much personal freedom as is possible—because of the freedom of conscience and of secular or religious worldviews—state arrangements begin with individuals and only secondarily treat people as relational beings who are dependent on and responsible for one another and take care of one another spontaneously. Because the state is made responsible for the costs of daily care, Western states have severe financial problems in paying for this care for all those who cannot look after themselves.[2] Therefore, the much greater personal freedom of the West makes people more dependent on public care than the extended family "system." One could perhaps say that extended family cultures have problems with personal freedom and individualistic cultures have problems with mutual care. This will touch especially on the role of women.

The difference between both solidarity systems is reflected in the role of women and the religious-cultural attitudes in issues like the termination of pregnancy as well. For many Muslims, marriage particularly aims towards starting a family. Refraining from having children is not an option. In many states around the Mediterranean, premarital genetic screening for thalassaemia, for instance, is offered or even mandated, and carrier couples can decide if they want to go through with the marriage. Different reports show that in some countries such as Jordan, people are actively frightened into marrying, whereas in other countries carrier couples are offered reproductive options such as abortion after prenatal diagnostics or IVF with preimplantation genetic diagnosis. The pursuit of health is highly valued in Islam, and preventive measures are considered important by most people as long as they are in line with the value of being a good Muslim. Although abortion is highly debated, it is not altogether prohibited by all Muslim schools (see Hegab). Therefore, we cannot simply assume that Muslims will never terminate pregnancies (see Nasser, Mansour, and

---

[2] The Netherlands used to have the most elaborate care system in the world, but the costs especially of care for people who need permanent care and support are growing exponentially and becoming too large a part of the state budget. For more background, see, e.g., Van Asselt *et al.* 2011: 46. In 2013 the Dutch government decided to let people contribute more to the costs of the public care they need.

Serour). When the mother's life is in danger, abortion could be allowed. When looking at the importance of family as caregivers for each other, that refraining from having children is not an option makes total sense.

Commonalities

We already discovered commonalities in practical argumentation beneath the surface of both paradigms, especially the idea of the dignity of every individual—which even has a common historical root in the revelation, both in "the West" and in Islamic/Arabic cultures. In both paradigms a more "conservative" and a more "liberal" or stricter and a more open interpretation can be pointed out (see Salem and Soeteman). Both paradigms have more in common, such as the way in which they construct arguments to choose between two complex options. Islamic moral reasoning accepts "the argument of the lesser evil"— which is accepted in Western moral reasoning as well. For both the rule "do as little harm as is possible" obtains. This principle implies that in serious dilemmas in operations or other treatments the quality of life will be a valid consideration. A higher obligation can invalidate the lower one. This argument is used to approve of organ donation from a healthy to a sick person. Some of the Muslim scholars stress that "necessity knows no law"—as the Western saying goes—and what is forbidden— haram—becomes halal in extreme situations: "necessity makes the prohibited lawful."

We see that Arab-Islamic authors refer to Scripture as the authoritative source in argumentation. The Western authors who write deliberately as believers—Muslims or Christians— do not refer straightforwardly to an authoritative source but to more generic terms like dignity, respect for life, and the integrity of the person. In their culture straightforward reference to religious sources is a conversation stopper, and therefore they look for terms on a more general level—which does not imply that their religious ideas do not provide the inspiration for their own views as they do for other members of their religious communities (cf. Boer, Schroten, and others). They look for a kind of "middle way" between breaking off discussion with their colleagues and speaking in purely secular terms (cf. Vroom 2013).

Law, Rules, Counseling, and Decisions

We have noticed that Islamic law varies from country to country and has been influenced deeply by common law and cultures in a more general sense (Salem). Some Islamic countries allow for the termination of pregnancy after rape (Hegab). In Egypt and other Islamic countries, the law has been strongly influenced by *shari'ah*. The ruler enacts his own laws but has to look over his shoulder to make sure the muftis do not protest too much. The "secular" laws in Western countries have to be valid for all. Nevertheless, state-church relations and rules for medical ethics vary widely in Europe. Just as in Islamic countries, these differences can only be understood from the perspective of the varying histories of European countries (and the USA).[3] Nevertheless, in the West freedom of religion implies that the law is the same for all inhabitants. Therefore, the law can provide criteria for treatments and research and leave further decisions to the individual: this is the right to moral independence (Soeteman). Autonomy implies that the patient has the last word but lives and dies among other people (cf. Ten Kate).

Nevertheless, the law prohibits acts and limits the legitimacy of some treatments. Therefore, in the West as well law is paternalistic and does not declare that "all is permitted." Soeteman distinguishes between soft and hard paternalism; even acts that do not harm others are sometimes forbidden. We will skip the philosophical question of the grounds on which the state (the community at large) has the right to deny certain rights to people.[4]

---

[3] For the complex situation in the USA, see Feldman 2005: 306.

[4] It can be argued that northwest European culture has some very basic and long-lasting insights on the value of life, shared by the large majority of the population (that are felt to be "humane"). Cultures in the USA and eastern Europe differ in several respects—which results in other criteria for abortion, palliative sedation, etc. These state-bound cultural backgrounds explain as well why the Turkish Islamic community in the West (and for that sake the Moroccan community, etc.) has other thoughts about some medical ethical issues

Beneath the general level of the law, we saw in both the Arab-Islamic and Western chapters that the medical specialists themselves, together with ethics/*fiqh* professors, made decisions on what may be done and what not. The chapters offer descriptions of rules for the treatment of people in the last phase of their lives and for organ donation. Laws and other rules imply that the medical doctors inform the patients about whatever they need to know. In practice, this implies that counseling depends on trust: the patient has to trust the specialist. Therefore, the medical community in the West has also established rules for good counseling (Cornel, Ten Kate)—rules that in practice are also followed largely in Islamic spiritual care (Karagül). So the decisions of the patients are made in consultation with a group of people, including spiritual caregivers—although the patient always has the right to refuse a treatment.

Final Comments

The main yield of the comparison of the "Western" and the "Arabic-Islamic" chapters in this volume is insight into the positions on medical ethical issues on both sides. There are clearly opposed rules—in relation to euthanasia and the use of sperm, eggs, and organs that do not come from parents or family members. Fundamental differences are those between legal ideas that presuppose individual freedom or the *Sunnah*, and social organization whose basis is the individual or the extended family. Nevertheless, beneath the surface of these differences lie fundamental human notions on the value of life, the dignity of the individual, and solidarity. Therefore, in many cases cooperation between medical staff and researchers is possible on the practical level, and families with Christian, Muslim, and secular family members will be able to find a treatment to which all can consent—if they learn to look beneath the surface.

---

than the majority of the ("Western") population; cf. the first part of the chapter by Arslan Karagül.

Bibliography

Feldman, Noah. (2005). *Divided by God: America's Church-State Problem—And What We Should Do About It*. New York: Farrar, Straus and Goroux.

Van Asselt, Evert Jan *et al.* (2011). *Health Care Reforms in an Ageing European Society, with a Focus on the Netherlands*. Brussels: Centre for European Studies. http://thinkingeurope.eu/sites/default/files/publication-files/healthcare reforms.pdf.

Vroom, Hendrik M. (2013). "Religious Insights in the Public Debate." in: Hendrik M. Vroom. *Walking in a Widening World: Understanding Religious Diversity*. AmSTaR Series. Amsterdam: VU University Press. Pp. 276-94

Index of Subjects

Index of Names

Contributors

Tineke Abma is Professor of Medical Humanities at VU University Medical Center Amsterdam.

Marzouk Aulad Abdellah is Assistant Professor of Ethics and Fiqh, Center for Islamic Theology, VU University Amsterdam.

Edien Bartels is senior researcher emeritus at the Department of Social and Cultural Anthropology of the Faculty of Social Sciences, VU University Amsterdam.

Theo Boer is Senior Lecturer in Ethics, Protestant Theological University, Groningen.

Pascal Borry is Assistant Professor of Bioethics at the Centre for Biomedical Ethics and Law of the University of Leuven.

Martina C. Cornel is Professor of Community Genetics and Public Health Genomics, VU University Medical Center, Amsterdam.

Mohammed M. I. Ghaly is Assistant Professor of Islamic Studies at the Institute for Religious Studies, Leiden University.

Ahmed Ragaey Ahmed Ahmed El-Gindi is Adjunct Secretary-General of the Islamic Organization of Medical Studies (IOMS), Kuwait.

Mostafa Hegab is Professor of Obstetrics and Gynaecology at the Faculty of Medicine, Al-Azhar University, Cairo.

Arslan Karagül is Assistant Professor of Islamic Spiritual Care, Center for Islamic Theology, VU University Amsterdam.

Leo P. ten Kate is Professor Emeritus of Clinical Genetics, VU University Medical Center, Amsterdam.

Serag El Din Mansour is Professor of Obstetrics and Gynaecology and Deputy Director of the International Islamic Center for Population Studies and Research, Al-Azhar University, Cairo.

Ayman Nassar is Professor of Obstetrics and Gynaecology and Director of the Al-Azhar ART Unit, Al-Azhar University, Cairo.

Ahmed Ragaa A. Ragab is Professor of Reproductive Health, International Islamic Center for Population Studies and Research, Al-Azhar University, Cairo.

Mostafa Fouad Hussein Salem is Professor of International Law, Al-Azhar University, Cairo.

Karin Schipper is a postdoctoral researcher in the field of the psychology of health care in the Department of Medical Humanities of the VU University Medical Center, Amsterdam.

Egbert Schroten is Professor Emeritus of Ethics of the Protestant Theological University, Utrecht (presently Amsterdam).

Gamal I. Serour is Professor of Obstetrics and Gynaecology and Director of the International Islamic Center for Population Studies and Research, Al-Azhar University, Cairo.

Arend Soeteman is Professor Emeritus of the Philosophy of Law, Faculty of Law, VU University Amsterdam.

Oka Storms is a doctoral student in the Department of Social and Cultural Sciences at the Faculty of Social Sciences, VU University Amsterdam, and is now an expert on informal care at MOVISIE (http://www.movisie.nl/)

Marieke E. Teeuw is a physician and researcher in the Department of Clinical Genetics, Section Community Genetics, EMGO Institute for Health and Care Research, VU University Medical Center, Amsterdam.

Petra Verdonk is Assistant Professor in the Department of Medical Humanities of the VU University Medical Center, Amsterdam.

Hendrik M. Vroom is Professor Emeritus of the Philosophy of Religion in the Faculties of Theology and Philosophy, VU University Amsterdam, and was coordinator of the VU Center for Islamic Theology.

Guido de Wert is Professor of Biomedical Ethics, Faculty of Health, Medicine and Life Sciences, University of Maastricht, Maastricht (Netherlands).

CPSIA information can be obtained at www.ICGtesting.com
Printed in the USA
LVOW06s1809061113

359782LV00005B/51/P